Graham Greene
Revised Edition

Twayne's English Authors Series

Kinley E. Roby, Editor

Northeastern University

TEAS 3

GRAHAM GREENE
(1904–   )
*Photograph by Karsh. Reproduced by
permission of Simon and Schuster.*

Graham Greene
Revised Edition

By A. A. DeVitis
Purdue University

Twayne Publishers • Boston

Graham Greene, Revised Edition

A. A. DeVitis

Copyright © 1986 by G.K. Hall & Co.
All Rights Reserved
Published by Twayne Publishers
A Division of G.K. Hall & Co.
70 Lincoln Street
Boston, Massachusetts 02111

Copyediting supervised by Lewis DeSimone
Book production by Lyda E. Kuth
Book design by Barbara Anderson

Typeset in 11 pt Garamond by Modern Graphics, Inc.,
Weymouth, Massachusetts

Printed on permanent/durable acid-free
paper and bound in the United States of
America

Library of Congress Cataloging in Publication Data

DeVitis, A. A.
    Graham Greene.

    (Twayne's English authors series; TEAS 3)
    Bibliography: p. 204
    Includes index.
    1. Greene, Graham, 1904–   —Criticism and
interpretation.   I. Title.   II. Series.
PR6013.R44Z632   1986   823'.912   85–17612
ISBN 0–8057–6911–0
ISBN 0–8057–6928–5 (pbk.)

Contents

About the Author

A. A. DeVitis received his doctorate from the University of Wisconsin in January 1954. He joined the English department of Purdue University in September 1953 and now holds the rank of professor. He has taught courses of all kinds in the years he has been there.

Besides having written a critical study on Greene in 1964, of which this book is an expansion and an updating, he has written on Evelyn Waugh, Anthony Burgess, and, with A. E. Kalson, a study of the prolific author J. B. Priestley.

His articles and book reviews, mostly on modern and contemporary British fiction, have appeared in such periodicals as *Contemporary Literature, College English, Twentieth Century Literature, Western Humanities Review, Saturday Review,* and the *Journal of Modern Literature.*

Preface

"It is only the infinite mercy and love of God that has prevented us from tearing ourselves to pieces and destroying His entire creation long ago," says Thomas Merton in *The Seven Storey Mountain*. And he then states: "People seem to think that it is in some way a proof that no merciful God exists, if we have so many wars. On the contrary, consider how in spite of centuries of sin and greed and lust and cruelty and hatred and avarice and oppression and injustice, spawned and bred by the free wills of men, the human race can still recover, each time, and can still produce men and women who overcome evil with good, hatred with love, greed with charity, lust and cruelty with sanctity."[1] Compare Bertrand Russell who writes in *The Impact of Science on Society:*

There are certain things that our age needs, and certain things that it should avoid. It needs compassion and a wish that mankind should be happy; it needs the desire for knowledge and the determination to eschew pleasant myths; it needs, above all, courageous hope and the impulse to creativeness. The things that it must avoid, and that have brought it to the brink of catastrophe, are cruelty, envy, greed, competitiveness, search for irrational subjective certainty, and what Freudians call the death wish. The root of the matter is a very simple and old-fashioned thing, a thing so simple that I am almost ashamed to mention it, for fear of the derisive smile with which wise cynics will greet my words. The thing I mean—please forgive me for mentioning it—is love, Christian love, or compassion. If you feel this, you have a motive for existence, a guide in action, a reason for courage, an imperative necessity for intellectual honesty. If you feel this, you have all that anybody should feel in the way of religion. Although you may not find happiness, you will never know the deep despair of those whose life is aimless and void of purpose; for there is always something that you can do to diminish the awful sum of human misery.[2]

Although Merton would disagree with Russell's statement concerning the place of formal religion in everyday life, he would accept the spirit in which it was written; for, mutually, they advocate love and compassion, and oppose them to hate.

In this book I have endeavored to explain what use Graham Greene makes of religious subject matter and religious belief. Since the religious idea informs much of his work, I have, by analyzing the place of religion in the overall pattern of his novels, traced—as far as possible—the development of his thought as it affects his art.

Since the 1930s writers have demonstrated a preoccupation with religious themes. Wherever possible I have drawn parallels and pointed out similarities. André Gide from his *Pastoral Symphony* to *The Counterfeiters* shows a penetrating awareness of the place of religion in contemporary life. His *Journals* may be opened at almost any point to reveal how the "arch heretic"—as Mauriac and Maritain consider Gide—fought a personal battle with God that was reflected in his novels. This conflict is revealed in all its aspects in Gide's correspondence with Paul Claudel, himself one of the most important of the writers in France who made use of religious subject matter. Claudel's dramas are strange and enchanting: in *Tidings Brought to Mary,* for example, he makes use of a "virgin" birth to test the faith of a medieval community. François Mauriac, in my opinion the most brilliant of modern novelists, followed the teachings of his Church and created some of the most penetrating studies of hypocrisy, greed, and lust ever written. His affiliation with Graham Greene is discussed later on. Georges Bernanos and, earlier, Léon Bloy, as well as Claudel and Mauriac, wrote within a frame of reference that is specifically Catholic; they are seriously read, challenging comparison with their English contemporaries. In the United States William Faulkner, in a nebulous manner, paralleled the European interest in the Christian myth. *Light in August* makes Joe Christmas, a thirty-three-year-old scapegoat, its protagonist, while *The Sound and the Fury* vaguely follows the occurrences of Easter week. There are many more writers, chief among them, Flannery O'Connor, who yet find the basic fabric of Christianity stimulating material for fiction.

An important point to consider is that Greene reflects a widespread interest in religious themes within the limits of his techniques and backgrounds. My problem in this study was not to define Greene's religious beliefs, but rather to evaluate his success or failure in having used artistically and imaginatively the properties of Roman Catholicism. I therefore addressed myself to the task of searching out motifs and patterns—showing how Greene uses certain themes and modifies them, and to what purpose and with what effect. My discussion relies principally on internal evidence. By analyzing plots, characters, and situations, I have endeavored to define the basis of the appeal that both the "entertainments" and the novels have. I did not minimize such other considerations as symbolism and technique but attempted to show how these sometimes dominated the religious theme or were, as is usually the case, controlled by it.

Since the religious theme becomes clearly apparent in the novels beginning with *Brighton Rock,* I have devoted much more space to Greene's publications since 1938, the date when this curious and fascinating book first appeared. Ultimately, I think, Greene's reputation will rest on the books written since 1938; and his contribution to English letters will be most clearly evidenced by them. I have gone through the early work, endeavoring to show how Greene's craftsmanship has been constantly improving, but how his thinking has remained fairly much the same. Part of the plan of this study is to show how Greene's Catholicism is not one stance, but a variety of stances—not always, perhaps, compatible with the strictest and narrowest interpretations of his faith. The works before 1938, it seems to me, are of interest not only as fictions but frequently as preliminary sketches and as tentative efforts for those more serious works that beguile and enchant Greene's readers. And, of course, I am enthusiastic about Greene—he has enlarged the scope of the English novel.

I have also endeavored to show in the opening chapter those factors common to many novels originating in the 1930s and the 1940s. I have done this for two reasons: first, to show how Greene is very much of his era; second, to show how in his own way he reacts to the forces of tradition of English literary history. Although Greene is very much in the current Continental literary swing, constantly challenging comparison with those other writers who make use of religiously oriented subject matters, he is first and last, in my opinion, an English novelist.

Many parallels have been drawn between Greene and Mauriac, and many of these provoke analysis. I have tried to show how these two writers are alike, concentrating specifically on Greene, how he has improved as a craftsman from understanding and appreciating the problems of his French contemporary.

In undertaking the revisions and updating for this study of Greene I discovered that I had not much changed my mind about his contributions to modern literature. If anything he has improved technically as a novelist as his subject matter has dealt less specifically with religious matters. I have, however, corrected to my best ability errors of fact and mistakes of judgment. I am indebted to my students at Purdue University who read Greene with me over the years in many classes for these modifications of judgment. They read Greene with enthusiasm, sometimes with anger, but never with apathy. If they are indication of Greene's lasting value as a novelist, he will be around for a very long time.

I should like to thank Professor John Pick of *Renascence* for having published a preliminary study of Greene's entertainments and of *The Heart of the Matter* and of *The Comedians* in that periodical; and also Mr. Robert Evans and Mr. William Jerome Crouch of the University of Kentucky Press for having published a preliminary study of the Greene-Mauriac affiliation in their collection of Graham Greene criticism, and Professor Peter Wolfe for publishing an early study of the novels since about 1960 in his *Essays on Graham Greene.*

A. A. DeVitis

Purdue University

Acknowledgments

I should like to thank the Bodley Head Press and William Heinemann Ltd. for permission to quote from their Collected Edition of Greene's works. I have used these texts whenever possible, taking into account, as much as the scope of this work permitted, those changes that Greene incorporated into this edition. I should also like to thank Simon and Schuster for allowing me to quote from their editions of Greene's latest works.

Chronology

1941–1946   Employed by Foreign Office; duty in Africa.

1943   *The Ministry of Fear*, an entertainment.

1947   *Nineteen Stories*.

1948   *The Heart of the Matter*, a novel. Trip to Czechoslovakia.

1950   *The Third Man* and *The Fallen Idol*, both entertainments.

1950–1951   Trip to Africa.

1951   *The Lost Childhood and Other Essays*. *The End of the Affair*, a novel.

1952   Received Catholic Literary Award for *The End of the Affair*.

1953   *The Living Room*, Greene's first drama.

1954   *Twenty-One Stories*.

1954–1955   Trip to Indochina.

1955   *Loser Takes All*, an entertainment. *The Quiet American*, a novel. Trip to Poland.

1957   *The Potting Shed*, a drama.

1958   *Our Man in Havana*, an entertainment. First trip to Cuba.

1959   *The Complaisant Lover*, a drama. Trip to Belgian Congo.

1961   *A Burnt-Out Case*, a novel. *In Search of a Character: Two African Journals*, accounts of two trips taken at different times. Trip to Moscow. Elected Honorary member of American Institute of Arts and Letters; later resigned.

1962   Honorary Doctor of Literature, Cambridge.

1963   *A Sense of Reality*, stories. Honorary Fellow, Balliol College, Oxford.

1963–1964   Trip to Haiti and Santo Domingo and the United States.

1964   *Carving a Statue*, a drama.

1966   Trip to Cuba. *The Comedians*, a novel. Named Companion of Honour in the New Year Honours List.

1967   *May We Borrow Your Husband and Other Comedies of the Sexual Life*, stories.

1969   Trip to Paraguay. *Travels with My Aunt*, an entertainment. *Collected Essays*.

1971   Trip to Chile. *A Sort of Life*, autobiography.

1973   *The Honorary Consul*, a novel.

1974   *Collected Stories. Lord Rochester's Monkey*, a biography.

1975   *The Return of A. J. Raffles*, a drama. *An Impossible Woman, The Memories of Dottoressa Moor of Capri*, for which Greene served as editor.

1976   First of several trips to Panama.

1978   *The Human Factor*, a novel.

1980   *Ways of Escape*, autobiography. *Doctor Fischer of Geneva or The Bomb Party*, a novel.

1981   *The Great Jowett*, a radio play.

1982   *Monsignor Quixote*, a novel. *J'Accuse: The Dark Side of Nice*, a pamphlet.

1983   *Yes and No*, a one-act play. *For Whom the Bell Chimes*, a farce.

1984   *Getting to Know the General: The Story of an Involvement*, a memoir.

1985   *The Tenth Man*, a novel.

Chapter One

The Catholic as Novelist

"Fate willed me to be a
writer and I write about
rootlessness"

In the first published version of Evelyn Waugh's *Brideshead Revisited* (1945), Charles Ryder says:

I had no religion. I was taken to church weekly as a child, and at school attended chapel daily, but, as though in compensation, from the time I went to my public school I was excused church in the holidays. The view implicit in my education was that the basic narrative of Christianity had long been exposed as a myth, and that opinion was now divided as to whether its ethical teaching was of present value, a division in which the main weight went against it; religion was a hobby which some people professed and others did not; at the best it was slightly ornamental, at the worst it was the province of "complexes" and "inhibitions"—catch words of the decade—and of the intolerance, hypocrisy, and sheer stupidity attributed to it for centuries. No one had ever suggested to me that these quaint observances expressed a coherent philosophic system and intransigeant historical claims; nor, had they done so, would I have been much interested.[1]

On the whole, the nineteenth century left to the twentieth a growing uneasiness in the face of the materialistic advances of science and the rising influence of the middle class. Moral and political ideas succumbed to the influence of Lenin and Marx, and the human personality found itself subjected to the analyses of Jung, Adler, and Freud. T. S. Eliot detected a death wish in Western civilization, defined it, and set forth in *The Waste Land* (1922) the most comprehensive set of symbols for characterizing the period of the early twentieth century. Some, like H. G. Wells, however, maintained faith in the machine.

Few serious thinkers were in the main able to maintain orthodox religious belief in the face of confusion or seeming chaos. There

1

seemed no place for the disenchanted to turn, and it became fashionable to be psychoanalyzed in order to understand how the personality reflected the order of the day. In the late 1920s and early 1930s, there came a depression following upon the inflation and the mad good times of the post—World War I period. Economic catastrophe a reality, the hopes of Shaw and the Fabians dimmed in the tide of Spanish fascism, and, later, German totalitarianism. The predicament in which man found himself seemed almost beyond solution.

In the first quarter of the twentieth century, the artist's concern was with form, style, and technique. Virginia Woolf in her criticism rebelled against the naturalism of the nineteenth century, and in *The Common Reader* (1925), she demonstrated an antiintellectual approach to literature. She preferred to analyze the text in the fashion of the late Romantics, dismissing the Victorian standards of scholarship and history. She watched Mrs. Dalloway through a day of her life, and in that one day Woolf told her readers all they needed to know concerning her heroine, and Mrs. Dalloway's existence did not include God. Clarissa Dalloway could feel sorry for Septimus Warren Smith, but the causes of his dilemma were for her and her creator primarily psychical, social, and economic; indeed, God had no place in the pattern of Mrs. Dalloway's thoughts, even as she glimpsed death. Lily Briscoe in *To the Lighthouse* (1927) concerned herself with the representation of Mrs. Ramsey as a splotch of paint on her canvas. Mrs. Ramsey sought to hold the moment of harmony at the dinner party, and for one moment it did occur to her to think of God, but she dismissed the thought immediately. Greene has said that Virginia Woolf's characters, as a result of their rationalism, "wandered like cardboard symbols through a world that was paper-thin."[2] Bernard Blackstone says of Woolf's religion: "Virginia Woolf's aversion from Christianity springs first . . . from her hatred of hypocrisy. It springs also from her sensitiveness to unpleasantness and pain. These things are, artistically, outside her scope. She knows they are there; and . . . she is ever too acutely conscious of them. They contradict her vision of beauty and significance."[3]

E. M. Forster in a *A Passage to India* (1924) and especially in *Howards End* (1910) described the Philistinism that Matthew Arnold had defined in *Culture and Anarchy*. The Schlegels he represented as Sweetness and Light, and Mr. Wilcox became Material Progress. In Howards End, Mrs. Wilcox's home, Forster symbolized the forces of tradition. The unseen presence of Mrs. Wilcox hovering over the house speaks of God, but very obliquely. It is tradition in *Howards End* that is important.[4]

Arnold Bennett and John Galsworthy carried on in their realistic fashion, but their realism seemed to imply no God in the world. Galsworthy's *The Forsyte Saga* (1922) moved the Forsytes out of the Victorian era, through the Edwardian lull, and into the twentieth century in which not even Soames's property was valuable any longer. Bennett's *The Old Wives' Tale* (1908) traced the development of two sisters in mundane, realistic description that often sprang into a vitality all of its own, but neither Sophia nor Constance paid any more than lip service to God.

A few like D. H. Lawrence reacted violently to the severe and unyielding strictures of nineteenth-century orthodoxy. In his rebellion were contained the seeds of a religious search, for Lawrence sought to revitalize mankind by returning to the springs of feeling. He looked in *The Plumed Serpent* (1926) for king-gods, and in *The Man Who Died* (1928), he took the Christ myth and infused his own ideas of sex into it. Christ, he decided, had not been a whole man because he had not found his polarity in woman. So Lawrence raised him from the tomb and sent him out searching for a complement. Lawrence believed that he found represented in the art and life of the Etruscans an epitome of civilization; and it was their appreciation of life, of vitality, of meaningful existence that he attempted to incorporate into his final work.[5] He traveled the world looking for a race still expressive of dark and vital blood; and in Mexico he thought he found untrammeled feelings and vital meaning springing from a belief in the ancient king-gods of the Mexicans. Lawrence's search was in fact a real one. Having inherited the disillusionment of the nineteenth century, he felt it necessary to find a substitute religion. That which he formulated, unfortunately, most people in his own time found distasteful, choosing to misunderstand his exaltation of sex.

James Joyce rejected Irish Catholicism, and by doing so turned himself, perhaps paradoxically, into the most Catholic of writers. In *A Portrait of the Artist as a Young Man* (1916), he traced his own spiritual awareness in the character of Stephen Dedalus; and, like Stephen, Joyce concluded that to remain faithful to his artistic vision he would have to leave Ireland. *Ulysses* (1922), his magnificent tour de force, worked in terms of multiple myth as it traced Stephen's rebellion against his God and his country still further. Into *Ulysses* Joyce put all the paraphernalia of psychoanalysis, of Jung and Freud, and fused it with a stream-of-consciousness technique; and, once and for all, he indicated the limitations of that device in the soliloquies of Mollie and Leopold Bloom.

In the 1930s a group of poets picked up the threads of a passive idealism and began to take stock; they looked about them and saw to what monstrous size the social organism had grown. W. H. Auden, Stephen Spender, and C. Day Lewis began to advocate English socialism. They preached decentralization of industry so that the social unit might be made smaller and man might again communicate with man. Cecil Day Lewis's *A Hope for Poetry* (1934) became for them a manifesto of their hopes and beliefs. They sought to revitalize poetic metaphor by drawing images from the machine, and they tried to re-educate the masses to understand the dangers of capitalism. They claimed literary descent from Gerard Manley Hopkins, T. S. Eliot, Wilfred Owen, and D. H. Lawrence. From the debris of a nineteenth-century pessimism that had led the early twentieth century to wish for death, they sought for new meaning, a new order. They looked for a way out of the waste land. Eliot in his poetry had defined the era; they took up the battle from there. Meanwhile Eliot clarified his beliefs in his literary criticism. In *After Strange Gods* (1934), he showed himself aware of the confusion frequently apparent in the writings of the nineteenth-century sages. He praised George Eliot for her insights into human motivations, for example, but he deplored her individualistic morals. He insisted that the writer, to be faithful to society, had to remain within an orthodox conception of history and tradition. He pointed out that when morals cease to be a matter of tradition and orthodoxy personality becomes alarmingly important.[6]

Eliot found Thomas Hardy's extreme emotionalism a symptom of decadence, for Hardy's personality was "uncurbed by any institutional attachment or by submissions to any objective beliefs. . . ."[7] He deplored Lawrence's eccentricity in setting up for himself a system of gods opposed to the Church. To Lawrence, Eliot said, any spiritual force was good; and evil resided only in the absence of spirituality.[8]

Eliot, in other words, reasserted the validity of the orthodox teachings of his Anglican Church. He found in the wisdom and traditions of the Church an answer to the ills of the waste land and a measure upon which to base one's spiritual awareness. Furthermore, Eliot found it essential for the artist to point out the difference between good and evil, insisting that awakening men to the spiritual life was a great responsibility: "It is only when they [men] are so awakened that they are capable of real Good, but . . . at the same time they become first capable of Evil."[9] The artist had become aware once more that art could not exist for itself alone.

The return to orthodoxy found very real opponents in the political theories prevalent in the 1930s. William York Tindall in *Forces in Modern British Literature: 1885–1946,* describes the influences that marked English literature after World War I: "Disenchantment and its effects, the cynical, the disgusting, and the grotesque, though products of the first World War, existed before it as products of science and bourgeois self-contemplation. With these effects came others, the comic, the ironic, and the fantastic, the last of which appears an attempt of the disenchanted to rediscover enchantment. Attitudes of disenchantment, found at their happiest in the work of Huxley and young Waugh, occur so abundantly that, like politics and religion, they discover the times."[10]

The 1930s largely continued to lament a world in which physics had displaced metaphysics and limited reality to matter. The return to religion, paralleling the trend to communism and socialism, indicated a desire to reunite matter with spirit. It indicated the fact that religion was at long last catching up with science: "The reunion of matter and spirit symbolized union of self and world and, beyond this, of the unconscious with the conscious. Religions offered ends and means," writes Tindall.[11] The opponents to orthodoxy in the 1930s were the Fascist and Communist ideologies.

André Gide, in his *Journals* from 1928–39, best typifies the attitudes that opposed the march back to religion. In Arcachon on the tenth of August, 1930, he wrote in his journal: "The great grievance one can have against the Christian religion is that it sacrifices the strong to the weak. But that strength should strive to find its function in bringing help to weakness, how can one fail to approve this?"[12]

The conflict seemed one between a cult of power and a religion of love. To approve the teachings of the Church and to accept the teachings of Marx and Lenin appeared incommensurate, for love and violence were totally incompatible. Fascism and, to many, communism advocated strength and the strong man, whereas capitalism allowed for meekness and humility. Gide wrote in his journal for the ninth of January, 1933, in double-edged irony:

But I see only too well, alas, how and why capitalism and Catholicism are bound up together and the great advantage that capitalism can find in a religion that teaches a man whom society strikes on the right cheek to hold out the left, which benumbs the oppressed and soothes him with hopes of an afterlife, transfers rewards to a mystical plane, and lets the oppressor enjoy a triumph which it persuades the oppressed to be but illusion. How could the man who knows that Christ said: "happy those that weep" fail to take advantage of Catholicism, and how could "those that weep" not accept submission if they know that "the last shall be first?" Theirs is the kingdom of God; the possessors leave it to them if it is well understood that those that weep will leave to the possessors the kingdom of this earth. Everything therefore is for the best and no one has anything to complain about. Christ remains on the side of the poor, to be sure; the rich leave him on their hands. The poor almost thank them for this. They know that they have "the better part." And probably Christ did not want this. In his time the social question could not be raised. Replying to a specious question, he said: "Render unto Caesar. . . ." So much has been rendered unto Caesar that there is nothing left but for him. But the poor know that everything they give up here below will be "returned to them an hundred fold." One cannot imagine a better investment!

And the rich still find a way of conciliating Christ (or of reconciling themselves with him) by making a point of being "charitable." For, after all, they have kindness—which will allow them, they hope, while keeping all their advantages "here below," not to allow themselves to be dispossessed of all hope of still being, after death, on the right side. [13]

Yet Gide was forced to admit that there was value in tradition and that systems that endeavored to build by destroying had their limitations. It was absurd, he wrote, to condemn the past in the name of the future and not to realize a filtration, a succession. He insisted that only by thrusting out a foothold into the past could the present spring into the future. [14] This statement, in all its force, coming from the advocate of the gratuitous act—the act committed for no real reason except to gratify the individual lust—indicates how far Gide had gone since his earliest works. The reliance on tradition, although Gide would never agree with the teachings of any church, indicates that the *enfant terrible* in his maturity came to realize the necessity of restricting individual conduct.

Religion, then, offered once again a basis for meaning in a topsy-turvy world to those who would accept its teachings. Not only that, but God suddenly became popular. The interest in psychoanalysis and Freud found a close rival in religion.[15] It became fashionable to be converted to either Anglicanism or Roman Catholicism. One was required to show an intense interest in the forms of worship to be in the literary swing. What is important, however, is that those writers who wrote about religion took their work seriously. They wrote for society, and they had a message to deliver. The message spoke to the point that man could put his garden to rights and reclaim the desert waste it had become since science had, seemingly, moved God out of the Church. Graham Greene and Aldous Huxley and Rex Warner and Evelyn Waugh and Christopher Isherwood and W. H. Auden and many more fell into the pattern of conversion defined and illustrated by Eliot from *The Waste Land* through *Ash Wednesday* (1930) to the *Four Quartets* (1935–42).

The writers of the 1930s, following a pattern implied by T. S. Eliot in his own work and using the imagery and motifs of *The Waste Land,* looked about them and decided that something had to be done about society. They realized that their function as writers was momentous, and they understood that their responsibility was a matter of moral responsibility. Graham Greene wrote to Elizabeth Bowen and V. S. Pritchett:

> First I would say there are certain human duties I owe in common with the greengrocer or the clerk—that of supporting my family if I have a family, of not robbing the poor, the widow or the orphan, of dying if the authorities demand it (it is the only way to remain independent; the conscientious objector is forced to become a teacher in order to justify himself). These are our primitive duties as human beings. . . . I would say that if we do less than these, we are so much the less human beings and therefore so much the less likely to be artists. But are there any special duties I owe to my fellow victims. . . . I would like to imagine there are none, but I fear there are at least two duties the novelist owes—to tell the truth as he sees it and to accept no special privileges from the state.[16]

By "truth" Greene meant that the novelist had to describe accurately, and that the authenticity of his observations depended on the validity of the emotion he was describing. For his own writing, Greene took Cardinal Newman as a guide. As a Catholic he main-

tained, with Newman, that he had to write about good as well as
evil and that it was his responsibility as an artist to awaken sympathetic comprehension not only for the evil but for "smug, complacent, successful characters" as well (48).

Greene realized that it was his duty as a novelist to be a thorn
in the side of Roman Catholic as well as social and political orthodoxy, and a questioner of the complacent who accepted religious
dogma and political ideology blindly, in order to reawaken the reader
to a comprehension of the essential mystery of life: "Sooner or later
the strenuous note of social responsibility, of Marxism, of the greatest material good of the greatest number must die in the ear, and
then perhaps certain memories will come back, of long purposeless
discussions in the moonlight about life and art . . . (49). For Greene
the writer "just as much as the Christian Church," became the de-
fender of the individual (49). Greene's own answer to fascism and
terror was his Roman Catholicism. And it is his Roman Catholicism
that informs his novels.

Rex Warner, in a paradoxical and sometimes contradictory manner, concurs with Greene's analysis of the function of the artist in
society:

> This is what may be called the political task of literature—to hold the
> mirror up to nature, to show men how they live and what is meant by
> their own words and manners, to investigate everything under the sun,
> to retain the tradition of the past, and to explore the future, to instruct,
> to criticize, to delight, to create and to reveal. In these activities, as in
> all others, the writer may be greatly helped or greatly hindered by the
> society in which he lives. The more he can co-operate with this society,
> the happier, as a rule, he will be. Yet, though his work is conditioned
> by his social group, it is not determined by it. And there is a sense in
> which it is true to say that his work must be, whether he is conscious of
> it or not, always disruptive of any State organization. For his loyalties as
> a writer are something wider and deeper than any State can be.[17]

In his works Greene does not insist on his faith as a unique way
out of the problems of the religious doubt, the political and social
unrest that characterize the times. To do so would make him a
Catholic writer instead of a writer who happens to be a Catholic, a
distinction on which he insists. He has, however, in over fifty years
of writing fiction presented characters whose preoccupations and
motivations reflect a private interpretation of Roman Catholic val-

ues. As his private understanding is reflected in the actions of his characters, however, it becomes for his reader a statement of belief that provides an understanding, however limited, of the various concerns that make up for him the complex of thought and action called life.

In his works Greene insists on the inviolable dignity of the individual—only that, but it is everything. He insists on the individual's right to live in accord with the highest promptings of his conscience, whether those promptings be political, religious, or social. The usual tendency is to read his works as those of a writer whose themes are exclusively religious, but Greene's novels are as provocatively political as they are religious. Indeed, when he is at his best the political, social, and religious threads form a nexus that convinces by virtue of its truth to the human experience.

For several weeks, as a prank while he was a student at Oxford and to win a free trip to Moscow, Greene belonged to the Communist party. He revealed his membership several years later as a gesture to curtail the influence of the CIA, but discovered later that the revelation had produced the annoying result of making him suspect to the United States State Department, who then limited his travel in the United States, a curtailment that was lifted during the Kennedy administration. Greene, however, admits real sympathy for the Communist ideology. Perhaps its more idealistic notions appeal to his sense of social betterment, but he is no more pleased to be referred to as a writer of the Left that he is to be called a Catholic writer. In *The Other Man,* his conversations with Marie-Françoise Allain, he admits that the confrontation between communism and Catholicism is a very powerful force in world politics, and that he is perhaps somewhat naively looking for "Communism with a human face,"[18] a consideration that affects *The Human Factor* (1978) and other works as well.

In his fiction Greene deals with political issues because for him politics is "in the very air we breathe, like the presence or absence of a God" (84). But his novels do not in any way become illustrations of his political leanings, which are to the Left and far from the Right, any more than they are illustrations of the dogmas of his adopted faith. Greene is, quite simply, aware of the fact that few people act and live with a full awareness of the philosophical or theological promptings that propel them. His characters, in other words, exist as individuals, and their actions are rarely in complete accordance with ideologies of which they may, or may not, be aware. For Greene the actions of individuals qualify philosophy and theology, rarely the reverse.

Greene does not in his novels advocate any specific political beliefs. Rather he is concerned with what Robert Browning called in "Bishop Blougram's Apology" the "dangerous edge of things." Allain warns, correctly, that it would be wrong to take Greene "on trust" in matters of commitment: "One would do better to watch out for what he has called 'divided loyalties': These are revealed in his life, as seeds of revolution, sown all the more deceptively in that they do not correspond to any logic but his own" (72). Add to this Greene's remark made at the University of Hamburg in 1969 that "the storyteller's task is 'to act as the devil's advocate, to elicit sympathy and a measure of understanding for those who lie outside the boundaries of state approval,' "(73), and the dialectical nature of his thought as it affects his art becomes more understandable.

The cleavage between the extremes of established belief and its rejection Greene has accepted as a "constant" in his life and work. "Perhaps it was the only way to exorcize the evil," he says to Allain. He would not be a good recruit for communism for he would be pulled between loyalty and betrayal, "the mind's contradictions, the paradox one carries within oneself" (21). With Tom Paine, he insists that "we must guard even our enemies against injustice, whether it's perpetrated by a democratic government or by a dictatorship" (106).

In his fiction Greene acts in much the same manner as a devil's advocate, challenging his readers to understand and sympathize with the emotional, religious, and social predicaments of his characters. He admits to Allain that only one of his novels was conceived on one side of his loyalties: *The Comedians* was written with "the intention of expressing a point of view and in order to fight—to fight the horror of Papa Doc's dictatorship" (78), which, strangely, makes that novel the most problematic of all his works. The protagonist Brown is fully aware of the evil palpable in Papa Doc's Haiti, and he accepts it as the order of the times, failing to commit himself, either ideologically or emotionally, to a counter force. In the majority of the novels, however, the individual, usually haunted by the past or pursued by intolerable forces in the present, comes to a point where he confronts either himself or the status quo; and in so doing reveals his measure of heroism, even though his cause may be lost in human terms. Yet the individual in standing for his beliefs allows for an appreciation of the truth behind the stand. In *The Comedians* Brown first accepts the status quo, then flees from it; by doing so he confirms the ascendancy of darkness in the political milieu.

In the majority of his works Greene is, for the most part, determined to play fair with forces on both sides of the dangerous edge. As a novelist he skirts the perimeters of what can, consequently, be termed good and not-good in order to render the highest kind of justice to both camps. "The novelist's station," he says to Allain "is on the ambiguous borderline between the just and the unjust, between doubt and clarity, but he has to be unscrupulous . . . and I've been misunderstood' (79–80). In his novels the borderline becomes the most compelling of the symbols he brings from personal experience, whether it is a green baize door or the frontier between nations.

Greene's concern since the publication of his first novel, *The Man Within* (1929), a work he professes to dislike, has been with the individual's struggle with things as they are, and the arena of combat has always been political, religious, and social. Justice has been his major preoccupation; yet he says, "In fact I don't fight injustice, for my aim is not to change things but to give them expression" (78). As a private man, nonetheless, Greene has fought injustice, expressing his opinions as a writer in indignant letters to the *Times,* in journalistic essays, and in action. He resigned, for example, from the American Institute of Arts and Letters as a protest against Vietnam and asked other writers to follow his lead. He objected to the archbishop of Paris who forbade prayers at Collette's grave. His controversial pamphlet *J'Accuse: The Dark Side of Nice* (1982) was written to champion the cause of his friend Martine Cloetta against organized fear and coercion. He numbers Castro among those he admires, although he fears his authoritarianism. He objected to the naïveté and hypocrisy of American foreign policy before and during the Vietnam crisis. He admits to having been a moderate helper of the Sandinista cause in Central America (78–79); and he likes to be in places where genuine changes can occur, which may account for the fascination that Central and South America exert in his later works. And in *Getting to Know the General: The Story of an Involvement,* an account of several trips to Panama at the invitation of General Omar Torrijos, Greene quite readily admits that what intrigues him

about Central and South American countries is the mixture of politics, idealism, and religion that informs the lives and spirits of the
people. In Torrijos Greene found a kindred spirit, a man of seeming
contradictions skirting the dangerous edges of political and social
upheavals, a man of good humor, obsessed by death, a romantic
who was yet a practical politician, a lover of women who upheld
the traditions of family and religion. The memoir in fact tells Greene's
readers more about Greene the man than do *A Sort of Life* and *Ways
of Escape,* the more straightforward accounts of his life.

There has been a tendency among Greene's readers from the
beginning of his career to read his characters as spokespersons of his
private beliefs. *The Power and the Glory* in 1940 earned the disapproval of the more orthodox members of the Roman Catholic Church;
and some readers later felt that Querry and Fowler in *A Burnt-Out
Case* (1961) and *The Quiet American* (1955) reflected his own loss of
faith and his disapproval of an American foreign policy that had
not yet been promulgated in Indonesia in the latter. The heart of
the matter is that Greene exists in the majority of his characters,
in some measure, as he renders them the fairest justice he can. There
are exceptions, however—Parkinson and Rycker in *A Burnt-Out
Case,* for example, are characters who require no justice whatsoever.

Since his first novels Greene's career has involved him in political
and social concerns that have taken him ever farther from the Roman
Catholicism he learned from his instruction by Father Trollope in
Nottingham when he decided to look into Catholicism because a
young woman, who would later become his wife, had criticized his
understanding of the doctrine of the veneration of the Virgin. Greene
has moved from an academic understanding of Roman Catholic
doctrines to an ever-widening humanism, one that confirms his
place within the tradition of English letters and marks him as one
of the most compelling of our modern authors.

In *The Emperor's Clothes,* an attack on the dogmatic assertions of
writers who use religion as background and rationale for their works,
Kathleen Nott says about the novelist who writes from a Roman
Catholic point of view: "It seems to be much easier for Catholic
writers who are born Catholic, for instance Mauriac, to stick to
psychological truth than it is for converts. This may be because it
is much easier to ignore Catholic theory when it is acquired below
the age of reason. Anglo-Saxon writers probably have a special dis-
advantage in this respect."[19]

Nott aims her barb directly at Greene and Evelyn Waugh, both converts to Roman Catholicism, the former in 1926 and the latter in 1930; and she goes on to observe that she finds the situation described in Greene's *The Power and the Glory* credible because the actions of the characters result from the interplay between a sentimental-religious education and the concrete circumstances of socialistic, government intolerance. But for *The Heart of the Matter* (1948) and *The End of the Affair* (1951) she has no sympathy, finding the situations described in these books factitious: "To be artistically satisfying the situation must be objectively described. The author must not imply that, for esoteric reasons, he knows more about the answers to the problem than the characters do. You can write a human book about a Catholic if you do not at the same time write a book about Catholic theories of human nature."[20] Indeed, Nott puts her finger on the point that has given rise to much of the controversy excited by the religious provocations portrayed by both Greene and Mauriac in their works.

Since the publication of *Brighton Rock* in 1938 the framework of Greene's novels, with few exceptions, has been Roman Catholicism. Writing for an audience primarily Protestant in orientation, Greene has faced obstacles as a novelist that Mauriac, who acquired his religious training "below the age of reason," did not. Yet both these novelists confronted identical problems regarding their artistic and religious integrity. Ultimately, both as artists have concerned themselves with the capacity of the human heart for sacrifice and greatness within a world governed by a God who seems unreasonable, hostile, and oftentimes indifferent; and both have grappled in their works with the all-pervasive nature of grace, the incontestable mystery of good and evil, and the difficulty of individuals to distinguish between the two.

The fact, however, that these writers—one born a Roman Catholic, the other a convert to Roman Catholicism—deal in their fictions with the predicaments of human beings within a framework of morality that is labeled Roman Catholicism does not necessarily mean that they are novelists who have allowed an appreciation of the orthodoxy of their beliefs to govern the artistic conception of their works. It would be just as foolish to label Homer a Greek theologian because Odysseus and Agamemnon are Greeks and concerned with the caprices of the deities. Furthermore, both Greene and Mauriac have been conscious of the difficulties of their positions

as artists and have written perceptively and persuasively on the
nature of their responsibilities to both their craft and their faith.
Both have been accused by their critics of "conniving" with the
devil in portraying their themes.

Speaking within the defined limits of Thomistic philosophy,
Jacques Maritain discusses in *Art and Scholasticism* the problem of
evil in the world and the novelist's responsibility to his audience.
The novelist's purpose, he says, is not to mirror life as the painter
does, but to create the experience of it. The novel, of course, derives
its rules of conduct from the real world; but, as art, its validity
depends on the quality of the life-experience it creates. It becomes
the responsibility of the novelist to understand with what object he
portrays the aspects of evil that form the materials of the true art
work: "The essential question is *from what altitude* he depicts and
whether his art and mind are pure enough and strong enough to
depict it without connivance. The more deeply the modern novelist
probes human misery, the more does it require super-human virtues
in the novelist."[21]

According to Maritain the only writer who can be a complete
artist is the Christian, for only he has some idea of the potentialities
of man and of the factors limiting his greatness. The Christian writer
who approaches his craft honestly portrays those universal truths
that are valid within a Christian configuration of morality and ethics.
If the artist finds himself in too much sympathy with misery and
suffering, his pity may lead him to censure the forces of divinity
that make themselves apparent in the phenomenal world. Such art
becomes destructive, even self-destructive, for it defeats any moral
end. It is for this reason that Maritain found the influence of Gide
pernicious, for much of Gide's work seemingly exalts a gratuitous
act without consideration of its moral and ethical ramifications. But
neither Greene nor Mauriac, many of their Catholic readers insist,
has maintained a suitable "altitude."

Graham Greene has been accused by his critics and fans alike of
"conniving" with his characters against his faith; he has been called
a Manichaean, a Jansenist, a quietist, an existentialist, and other
names as well. Many commentators have made an attempt to abstract
his personal convictions from the world of his invention, insisting,
understandably enough, on a prerogative of philosophical and religious speculation, failing to understand that in his novels, and
often in his entertainments, Greene describes a human condition,

and that the experience of life developed within that condition is not necessarily representative of a religious bias. Greene himself says in a letter to Elizabeth Bowen and V. S. Pritchett:

If I may be personal, I belong to a group, the Catholic Church, which would present me with grave problems as a writer were I not saved by my disloyalty. If my conscience were as acute as M. Mauriac's showed itself to be in his essay *God and Mammon,* I could not write a line. There are leaders of the Church who regard literature as a means to an end, edification. I am not arguing that literature is amoral, but that it presents a different moral, and the personal morality of an individual is seldom identical with the morality of the group to which he belongs. You remember the black and white squares of Bishop Blougram's chess board. As a novelist, I must be allowed to write from the point of view of the black square as well as of the white: doubt and even denial must be given their chance of self-expression, or how is one freer than the Leningrad group? (31–32).

In the majority of his works, Greene creates an experience of life—to use Maritain's phrase—in which the religion of the chief actors is Roman Catholicism. As do the characters of Henry James, a writer whom he much admires, Greene's make a place for themselves within the life-experience, exciting the pity and curiosity of the reader as they move within the boundaries of a problem that often seems to admit no earthly solution. Were Greene to force his people to react to the conditions in which they find themselves as good and true Catholics, if the solution for their unhappiness were brought about in terms of religious dogma, then indeed the results would be bad art—if art at all. And it is precisely this dilemma that he addresses in his play *The Living Room* (1953). But the novelist who retains his faith as a man can be allowed a point from which to explore evil. If a novelist were to glorify good and refuse to recognize the beauty of evil, the beauty that Lucifer carried with him when he fell, if he were to attest only a religious certainty, he would be, as Greene says, "a philosopher or religious teacher of the second rank."[22]

The fact is that Greene is primarily a novelist; he is neither a theologian nor a philosopher. In his travel book *In Search of a Character,* he writes: "I would claim not to be a writer of Catholic novels, but a writer who in four or five books took characters with Catholic ideas for his material. Nonetheless for years—particularly after *The*

Heart of the Matter—I found myself hunted by people who wanted help with spiritual problems that I was incapable of giving. Not a few of these were priests themselves."[23] Greene also states in his essay on Henry James in *The Lost Childhood* that "The novelist depends preponderantly on his personal experience, the philosopher on correlating the experience of others, and the novelist's philosophy will always be a little lop-sided."[24]

Ultimately Greene concerns himself with the problems of good and evil not so much as they exist within the Catholic Church but as they exist in the great world. His novels deal primarily with fallen man; and at least two of them, *The Power and the Glory* and *The Heart of the Matter,* afford the possibility of heroic action. Although Catholicism pervades the plots of his novels, Greene is not concerned in justifying the activities of that religion. Greene chooses to deal with the seedy, the unlikable, the unhappy—those in whom he feels the strange power of God. When he does choose to work with sainthood, his work suffers, as does *The End of the Affair.* Perhaps Mauriac explains the failure when he writes in *God and Mammon:*

Why should not we portray saints just as Benson, Foggazaro, Boumann and Bernanos did—or tried to do? On the other hand it could be maintained that on this point of sanctity the novelist loses his rights, for if he tries to write a novel about sanctity he is no longer dealing purely with men, but with the action of God on men—and this may be an extremely unwise thing to try to do. On this point it seems that the novelist will always be beaten by reality, by the saints who really have lived.[25]

In his conversations with Allain, Greene, in a sense, comments on Maritain's statement concerning the "altitude" from which the artist creates: "I detach myself from my emotions at the moment of writing" (81), he says. He observes that Mauriac's loyalty to the Roman Catholic Church made him into too scrupulous a writer "in a theological rather than a moral sense" (80). Later he says, perhaps paradoxically, that he himself does not write his novels to be read but "for his own relief": "Novelists who write for a public are, in my opinion, no good: They've discovered who their readers are, and, in submitting to their judgment, they're dishing up things like short-order cooks. But a writer has to be his own judge, for his novels contain faults which he alone can discern" (115). In denying a commercial intention, Greene repeats, nevertheless, his conviction that art must be free of all obligation if it is to render justice to an experience of life, whether created to relieve doubts or neuroses or inhibiting allegiances. Of course, it must please Greene that his works are widely read and that he can live by them. He is no Kafka, who asked Max Brod to destroy his manuscripts. Whatever he says, he publishes his books, they sell, and they make for him a living doing what pleases him most.

When Greene is concerned with fallen man and the possibility of redemption, he is at his best, choosing deliberately to create his experience of life in uncharted theological waters. But at the end of the life-experience he reestablishes his direction and relocates his port. To do this Greene frequently uses a spokesman of the Church of which he is a member: the priest who comforts Louise Scobie at the end of *The Heart of the Matter,* Father Browne in *The Living Room.* These characters are not merely plot contrivances as they at first appear; rather, they reestablish ethical norms of behavior and a proper religious perspective after the passions of men have spent themselves. As in Elizabethan and Jacobean drama, order is reestablished before the reader is released. In *Hamlet* the audience leaves the theater with the knowledge of Fortinbras's confirmation of a divine chain of being in Denmark. The trick is one that Greene learned from his study of the drama, and he puts it to capital use in his melodramatic pieces.

Born in 1904, Graham Greene attended Berkhamsted School in Hertfordshire, about twenty-five miles northwest of London, where his father was a teacher. The elder Greene had left Oxford intending to become a lawyer but instead had become a schoolmaster. Later he became headmaster. The boy Graham, one of six children, hated the town and the school. To escape from the all-pervasive eyes of the school authorities, he took to solitary walks forbidden by the rules; once he ran away and hid on the common where he was found by his sister.

Of these early years, during which he flirted with suicide, taking an overdose of aspirin, playing Russian roulette, drinking chemicals, he has written poignantly in "The Lost Childhood" and "The Revolver in the Corner Cupboard," as well as in two books of autobiography, *A Sort of Life* (1971) and *Ways of Escape* (1980). In *A Sort of Life* he describes his early years with his brothers and sisters in Berkhamsted, its castle and its common dominating the land-

scape, to which he returned in *The Human Factor*. He describes his
early fear of bats, of fire, of drowning, of the witch lurking in the
linen cupboard. He describes his sister's dead pug, placed by his
nurse in his perambulator as a handy means of returning the carcass
to the house, an image that haunts *The Ministry of Fear* (1943). He
tells of his family's visits to his uncle's large house with its adjacent
walk, garden, pond and island, the setting for "Under the Garden"
(1963). And he speaks of the telegrams he once received in reverse
order, the first informing him of his father's death, the second of
his father's illness, giving rise to one of the most moving sequences
in *The Heart of the Matter*.

The relative peace and security of living with his family in the
headmaster's house ended rudely when Greene moved into the school
precincts, where the lack of privacy and the offensiveness of the
other boys upset and confused him. He took to solitary walks on
the common, reading Racine and Ruskin and the adventure books
that gave him the greatest pleasure; at least once he stole a book
from the local bookseller. Because of his unhappiness, his brother
Hugh, studying to be a doctor, suggested that he be sent to an
analyst. The Greenes chose Kenneth Richmond, who employed
Freud, Jung, and Adler eclectically to bring about his cures, relying
heavily on the interpretation of dreams. Greene schooled himself to
remember his dreams, and began to keep a dream notebook, a
practice that he has continued off and on throughout his life. Dreams
consequently figure in much of the fiction, sometimes as a means
of adding to a character's motivation, sometimes suggesting a fluid
form, as in the stories "The Root of All Evil" (1967) and "A
Discovery in the Woods" (1963). When he could not remember a
dream to please his analyst, he invented one, sometimes bringing
a pig into the narration, which may explain the pig incident in the
funniest of his short fictions, "A Shocking Accident" (1967).

At seventeen he went to Balliol College, Oxford, where the atmosphere was not so much that of *Brideshead Revisited* as of Maclean
and Philby's Cambridge. He became immersed in the literary life
of the college, editing the *Oxford Outlook,* learning to enjoy bitter
beer. Besides flirting with communism, he offered to spy for the
Germans on the French who were attempting to set up a Palatine
Republic between the Moselle and the Rhine despite the articles of
peace arranged at the end of World War I. He admits to Allain
that he has some scruples over the offer, but then adds meaningfully:

"I suppose too that every novelist has something in common with a spy: he watches, he overhears, he seeks motives and analyzes character, and in his attempt to serve literature he is unscrupulous" (143).

At the age of twenty he published his first book, *Babbling April* (1925), which he describes as a "dreadful collection of verse" (153). Knowing that he would become a writer, his family supported him tacitly in his endeavor. In 1927 he married Vivien Dayrell-Browning, a Roman Catholic; his conversion he has described in *The Lawless Roads* (1939) and *A Sort of Life* (1971). The marriage produced two children. Greene is characteristically reluctant to talk or write about his personal life. Unlike his cousin Christopher Isherwood who tells all, Greene tells little or nothing about those he has known and influenced in his life. He considers himself a private person and speaks to answer only those questions that affect his art.

In 1929 Heinemann accepted his first novel, *The Man Within,* which was well received in England but was a failure in the United States. This novel was followed by *The Name of Action* (1930) and by *Rumour at Nightfall* (1931), two works that Greene has withdrawn from his bibliography and has encouraged his readers to forget. In 1932 *Stamboul Train* was published, and Greene became a popular success. From 1935 to 1939 he was film critic for the *Spectator* and *Night and Day,* and this post may account for the use of cinematographic techniques characteristic of much of his early work. The majority of his novels have been made into films; ironically the one that he wrote with cinema effects in mind, *It's a Battlefield* (1934), has not. Greene has traveled extensively, in Africa, in Mexico, in Asia, in South America, and the observations made on these trips have been published in *Journey Without Maps* (1936), *The Lawless Roads, In Search of a Character: Two African Journals* (1961), *Ways of Escape* (1980), and *Getting to Know the General* (1984); and he has referred to his travels in the introductions to his Collected Edition as they affect the genesis of his plots and characters.

Something has been said of Greene's early preoccupation with evil, or what Kenneth Allott and Miriam Farris, his first important critics, call in their study the "divided mind." Greene himself has a great deal to say on the subject. In the revealing biographical sketch, "The Lost Childhood," he gives some indication of his precocious interest in good and evil. His early reading had been in Anthony Hope, Rider Haggard, and John Buchan, stories of violence and adventure told with gusto and emphasized by melodrama. In the writings of Haggard and Marjorie Bowen, he says, he learned that people were not all as good as Allan Quartermain nor as evil as the witch Gagool. From *The Viper of Milan* he experienced the fascination of evil, its reality, and found its place in his own life:

As for Visconti, with his beauty, his patience and his genius for evil, I had watched him pass by many a time in his black Sunday suit smelling of mothballs. His name was Carter. He exercised terror from a distance like a snowcloud over the young fields. Goodness had only once found a perfect incarnation in a human body and never will again, but evil can always find a home there. Human nature is not black and white but black and grey. I read all that in *The Viper of Milan* and I looked round and I saw that it was so.[26]

This preoccupation with evil, with what he has called the black and the grey of human life, came upon Greene as a child. His early reading determined the pattern of his writing: "Imitation after imitation of Miss Bowen's magnificent novel went into the exercise books," he says somewhat hyperbolically, "stories of sixteenth-century Italy or twelfth-century England marked with enormous brutality and a despairing romanticism. It was as if once and for all I had been supplied with a subject."[27] He writes:

religion might later explain it to me in other terms, but the pattern was already there—perfect evil walking the world where perfect good can never walk again, and only the pendulum ensures that after all in the end justice is done. Man is never satisfied, and often I have wished that my hand had not moved further than *King Solomon's Mines*. . . . What is the good of wishing? The books are always there, the moment of crisis waits, and now our children are taking down the future and opening the pages.[28]

The concern with evil was not only discovered in his reading: in both *The Lawless Roads* and *A Sort of Life* he speaks of his boyhood at his father's school in Berkhamsted. There he lived on the border— between the school dormitories and the family rooms:

One became aware of God with an intensity—time hung suspended— music lay upon the air. . . . There was no inevitability anywhere . . . faith was almost strong enough to move mountains. . . .
    And so faith came to one—shapelessly, without dogma, a presence above a croquet lawn, something associated with violence, cruelty, evil

across the way. One began to believe in heaven because one believed in hell, but for a long while it was hell only one could picture with a certain intimacy—the pitchpine partitions in dormitories where everybody was never quiet at the same time: lavatories without locks: "There, by reason of the great number of the damned, the prisoners are heaped together in their awful prison . . .": walks in pairs up the metroland roads, no solitude anywhere, at any time. The Anglican church could not supply the same intimate symbols for heaven: only a big brass eagle, an organ voluntary, "Lord dismiss us with thy blessing," the quiet croquet lawn where one had no business, the rabbit and the distant music.

Those were the primary symbols: life later altered them. . . . The Mother of God took the place of the brass eagle: one began to have a dim conception of the appalling mysteries of love moving through a ravaged world—the Curé d'Ars admitting to his mind all the impurity of a province: Péguy challenging God in the cause of the damned. It remained something one associated with misery, violence, evil, "all the torments and agonies," Rilke wrote, "wrought on scaffolds, in torture chambers, mad-houses, operating theatres, underneath vaults of bridges in late autumn. . . ."[29]

Greene has written about this period in the essay "The Revolver in the Corner Cupboard," describing his psychoanalysis as "perhaps the happiest months of my life," and of the boredom that followed upon his correctly "orientated" and "extrovert" interest in life.[30] Boredom became and remained for him a problem; his journeys to the earth's trouble spots, his taking of opium, even his writing have been for him means of evasion. His early obsessions with evil, with violence and brutality, and with the unhappy found expression in the people of his novels. He could find no meaing in the Anglican service. He found in the Catholic Church a "hint of an explanation," to use his own term, for the fears he had discovered as a child.

The pattern of melodrama, the keynote to much of Greene's work, was set by his early reading. His precocious awareness of good and evil indicated to him his own place in a moral dilemma. His conversion to Roman Catholicism seems to have been a logical step in an intellectual development; in the forms of the Roman Catholic Church he found a measure of an answer to the problems that vexed him once he left the family rooms at Berkhamsted and entered the school. The Catholic Church offered an explanation for suffering and misery, for crime and brutality; it offered a hint as to why a fifteen-year-old girl and twenty-year-old boy were found headless on a railwayline, why Irish servant girls met their lovers in ditches, and why the professional prostitute tried to keep the circulation going under her blue and powdered skin.

It only remains to consider Greene's present position vis à vis his adopted faith. Rumors from time to time have filtered through the popular press that he has lost his faith, that he has recovered his faith, that he has become an existentialist, that he has become a film actor. His accounts of his conversion suggest that he came to Roman Catholicism almost passively. In *A Sort of Life* he says that he was attracted to Catholicism because it allowed for abstract discussion, and not because it offered convincing "proofs" for the existence of God. He retells an anecdote told him by his friend Antonia White, who once asked a priest to detail for her the arguments for the existence of God, to which he replied that he had forgotten. "I have suffered from the same loss of memory," Greene writes, "I can only remember that in January of 1926 I became convinced of the probable existence of something we call God, though I now dislike that word with all its anthropomorphic associations and prefer Chardin's 'Omega Point'. . . ."[31] He rightly complains about those who have discerned in the reluctant Catholic Morin of "A Visit to Morin" (1963) aspects of his own loss of commitment, arguing, convincingly, that Morin's loss of belief reflects Querry's neuroticism in *A Burnt-Out Case* (1961) and not his own religious attachment. Yet his words to Allain echo Morin's: "Faith is above belief. Belief is founded on reason. On the whole I kept my faith while enduring long periods of disbelief. . . . My faith remains in the background, but it remains" (163).

Greene's interest in theology since his conversion has continued, a fact that he acknowledges in his author's note to *Carving a Statue*. He has moved from St. Thomas Aquinas and St. Francis de Sales, from the English theologians D'Arcy and Martindale to Teillhard de Chardin; and he reads Edward Schillebeeckx and Hans Küng, whom he considers Christian rather than Catholic theologians. He admits to Allain that reading Schillebeeckx brought about in him a reaction other than the one Schillebeeckx was looking for. He suddenly felt reviving in himself "a deep faith in the inexplicable, in the mystery of Christ's resurrection" (159).

Greene claims not to believe in hell, saying that God's justice is a mathematical consideration deriving from total knowledge: "If God exists—I'm not convinced He does—He is omniscient; if He is omniscient, I can't bring myself to imagine that a creature conceived by Him can be so evil as to merit eternal punishment. His grace must intervene at some point" (151)—which is the object of *Brighton Rock* (1938): that grace may be the thunderous wings that beat against the windscreen of the car that carries Pinkie to Peacehaven, that "between the stirrup and the ground" Pinkie may find the peace that he strives for as he lashes out at a society that he has rejected and been rejected by. And Greene confesses to Allain that he hopes that God is "still dogging my footsteps" (154). Not only does he reject hell, he also modifies the Catholic notion of purgatory: "It's what we—you and I—are living through at this moment" (22), a consideration that strongly influences the subtext of such later novels as *The Honorary Consul* (1973) and *Doctor Fischer of Geneva* (1980).

Greene admires Pope John XXXIII for having enlarged the humanistic scope of the Church, he feels that Paul VI was overly solicitous of the Curia, and he has great respect for John Paul II for his knowledge of politics and of life as it is lived, yet he criticizes his stand on the marriage of priests. In other words Roman Catholicism remains for him a point of reference, and the subtext of his art can be understood as the stances that he as controlling author takes as he observes his characters in their struggle to verify their humanity. "The writer plays God until his creatures escape him and, in their turn, they mold him," he tells Allain, adding, "It is the 'human factor' that interests me, not apologetics"(150).

Greene's present position within his Church might, consequently, be described as "semilapsed." He confesses to Allain that there was a time when he considered himself a practicing Catholic. He still attends Sunday mass, however, but no longer finds the practice comfortable: "It's no longer said in Latin; and all my education after my conversion was bound up with the mass in Latin" (161).

The essential fact is, despite the provocative nature of the propositions sketched above, that Greene is a storyteller first and last. Private concerns demand consideration from his readers only insofar as they are reflected in his texts. His chief preoccupation as an artist is still with fallen man and with the possibility of redemption. Since Greene rejects hell, it would appear that he rejects total evil. This he may do as a man, yet his characters act and live within an awareness of eternity, an awareness that produces a dialectical process in the novels frequently charted by the device of flight and pursuit as his characters vacillate between the extremes of good and evil, right and wrong.

So convincingly does Greene portray the difficulties of his characters to determine and verify their humanity that readers comment on them as though they are living beings. In just such a manner spectators have diagnosed for centuries the madness of Hamlet, while rivers of scholarly ink have been spilled in pursuit of a better understanding of his psychology, his times, and his ethics. The whiskey priest and Major Scobie and Sarah Miles and Eduardo Plarr are such characters. The confusion, both critical and private, that arises is based quite simply on the fact that their predicaments are so very human and so completely believable. Indeed Greene has contributed a remarkable gallery of mythic characters to the realm of literature.

Chapter Two
The Entertaining Mr. Greene

> "By melodrama I mean a
> measure of violence in the
> action"

When asked by Marie-Françoise Allain about the differences between his entertainments and novels, Greene replied that he had established the distinction in the thirties to satisfy his publisher, to make money for his growing family, and to avoid as much as possible the taint of melodrama in any novel that might follow. Parenthetically he added that he no longer considered melodrama "all that baneful" (140), and in the introduction to *A Gun for Sale* in the newly Collected Edition he humorously admits to having failed in subduing it in the novels from *Brighton Rock* to *The Comedians*.[1]

Greene's entertainments, chiefly *Stamboul Train* (1932), *A Gun for Sale* (1936), *The Confidential Agent* (1939), and *The Ministry of Fear* were primarily conceived as thrillers in the manner of John Buchan's *The Thirty-Nine Steps* (1915), a work Greene much admired. Following the composition of *The Ministry of Fear,* he told Allain, the novels and entertainments so came to resemble one another that the categorization no longer seemed relevant. The element of melodrama, common to both the entertainments and the novels, was to some extent justified as well as undercut by the more-than-melodramatic events of World War II, during which time Greene served his country actively as a member of the Colonial Office in Freetown, W. Africa. With the publication of *Travels with My Aunt* (1970) he formally abandoned the dichotomy "for it served no further purpose" (Allain, 140).

Brighton Rock, which appeared in 1938 on the eve of the war, began in Greene's mind as a thriller, but the work moved in quite a different direction and was finally called a novel. *Brighton Rock* in fact marks a dividing point, and the characteristics that at first distinguished the two categories, as Greene observes, became less apparent as other books appeared. In *The Man Within,* his first novel, Greene had demonstrated an interest in the divided self. The epigraph from Sir Thomas Browne, "There's another man within me that's angry with me," indicated his preoccupation with the problems of good and evil. In this novel Greene followed his protagonist, Andrews, from his boys' school onto a smuggling vessel where his father had been respected because of his strength and courage, and into a betrayal of Carlyon, his friend, the leader of the smugglers. In a foggy wood, reminiscent of Dante in the *Inferno,* the boy had come upon goodness—Elizabeth, the girl, keeping watch over the corpse of her stepfather who had been killed by the smugglers. At the end of the novel Andrews was forced to commit suicide not only for having betrayed the man within but as a way of reconciling the division in himself. From this surprisingly excellent novel, which Greene himself disparages, the reader became aware of a concern with good and evil as the gray and black of human life.

It was not until the publication of *Brighton Rock,* however, that this concern with the nature of good and evil found a frame of reference that is specifically religious. What had been before *Brighton Rock* a deeply felt religious outlook became with this novel a frame of reference within which the action developed. The novels before *Brighton Rock* had been "secular" in their outlook, those immediately following were "religious," for it was Greene's Roman Catholicism that gave coherence and meaning to the narratives. And Greene's readers and fans alike will concede the fact that the "novels" on which his reputation primarily rests afford a great deal of material that is at the very least beguilingly controversial.

But what of the entertainments? Much critical attention has been devoted to Greene the Manichaean, Greene the theologian, Greene the Jansenist, Greene the existentialist, Greene the quietist—and the list could be stretched on and on—, but somewhat less attention has been given to the nature and quality of the entertainments. Certainly they are thrillers; they lend themselves easily and brilliantly to the idioms of the motion picture, as Greene's list of credits shows; and they make money for him. Furthermore, a great many of his fans contend that the best of Greene is to be discovered in the entertainments; for in them he is intent on telling a good story, on keeping his readers in suspense, and on making the action that is, more often than not, a melodramatic chase, as original and exciting and breathtaking as possible. That Greene is a consummate

storyteller and that he knows how to maintain that elusive factor
called suspense make him a detective story writer of the highest
caliber, the equal of Raymond Chandler, Agatha Christie, Georges
Simenon, and S. S. Van Dyne, to name a few masters of the genre.
An investigation of the nature of the entertainments reveals Greene's
craftsmanship and also points out how, very often, the entertainments are preliminary studies for the more elaborate novels that
follow them.

In the preface to the Viking edition of *The Third Man* (1950),
perhaps Greene's most popular entertainment because of its brilliant
translation into a motion picture under the direction of Sir Carol
Reed, Greene refers to the happy ending that characterizes the
thriller type. But whether or not Greene's endings are happy in the
conventional sense is a matter for satiric comment, for the endings
of his entertainments are often as pessimistic and gloomy as those
of his novels. There is one thing, however, that does specifically set
the entertainments apart from the novels: the serious preoccupation
with religious and ethical problems that the novels pose. The entertainments may indicate the problems, but these are second to
the plot, action, and melodrama that distinguish them. Evelyn
Waugh, a Catholic writer of Greene's own stature, distinguished
between Greene's novels and entertainments in this way: ". . . the
'novels' have been baptized, held deep in under the waters of life.
The author has said: 'These characters are not my creation but God's.
They have an eternal destiny. They are not merely playing a part
for the reader's amusement. They are souls whom Christ died to
save.' "[2]

In the novels from *Brighton Rock* through *The End of the Affair,*
Greene creates, for the most part, an experience of life in which the
religion of the chief actors is Roman Catholicism; in the entertainments, however, religion seems to be superstition or, as is the case
with Raven, the protagonist of *A Gun for Sale,* a sense of loss, a
feeling of inadequacy, life without justice or pity. In the novels,
Greene expends more time and energy on characterization, and his
people react as human beings to the conditions in which they find
themselves; in the entertainments, the conditions are more often
than not contrived, and causality plays an all important part in the
unraveling of the action.

It is, to be sure, interesting to speculate as to the possible theological interpretations of the actions of certain characters in certain

novels. But it is essential to remember that these characters—Scobie, Sarah Miles, and the whiskey priest—exist as constructs in an invented experience of life. Yet if Greene feels that, by portraying individuals in tragic circumstances, and rubbing the side of his religion long and often enough, he becomes an indispensable opposition in an enlargement of the human spirit, more power to him. He says, "For to render the highest justice to corruption, you have to be conscious all the time within yourself of treachery to something valuable."[3] If the novelist, who happens to be a Catholic, does not flirt with heresy—as Greene's critics say he often does—he will not be able to understand the attraction of goodness. If he glorifies good by refusing to recognize the fascination of evil, if he desires only to attest the validity of his religion, he becomes, as Greene himself has said in an essay on Henry James, "a philosopher or religious teacher of the second rank."[4] Certainly Greene is neither!

Greene, as has been already observed, is a writer with a profound sense of evil in the world, and any reader of the essays included in *The Lost Childhood* knows that he had this sense long before his conversion to Roman Catholicism. His novels deal primarily with the fall of man; his entertainments deal with man—fallen or not—primarily in his relationship to other men, not to God. " ' Do you believe in God?' " Raven asks Anne Crowder in *A Gun for Sale*. " 'I don't know,' " she says. " 'Sometimes maybe. It's a habit, praying. It doesn't do any harm. It's like crossing your fingers when you walk under a ladder. We need any luck that's going' " (149).

Although a religious sense is present in the entertainments, one might say that religion and superstition are accounted as one. There is not in them that profound religious conviction that inspires Scobie to suicide in *The Heart of the Matter* and the whiskey priest to sainthood in *The Power and the Glory*. Yet Greene's novels, although they make use of the properties of Roman Catholicism, do not attempt to throw light on the teachings of the Church. What Greene is concerned with is the possibility of salvation within the tablets of the law of the Church. In allowing for personal salvation, Greene allows for heroism; and he does this by creating his experiences of life on the dangerous edge, that is, in those uncharted theological regions where the boundaries are blurred.

In *Brighton Rock,* the frame of reference within which the narrative develops is the hero's Roman Catholicism. The novel is in the tradition of the detective story, and in it Greene used the same conventions as in the entertainments that preceded it, *Stamboul Train* and *A Gun for Sale*. In these thrillers Greene drew heavily on the atmosphere and symbols of *The Waste Land*, and the sense of degeneracy and futility of Eliot's poem pervades both. These entertainments have a "happy" ending, provided the reader accepts Greene's peculiar conviction concerning the nature of the thriller, as mentioned above.

Stamboul Train

Stamboul Train was written deliberately to please an audience and to lend itself easily to the idioms of the motion pictures. "The devil looks after his own," Greene writes in his introductory note to the work in the Collected Edition, "and I succeeded in both aims, though the film rights seemed at the time an unlikely dream, for before I had completed the book, Marlene Dietrich had appeared in *Shanghai Express,* the British had made *Rome Express,* and even the Russians had produced their railway film, *Tarksib*. My film came out last and was far and away the worst. . . ."[5]

In *Stamboul Train,* Greene used a speeding train as the locale for a melodrama that traced Carleton Myatt, a merchant of currants, and Coral Musker, a pitiful chorus girl, through an intrigue that involved murder and a Balkan uprising. Within the action Greene sketched and outlined the theme of pity he was to use with such masterful effect in the entertainment *The Ministry of Fear* (1943) and the novel *The Heart of the Matter* (1948). As film critic for the *Spectator* and *Night and Day* he had learned a great deal concerning the technique of the cinema, the importance of melodrama, and the necessity of brisk and suspenseful action. Adapting the devices of the Hitchcock movie camera to the needs of the thriller, Greene used the train with great skill: the halts and stops, the melodramatic chase in Subotica, the inquisitive newspaperwoman, the lulls, the very lurch and speed of the train—all were contained within a narrative that kept pace with the engine itself. Using the moving-picture camera technique, he moved from point to point on the speeding train, developing his theme and characters on the way, emphasizing the violence, and defining his craft.

Myatt's gratitude to Coral, once she had given herself to him, had led him to promise her an apartment of her own in Constantinople; and he had felt responsible for her safety after she had unintentionally involved herself with Dr. Czinner, the revolutionist. Myatt had attempted to rescue her but had successfully pushed his pity aside when the task proved too much for him. As a result of his betrayal, Coral had fallen into the arms of Mabel Warren, the newspaperwoman; and Janet Pardoe, Mabel's friend, into his, Greene thus completing a figure eight pattern to lend unity to the action of the novel.

Held in abeyance primarily by the demands of plot and suspense, the religious sense was primarily portrayed through the points of view of the two principal characters, Coral Musker, the unattractive and kind-hearted chorus girl whose goodness is doomed, and the idealistic socialist Dr. Czinner, who is returning to Belgrade after five years of exile in England to stand with his friends against the fascist government represented by Colonel Hartep. Aware of the futility of his gesture as the speeding train approaches Subotica, Czinner remembers his Roman Catholic upbringing, his youthful denial of a "two-faced god, a deity who comforted the poor in their distress . . . and a deity who had persuaded them, for the sake of a doubtful future, to endure their pain, as they lowered their heads . . ." (132). Yet he unaccountably seeks to confess his sins to the Anglican clergyman, Mr. Opie, who is putting together a spiritual anthology, "something to take the place in the English church of the Roman Catholic books of contemplation" (138). In her simplicity and optimism Coral anticipates Rose of *Brighton Rock* while Czinner anticipates the idealistic lieutenant of *The Power and the Glory*. Despite these and other religious implications, the prevailing temper of the book is secular.

In the introduction to *Stamboul Train* Greene admits to a few points of "academic interest," an early passion for playwriting, and a conscious contriving of key scenes. "Often these scenes," he writes, "consisted of isolating two characters. It was as though I wanted to escape from the vast liquidity of the novel and to play out the most important situation on a narrow stage where I could direct every movement of my characters. . . . I thought it might be said that I reached the logical climax of the method in *The Honorary Consul* where almost the whole story is contained in the hut in which the kidnappers have hidden their victim" (xiii). He admits also to a "distant respect" for the young author in his twenties who conceived the character of Colonel Hartep, "whom I suspect survived into the world of Aunt Augusta" (xiii).

A Gun for Sale

A Gun for Sale is a thriller, fast-paced, tightly organized, economical, and exciting. Again Greene demonstrated his dexterity in handling suspense while adapting the devices of the Hitchcock camera to his materials. Like *Stamboul Train, A Gun for Sale* contains many of the devices of the mystery story: the chase, the confession, the betrayal.

Inspired by a commission set up in the thirties to look into the private manufacture and sale of armaments and by a biography of Sir Basil Zaharoff, called the Mystery Man of Europe, with whom the munitions manufacturer Sir Marcus shares a "family resemblance," the novel is set against a political climate of impending war. Running through the action as a harbinger of things to come is the word "Ultimatum."

The protagonist of the entertainment, James Raven, is, in the Conradian tradition, an antihero; he is bitter, antisocial, and desperate—all that the traditional hero is not. Opposing Raven is a strong and determined and unimaginative detective, Mather, who is in love with Anne Crowder, who, like Coral Musker of *Stamboul Train,* is a chorus girl in second- and third-rate provincial companies. Raven has many things in common with Pinkie Brown, the chief character of *Brighton Rock*—the same sordid background, the squalor of Paradise Piece and Nelson Place, the evil that comes with poverty. Both Raven and Pinkie bear the signs of their environment: Raven, his hairlip, Pinkie, his aversion to sex. But Pinkie is a Roman Catholic, Raven is not.

A Gun for Sale is in many ways a preliminary study for *Brighton Rock.* The similarity between the two characters is explicitly made in the mutual relationship they bear to the racetrack protection rackets. The murder of "Battling" Kite, the leader of Pinkie's gang, is recounted by Raven: " 'I was doing the races then. Kite had a rival gang. There wasn't anything else to do. He tried to bump my boss off the course. . . . I cut his throat and the others held him till we were all through the barrier in a bunch' " (154). And it is revenge for Kite's murder that forms the raison d'etre of *Brighton Rock.*

The action of *A Gun for Sale* moves against the Christmas season—against the cheap religious images, "the plaster mother and child, the wise men and the shepherds"—and against the betrayal of Christ by Judas. Raven makes an association with himself and the holy family for whom there had been no room at the inn. He is angered by the fact that the myth of the birth of Christ is perpetuated by a godless nation:

Love, Charity, Patience, Humility . . . he knew all about those virtues; he'd seen what they were worth. They twisted everything: even the story in there, it was historical, it had happened, but they twisted it to their own purposes. They made him a god because they could feel fine about it all, they didn't have to consider themselves responsible for the raw deal they'd given him. He'd consented, hadn't he? That was the argument, because he could have called down "a legion of angels" if he'd wanted to escape hanging there. On your life he could, he thought with bitter lack of faith. . . . (106)

The similarity between Pinkie Brown and James Raven is their common betrayal by society and the destruction of their innocence. Raven had seen his mother cut her throat, and Pinkie had witnessed his parents' Saturday night ritual of sex. Although both the entertainment and novel use conventional religious symbolism, in *A Gun for Sale* the symbolism is subordinated to the activity of the novel whereas in *Brighton Rock* it gives emphasis to the theme and helps push the action into the dimension of religious allegory.

A Gun for Sale also moves against a background of political intrigue. Hired by a fat man, called Cholmondeley or Davis, to murder an important and humanitarian minister of a small European nation, to incite enmity between England and that nation and insure the Midland Steel empire of Cholmondeley's employer, Sir Marcus, Raven is betrayed by both Cholmondeley and Sir Marcus. Flight and pursuit structures the novel as Raven attempts to identify his betrayers. Mather, the detective engaged to marry Anne Crowder, follows the trail Raven leaves with his counterfeit money, but he does not know that Raven is the murderer whose deed is exciting the country to war. Anne Crowder, as had her predecessor Coral Musker, becomes unintentionally involved in the action, her pity for Raven leading her first to befriend him, then to help him escape the police so he can destroy Cholmondeley and Sir Marcus if necessary and, as she thinks, prevent war.

It is through Anne Crowder that the Judas theme finds its most important development in the novel. The other betrayals do not discomfit Raven, since he trusts no one. His education had taught him to put his faith in no one, particularly in a woman. He cannot understand why Anne befriends him, and he instinctively mistrusts her. Anne herself is willing to take Raven as she finds him until she learns that he is the murderer of the old minister who had dedicated his energies to the prevention of war; and, when she and Raven part, she does not hesitate to betray him to Mather. Willing to befriend him as one of the oppressed, a champion of the poor, she rejects him when she sees him as an oppressor of his class. Raven dies in the knowledge of her treachery, and he associates his betrayal with that of Christ by the Jews. He thinks of the crèche he had seen on arriving in Nottwich. Anne had said to him, " ' I'm your friend. You can trust me!' " (206). But she had deceived him.

Within the symbolic structure of the entertainment, Raven is a scapegoat; the sins of the world are loaded onto his shoulders, a fact he is resentfully aware of. But for all its religious implications, the book remains predominantly secular in its outlook. With Raven, however, Greene comes near to the religious intensity that informs the novels beginning with *Brighton Rock*. Betrayed by Anne and the world, Raven reaches out for a God he doesn't believe in. Pinkie, his successor, believes in that same God; but he has rejected him. Allott and Farris say of Greene's world, "Where there is faith, in Greene, there is the profounder sense of evil and more helpless degeneration" (110). In *A Gun for Sale,* the unforgettable Acky, the unfrocked clergyman who finds some consolation for his defection in the genuine affection he shares with his grotesque wife, exists as an aspect of evil rather than an exponent of it. Acky's marriage to the ancient procuress is the union of lust and insanity; and thus the religious note is held in abeyance.

In their attitude to God, both Anne Crowder and Raven are near to Ida Arnold of *Brighton Rock* in that their religion has degenerated into superstition. Anne crosses her fingers when walking under a ladder because she needs any luck that's going, and Ida Arnold consults her ouija board to secure the sanction she needs to avenge Fred Hale's murder. The implied religious note of *A Gun for Sale*—Raven's likening himself to Christ, the "little bastard" betrayed by Judas—becomes in *Brighton Rock* the frame of reference that informs its structure and makes it a consistent allegory on the subject of good and evil, as allegorized in the boy Pinkie and the girl Rose.

Yet the subject matter of *Brighton Rock* is presented in the same melodramatic convention; the confrontations and the coincidences still form a portion of the structure. But the chase, the confession, the betrayal, all the devices are subjected to the dominating religious motif, and it becomes an important consideration to understand why damnation is possible for Pinkie Brown. *Brighton Rock* becomes a consistent allegory on the subject of good and evil, the religious framework allowing for the allegorical interpretations. The use of the sensational and the melodramatic permits Greene to present his theme in terms compatible with his religious thesis. The detective story framework sustains and is sustained by the allegory.

Greene makes brilliant use of the images of nature in order to define good and evil in the phenomenal world. The background of Brighton and the sea at once lend reality as they form the background for the allegory; the sea is as present as it is symbolic of continuity. The amusement areas where all is flash and glitter, artifice and tinsel, love songs and rock candy afford an admirable contrast of color for the stark drama of black and white played out against them. The storm in which Pinkie dies emphasizes the spiritual turmoil of the drama, but it does not purge. It exerts its peculiar influence on the reader who agrees with the priest, Greene's spokesman, that the mercy of God is "appalling" to contemplate.

The technique of the cinema camera prepares for the climaxes as Greene moves from scenes of color to scenes of unrelieved drabness, from scenes of purposeless activity to scenes of tense inactivity— Pinkie on the bed amid the remains of his sausage roll, Pinkie looking at the woman who is saved, Ida at the race track. The cinema technique allows the reader to follow the chase, to understand the panic, to savor the suspense.

The conception of *Brighton Rock* is a brilliant one—Graham Greene at his melodramatic best. Following upon *A Gun for Sale,* it demonstrates to what an extent the religious note animates the narrative. And yet the two books are much alike. The fact that *Brighton Rock* makes use of specific religious subject matter distinguishes it from an entertainment and makes it a novel—according to the definition cited above.

In the introduction to *A Gun for Sale* in the Collected Edition, Greene readily confirms the affinity between James Raven and Pinkie Brown, conceding Raven as a Pinkie "who has aged but not grown up," adding that Raven and Pinkie are the real Peter Pans of the world, "doomed to be juvenile for a lifetime. They have something of a fallen angel about them . . . ." (viii). Greene also admits to a certain pride in the manner in which he handled the air-raid practice scenes, and for Acky and Tiny, the unfrocked clergyman and his wife, "joined to each other by a selfless love" (viii). Acky and Tiny are in fact such memorably drawn characters that they all but run away with the work.

The Confidential Agent

Published in 1939 *The Confidential Agent* is secular in outlook in much the same sense as *Stamboul Train* and *A Gun for Sale;* and it exhibits the chief characteristics of the thriller form—revenge, flight and pursuit, the haunted hero, a sense of loss, of finality. The work was written in six weeks in 1938 while Greene was writing *The Power and the Glory,* a novel that seemed to offer no financial gains at the time. He wrote the entertainment in the mornings in a rented studio while he "ground on" with the novel in the afternoons.[6] To facilitate the composition he took benzedrine. "Each day I sat down to write with no idea of what turn the plot might take," he writes in the introduction; "I think that those benzedrine weeks were more responsible than the separation of war for breaking up my marriage" (ix). *The Confidential Agent,* he admits further, is "one of the few books of mine which I have cared to reread—perhaps because it was not really one of mine. It was as though I were ghosting for another man" (viii).

Greene himself offers an adequate explanation of the feeling of strangeness and familiarity when he refers to J. W. Dunne who, in *An Experiment with Time* (1927), posited that it is sometimes possible for an individual to see into the future in either dreams or states approaching dream. In both Greene's entertainments and novels dreams frequently anticipate plot events while serving to suggest Freudian or psychological levels of motivation through a reliance on meaningful symbolism, as do the references to the dead tomcat in *The Confidential Agent.* But *The Confidential Agent* may suggest something more, that prescient awareness to which Greene confesses to Allain in the *Conversations,* illustrating again Dunne's contention that past and future time exist in present moments of awareness:

Perhaps it is just as well for an author not to reread the books he has written. There may be too many hints from an unhappy future. Why in 1938 did I write of D. listening to a radio talk on the problem of Indo-

China? . . . . Six years were to pass before the war there began and eight
more before the problem became vivid to me. . . . . (xii)

Greene's protagonist in *The Confidential Agent,* D., is a middle-
aged scholar sent by his government, presumably Spain, to negotiate
a contract with British mine owners for badly needed coal. He is
balked by counteragents and in the end is defeated by them. Although he fails to secure the coal his country needs, he has the
satisfaction of knowing that the enemy will not have it either.

In the characterization of D., Greene enlarges on the theme of
pity which he had lightly sketched in both preceding entertainments. Myatt's concern for Coral and Anne's for Raven had been
briefly outlined but had been left undeveloped in order not to intrude
upon the action. In *The Confidential Agent,* D. is presented as a
middle-aged scholar who had at one time discovered an important
manuscript of *The Song of Roland.* The war, which seems to parallel
the civil conflict in Spain, had cut short his literary activities and
forced him to devote himself to his political party. He is alone, and
the death of his wife at the hands of fascists has paralyzed his feelings.
He has nothing to hold on to, not even belief in God. And he
cannot be certain of the integrity of the cause for which he fights.
"It's no good taking a moral line—my people commit atrocities
like the others," he says to Rose Cullen (67). Like Raven and Anne
and Ida Arnold, D. is unable to trust to the God of tradition; and
again it is this secular outlook that distinguishes the world of the
entertainment.

Although he thinks he is past all feeling, D. is touched by the
mute appeal of the child, Else, and by the unhappiness of the girl,
Rose Cullen, the daughter of Lord Benditch, D.'s contact for the
coal. He finds it impossible to feel love since the death of his wife;
but he can feel pity—and pity, according to Greene, can be a
corrosive emotion. D.'s pity leads him, eventually, to a "happy"
ending; he goes off at the novel's end with Rose into an uncertain
future.

D. is aware of evil in the world, but he is passive in the face of
it until Else is killed by the manageress of the hotel in which he
lives. (D. had entrusted his identity papers to the child, and she is
murdered because she remains faithful to the trust.) Once D.'s
humanity is aroused by the brutality and senselessness of the crime,
he is no longer the pursued but the pursuer. And like Ida Arnold,

he indulges in the pleasure of revenge: ". . . If you believed in God, you could also believe that it [the body of Else] had been saved from much misery and had a finer future. You could leave punishment then to God. . . . But he hadn't that particular faith. Unless people received their deserts the world to him was chaos: he was faced with despair" (138).

D. can give himself to the chase to satisfy his sense of outraged humanity; and so long as he adheres to the world's dictum regarding right and wrong, he can allow himself the luxury of revenge, an eye for an eye, a tooth for a tooth. There is no God, so vengeance is D.'s. But in the "religious" novels the issues are much more complex since Greene is concerned with the more comprehensive problem of good and evil; right and wrong become aspects of the universal dilemma. The secular attitude is, of course, present in all the novels; but in the entertainments it is the chief focus through which Greene develops his characters and his action. And yet by subduing the religious center, Greene does not minimize the religious sense. Ultimately, in all his writings—entertainments, novels, stories, plays—the final point of reference is God.

The Confidential Agent is not so successful an entertainment as *Stamboul Train*, nor does it demonstrate the conciseness and economy of *A Gun for Sale*. And its ending seems somewhat arranged, even considering the melodramatic contrivances of the plot. Greene allows D. to escape the web of evidence that has connected him with the murder of Else, the death of K., the political intrigue in which the government is involved—and all this is done to bring about the "happy" ending which, as he wryly implies in the preface to *The Third Man*, is one of the distinguishing features of the thriller. D. is rewarded for a humanity that nothing has been able to destroy in him—nothing had been able to dry up the spring of pity which responds to the pressure of Else's appeal. The typical Greene child, precocious and sad beyond her years, Else recognizes in D. a largeness of spirit, and her appreciation of his kindness leads to her sacrifice. Her faith engenders in D. a feeling of responsibility, as had Coral's in Myatt.

The Ministry of Fear

The Confidential Agent was followed by *The Lawless Roads,* a travel book in 1939 and by *The Power and the Glory,* a novel, in 1940.

The Ministry of Fear, an entertainment, appeared in 1943, and it stands in relation to *The Heart of the Matter* much as *A Gun for Sale* does to *Brighton Rock.* Like Greene's other entertainments, it is fast-paced, melodramatic, exciting—perhaps his best. It depends on coincidence for much of its action; and, unlike *Stamboul Train* and *A Gun for Sale,* it makes use of an actual war for its mise-en-scène: London at the height of the blitz.

First conceived as a thriller in the manner of Michael Innes that would be both funny and fantastic, *The Ministry of Fear* was begun in 1941 and written while Greene served in the British Colonial Office in Freeport, Sierra Leone, West Africa. Because of the interruptions occasioned by his duties, and perhaps because of the perspective of events at home understood from a distance, the work turned out to be in some measure fantastic but in no measure funny, although Greene admits to being happy while working on the book in the country he had learned to love since he first traveled in it in the early thirties, the voyage recorded in *Journey without Maps* (1936).[7]

The title, taken from Wordsworth's *The Prelude,* refers primarily to Fifth Column activities in wartime London but, on another level, to the complexities of human involvement: "It was a Ministry as large as life to which all who loved belonged. If one loved one feared" (258). Like *The Confidential Agent* it too employs dreams to anticipate events and to characterize its guilt-haunted protagonist, Arthur Rowe; but here the dreams more clearly serve a structural purpose. Some critics have found, following a Freudian bent, that the work in several ways resembles Greene's own career. In *The Aesthetics of Exploration,* for example, Gwen Boardman holds that the novel recapitulates in its use of event and dream "a return to childhood innocence, a period of artificial adolescence, and a violent act that propels . . . to the threshold of true maturity."[8] Be that as it may, the dreams lend a surrealistic quality to the action that suits not only the theme but also adds immeasurably to the ambiance.

In *The Ministry of Fear* Greene further develops the anatomy of pity, the emotion that he will use to larger and more comprehensive effect in *The Heart of the Matter.* Although a feeling for suffering and a sensitivity to ugliness and frailty characterize both Rowe and Scobie, the demands of the thriller form subsume the element of compassion, even though it is one of the most compelling aspects of the whole. In both the entertainment and the novel pity is portrayed as a corrosive sentiment that, if allowed to develop disproportionately, creates in its advocate a sense of responsibility that at once sets him apart from his fellow beings and, paradoxically, causes him to love them the more for being apart. What separates Rowe and Scobie is the element of pride, which Scobie has in abundance but which Rowe is too humble to be aware of. Scobie is, furthermore, a Roman Catholic, Rowe is not.

It is his sense of pity that makes Rowe capable of bearing pain but equally incapable of causing hurt to others. He becomes involved in the activities of a Fifth Column organization operating in bomb-torn London, an organization that uses as its front a charity, Comforts for Mothers of the Free Nations Fund. Unwittingly and unwillingly Rowe becomes a spokesman for humanity and the opponent of a power cult, the same cult to which the lieutenant subscribes in *The Power and the Glory*.

The entertainment is divided into four parts: The first deals with Rowe, the man who killed his wife. It sets the stage for the action and portrays the trapping incident, the fete; ironically, in the cake that Rowe wins in a raffle, the spy ring has placed the microfilm of secret naval plans. The second section deals with the happy man, the Rowe who has lost the memory of his past, the awareness of the pity that has propelled him since adolescence. The third begins his reorientation—Rowe slowly rediscovers what his beliefs and convictions are, and, since he is not reacquainted with the sense of responsibility that characterized him before, he is still happy. In the fourth and last section, called "The Whole Man," Rowe returns to Anna Hilfe, the woman who loves him, in complete knowledge of his past and her attempts to safeguard him from that knowledge. To portray these stages, Greene is forced to present his action chiefly from Rowe's point of view—to arouse and maintain the suspense factor so important to the entertainments. Willi Hilfe, the representative of the cult of power, is developed from the "outside."

In *The Power and the Glory*, Greene's portrayal of the lieutenant develops the motives of the power addict, particularly his antagonism to the Roman Catholic Church and all it represents to the power state. Greene gives expression to these views in the dramatic debate at the novel's end between the whiskey priest and his antagonist. The religion of power to which the lieutenant aspires is shown to be a thing of particular beauty. Violence and brutality, in the lieutenant's philosophy, are tools necessary to secure the operation of a new dispensation that offers as its sacraments food, shelter, education. In *The Ministry of Fear*, however, Willi Hilfe, the head of the Fifth Column, and Dr. Forrester, who runs the sanitarium where Rowe is taken, are minimally characterized and their philosophy of commitment to country and ideology is merely suggested. For purposes of the plot and the surprise ending, Willi emerges at the entertainment's end as Rowe's chief antagonist. The reader discovers along with Rowe that Willi had attempted to murder his sister Anna as well as Rowe, and that he had arranged for the murder of Jones, the inept detective. The reader is asked to accept the personification of evil as it is; and he does. The action develops with speed and ingenuity; such melodramatic contrivances as a séance, a fearful sanitarium, a "Roman death" in a fashionable tailor shop, a sensational suicide in a lavatory counterpointing the suspense generated by falling bombs, the constant threat from the enemy—indeed the puzzle itself—all excuse the many irregularities of characterization.

   Pity is, however, the dominant theme of the book. Arthur Rowe had killed his wife because he could not bear to have her suffer from an incurable disease. He cannot be certain whether he killed her to free himself of her pain or to relieve her of it. The courts had found him not guilty and had released him to a life of haunted awareness. He stumbles upon a fair, drawn to it "like innocence." He is reminded of vicarage gardens and of girls in cool summer frocks; he is reminded of security. He remembers a Charlotte M. Yonge book, *The Little Duke*, and Greene ingeniously uses phrases from it as epigraphs to set the mood of his chapters. The fair allows Rowe to set aside temporarily the misfortunes of twenty years that have taught him, a man "with a too sensitive mouth," to love too well: "People could always get things out of him by wanting them enough: it broke his precarious calm to feel that people suffered. Then he would do anything for them. Anything" (17). The pity that Rowe feels for ugliness and misfortune makes him a bondsman of his emotion. At a cry of unhappiness or alarm he is ready to commit himself to any course of action. He has a sense of God, but it is undefined. As a boy he had been taught to believe, but somehow he had lost his childhood faith, preferring to depend on his own feelings for assurance of love. But his own feelings exaggerate the sense of pity and make of him a victim to those who appeal to him.

   The religious sense is, perhaps, more explicitly portrayed in *The Ministry of Fear* than in Greene's other entertainments: for Rowe's sense of the loss of innocence is, inexplicably to him, somehow a sense of the loss of God:

Listening Rowe thought, as he so often did, that you couldn't take such an odd world seriously; though all the time he did, in fact, take it with a mortal seriousness. The grand names stood permanently like statues in his mind: names like Justice and Retribution. . . . But of course if you believed in God—and the Devil—the thing wasn't quite so comic. Because the devil—and God too—had always used comic people, futile people, little suburban natures and the maimed and warped to serve his purposes. When God used them you talked emptily of Nobility, and when the devil used them of Wickedness, but the material was only dull shabby human mediocrity in either case. (30)

This passage speaks pointedly to what is more often intimated: why Greene peoples his novels with the seedy, the unhappy, with "dull shabby human mediocrity," a world that, to Greene's dismay, has been called "Greeneland."

With the betrayal of childhood innocence comes the knowledge of the phenomenal world, and the Wordsworthian theme—"the clouds of glory"—is developed. Aware only of "simplicities," a child does not understand the sense of pity that occasionally overtakes him, as it had overtaken the boy Rowe when he had killed the rat to keep it from suffering, one of his earliest memories. The child, in Wordsworthian idiom, becomes father of the man. For Rowe the man is Arthur the boy; the boy had killed the rat, the man his wife. With his loss of innocence had come the realization that humanity cannot be loved in the abstract; only men and women can be loved. And this is the lesson that the whiskey priest learns in *The Power and the Glory* and that Beatrice in *Our Man in Havana* gives voice to.

The Arcadian interlude in the sanitarium after Rowe's memory has been lost becomes for him a period of reorientation into the world. The door between the ward where Rowe is being cared for and the part of the sanitarium where the "dangerous" patients are kept becomes symbolical of the past and the present, of responsibility and freedom, of illusion and reality. He rediscovers once through the door the idyl of his childhood, but he also discovers the necessity of love—its inevitability. If one loves men and women, Rowe remembers, then it becomes necessary to love and hate as they do, "and if that were the end of everything suffer damnation with them"

(150). Rowe's love for Anna Hilfe, his betrayer's sister, leads him inevitably toward suffering, loss, and despair. The sense of pity finds its man at the entertainment's end, and it is still the corrosive influence it had always been. The commentary on the theme is made by Prentice, the man from Scotland Yard: "Pity is a terrible thing. People talk about the passion of love. Pity is the worst passion of all: we don't outlive it like sex" (200).

Rowe's passionate pity is indeed, as is Scobie's, a form of egotism, for it insists that the individual assume responsibility for his fellow man without consulting God. It implies a lack of trust and of faith, but in *The Ministry of Fear* this point is left unexplored, since the book exhibits the characteristics of the entertainments. In *The Heart of the Matter,* this theme of necessity becomes more explicit. Both Rowe's and Scobie's responsibility for and concern with unhappiness characterize them to such an extent that they become, paradoxically, humble men, bondsmen to those they love. The parallel drawn with Christ is implicit. Major Scobie, like Arthur Rowe, is defined by his pity; but as a Roman Catholic, he is aware of God in the world. And it is religious conviction that distinguishes *The Heart of the Matter* from *The Ministry of Fear:* What in the entertainment is a religious sense becomes in the novel a religious theme.

The Third Man

Greene's next entertainment, *The Third Man,* was written in 1950 for the motion pictures. In the preface to the Viking edition, he explains that, before he could write a script for Alexander Korda and Carol Reed, he had first of all to develop the line of his story's action. *The Third Man,* never intended for publication, is the result. Greene admits that the motion picture is better than the story "because it is in this case the finished state of the story," an admission not wholly accurate.[9]

The Third Man contains in brief many of Greene's favorite themes. The entertainment describes the penicillin racket in Vienna immediately after World War II. Harry Lime, the black marketeer, summons his friend Rollo Martins, a writer of Western adventure stories, to describe the occupation of the city for the agency Lime runs; but Rollo arrives instead in time for Harry's funeral. He comes to suspect that Harry has been murdered, and he refuses to accept Colonel Calloway's explanation that Lime was implicated in the

rackets. Investigating for himself, Martins meets Harry's friends and
Anna Schmidt, his mistress. He learns from Harry's neighbor that
three men had carried the body to the pavement on the night that
Harry had been run over by a truck, but the police can account for
only two. The action of the entertainment depends on Rollo's finding
the third man.

Vienna under the four-power occupation allows Greene the opportunity to develop many of *The Waste Land's* images. The city
itself is reminiscent of Eliot's Unreal City, and the title of the book
owes as much to Eliot as it does to the Bible:

> Who is the third who walks always beside you?
> When I count, there are only you and I together
> But when I look ahead up the white road
> There is always another one walking beside you
> Gliding wrapt in a brown mantle, hooded
> I do not know whether a man or a woman
> —But who is that on the other side of you?[10]

The biblical reference, in the twenty-fifth chapter of Luke, is, of
course, to the travelers to Emmaus. They are accompanied on their
journey by a third man, and that man is Christ. In *The Third Man*,
the shadowy figure is ostensibly Harry Lime; symbolically, however,
it is Christ who accompanies Rollo Martins in his search, or rather
his sense of justice. Keeping one step ahead of the police, Lime had
falsified his death. So Rollo, looking for Harry's murderer, looks
for Harry. In his search he discovers that the man "he has hero-
worshipped now for twenty-five years, since the first meeting in a
grim school corridor with a cracked bell ringing for prayers," is, in
reality, a Peter Pan who has somewhere, somehow, replaced the
innocence of childhood with the evil of maturity (80).

The search motif in *The Third Man* parallels that in Greene's other
works—it is jointly a search of recognition and a search for meaning.
Once he realizes that Harry by selling adulterated penicillin causes
more suffering to those who already suffer, Rollo becomes the aggressor. The third man whom he seeks in reality accompanies him.
Such religious implications are, however, subdued, held in check
by the more important demands of the puzzle and the melodrama,
but they appear nevertheless. Both Harry and Rollo are ostensibly
Catholics, although they wear their religion with greater noncha-

lance than do other of Greene's characters. Their faith becomes important in the final action of the story, for Rollo's pity overwhelms his sense of justice, and he kills Harry rather than allow him to endure pain.

Within the pattern of the entertainment Lime is the exponent of the cult of power. In dealing in black-market goods, he not only puts himself above the law but presumes to judge individual humanity. Lime says to Rollo: "It's the fashion. In these days, old man, nobody thinks in terms of human beings. Governments don't, so why should we? They talk of the people and the proletariat, and I talk of mugs. It's the same thing. They have their five-year plans and so have I" (105). Gavin Lambert suggests that Lime, "with his schoolboy's criminal pride," sees himself "as the most honest person in a corrupt society," denying an essential fact of the characterization: that Lime has been brought up a Roman Catholic and, in Greene's world, this means quite simply that he knows better.[11]

One of the aspects of the entertainment's technique that has disturbed Greene's readers and critics is his use of Colonel Calloway, the Scotland Yard detective in charge of the British contingent in occupied Vienna, as narrator. Peter Wolfe has astutely observed in his study of Greene's entertainments that the first-person narration may simply be Greene getting into practice for the larger demands that point of view will entail in *The End of the Affair,* and then states that Calloway's observations make up in "clarity and judgement" what they lack in action.[12] *The Third Man* does in fact begin as a conversation or *récit* between Calloway and a shadowy listener first addressed as "you," suggesting by this beginning Ford Madox Ford's *The Good Soldier.* There is also an echo of Ford's opening sentence in the line, "If you are to understand this strange, rather sad story you must have an impression at least of the background . . . ." (12). The result is to transform Calloway into a narrator whose reliability is suspect; the reader is consequently alerted to interpret the truth of the events for himself. As Calloway reconstructs the events, he presents himself as something of a psychologist as he points out the mixture of romanticist and realist that he detects in Rollo. Later he details Rollo's amateurish but effective methods of detection, which in some ways are superior to his. The reader soon understands that Martins represents the spirit of the law and that Calloway, who should see himself only as the letter of the law, is part romantic himself. The two in fact connive at the story's end in an action that Calloway feels the need to justify: he chooses to forget "that bit" about Rollo putting a bullet through his friend Harry, whose final words Rollo has interpreted as "some sort of act of contrition, however inadequate" (116). The listener, referred to first as "you" and later as "reader," may be yet another third man whose compassionate understanding is being solicited. Thus the entertainment's religious sense is subtly extended to implicate the reader in its presentation of human justice and divine grace.

It would be unfair to condemn *The Third Man* as an inferior production. It is simple, economical, austere. If, as an entertainment, it does not measure up to the standard of Greene's earlier works, it must be remembered that the final version of the story is, as Greene says, the motion picture. The city of Vienna, its bombed-out houses, its sewers "a cavernous land of waterfalls and rushing rivers, where tides ebb and flow as in the world above" (148), indeed the region of the dead, formed a most suitable background for the portrayal of the Greene themes. The black and white photography and the strange music of the zither combined to make a strikingly excellent entertainment. The cogency of the themes found commensurate exposition in the visual techniques of the camera. And one can only say that "the finished state of the story" is as successful as any other Greene entertainment.

Loser Takes All

The End of the Affair, a novel published in 1951 following *The Third Man,* demonstrates Greene's growing concern with the craft of fiction. The melodramatic contrivances of *Brighton Rock* and the entertainments and the dramatic technique of *The Power and the Glory* and *The Heart of the Matter* are replaced by devices more consistent within the forms of the modern novel: the unreliable narrator, stream-of-consciousness, the time shift, the diary to explain motivation, the interior reverie, and the spiritual debate—all are used with extreme discretion as Greene tells his story about Sarah Miles, a woman who finds God and, possibly, sainthood. *The End of the Affair* is perhaps Greene's best constructed novel, although it may not be his most successful. It was followed by *The Living Room,* a drama, in 1953, and by *Loser Takes All,* an entertainment, in 1955. Like *The Third Man, Loser Takes All* was originally written for the films, but it is a far cry from the other entertainments.

In his introduction to the work Greene explains that he had just completed *The Quiet American* and was in the mood for an escape from the excesses of a politicized world. He planned *Loser Takes All* as an "amusing, agreeably sentimental *nouvelle*—something which neither my friends nor my enemies would expect."[13] The character of Dreuther was based directly on Greene's friend Alexander Korda, with whom he had worked on the films *The Fallen Idol* and *The Third Man*. Korda suggested the plot and Greene even appropriated scraps of Korda's conversation for dialogue.

Slight, easy-going, entertaining, *Loser Takes All* is a first-person account of a Monte Carlo honeymoon. A middle-aged accountant husband, Bertram, narrates how he and his bride Cary are invited by his employer, the Gom—short for Grand Old Man—to be his guests during their honeymoon. The Gom forgets to show up, and Bertram is forced to invent a system at roulette in order to live while waiting. The system works, and he becomes a comparatively wealthy man. He then pledges his winnings against a share of his company's holdings held by an important stockholder of his firm who is short of funds while trying his own system at the roulette tables. Bertram almost loses his bride, but he wisely chooses to lose the fortune he has won and to keep his wife. The Gom finally sails into the harbor in time to tell Bertram how to get back his wife, thus suggesting a God figure.

Loser Takes All is perhaps more a long story, lacking as it does the depth and flow of the early entertainments and novels. Nevertheless, it is important in the Greene oeuvre because it demonstrates that Greene can be lighthearted if he likes and can develop a theme that is primarily comic if he wants. Those expecting the intense gloom and pessimism of early Greene will be disappointed, for *Loser Takes All* and its successor entertainment, *Our Man in Havana* (1958), are both lighthearted and witty. And they are excellently done, for Greene is above all a craftsman of distinction. In many ways both entertainments look forward to one of Greene's sunniest books, *Travels with My Aunt* (1969).

There are in *Loser Takes All* mischievous comments on religious belief, on greed, on ambition, on the Trinity, on those who sell systems and those who play roulette with the same dedication that devils and theologians expend on human souls. But all such remarks are moderated by an overreaching charity and humor. Indeed Bertram emerges by the entertainment's end as one of Greene's most sensitive and sensible protagonists. What ultimately distinguishes the work is its enthusiastic insistence on the loving heart to give meaning and beauty to the mundane activities of life. Bertram decides not to gain the whole world but to accept gratefully the loving kindness of his childlike wife and perhaps thereby to save his soul. The first-person narration, kept in check by the lightness of the tale's sentiment, adds both charm and poignancy to the action.

Our Man in Havana

The idea for *Our Man in Havana,* a Secret Service comedy, first came to Greene when film director Alberto Cavalcanti asked him to write a movie script. The events of the comedy were originally set in Tallinn, the capital of Estonia, and the protagonist at first had nothing whatsoever to do with vacuum cleaners. The film venture came to nothing, but the plot remained in Greene's mind. When several years later he went to Cuba in the final stages of Batista's regime, he knew he had found the proper milieu for his thriller.[14]

Published in 1958, *Our Man in Havana* was for many of Greene's readers a blessed relief from the high seriousness that pervaded so much of his earlier work, apart from the slighter *Loser Takes All.* The entertainment is, among other things, a delightful satire with a serious edge, a complete change of pace for the artist, significant in that it illustrates the range of his creativity while offering the reader a thoughtful look at a flair for comedy latent in the earlier novels and entertainments and barely perceptible in a few of the stories. The irony, sometimes heavy-handed in earlier works, is apparent here, but it is controlled by the tone and intention of the whole.

Our Man in Havana is like the other entertainments: an economical, tightly constructed, exciting satire on the exploits of the British Secret Service abroad. But, unlike the other entertainments, it is amusing, witty; in short, entertaining. Chief agent for Phastcleaner vacuum cleaners, Jim Wormold, whose name is descriptive of his character as are those of other Greene characters, is one of the commercially unsuccessful, a group of people whom Greene dearly loves. Middle-aged, walking with a limp, early deserted by a beautiful wife but blessed with a beautiful daughter whom he has prom-

ised to bring up a Roman Catholic, although he himself has no
formal religion, Wormold finds his position in Havana difficult but
not impossible.

His chief difficulty is economic, for his daughter Milly has expensive tastes. She prays to her patron saints and makes novenas for
what she wants, and she usually succeeds, since Wormold can deny
her nothing. He feels that there is something theologically wrong
with her methods, but he is too kindly to remonstrate; and Milly
points out to him time on time that he is an "invincibly ignorant"
Protestant. Wormold solves his financial difficulties by becoming
a reluctant spy for the British Secret Service: he invents agents,
takes their names from the Country Club registry, and by borrowing
for them and for himself against an expense account manages to
secure Milly's future. Unaccountably Wormold's creations spring
to life, and he is forced to a reckoning. By fabricating facts and
passing them off as secret data, Wormold brings about the deaths
of a young aviator and his friend, Dr. Hasselbacher. A sense of guilt
leads him to avenge their deaths; and, luckily for him, he succeeds
without being technically responsible for the death of the counterspy
Carter, a name that hearkens back to Greene's dormitory days at
Berkhamsted school. Deported from Havana and back in London,
his exploits now known by his employers, Wormold wonders what
is to be done with him, for legally he is not guilty of espionage—
all his information had been invented and his one actual attempt
at espionage has proved a failure. To his embarrassment the Secret
Service presents him with a medal and makes him a temporary
instructor in the espionage school, an ironic reward for his bungling.

Anyone looking for deep philosophical and religious meaning in
Our Man in Havana will be disappointed, for Greene does nothing
more in the entertainment than entertain. The satire and the ease
with which he moves into the field of comedy make *Our Man in
Havana* significant within the oeuvre, and as an entertainment it
gains and fails as his previous efforts have gained and failed—it is
short in characterization but long in incident and detail. Nevertheless, Greene's criticism of the contemporary political scene is as
intelligent as ever it was in such early novels of social commentary
as *England Made Me* (1935) and *It's a Battlefield,* and it is tinged
with that pessimism and melancholy that the reader has come to
identify as a characteristic aspect of the Greene universe. He pokes

fun at stupid, bureaucratic procedure and—indirectly and rather amusedly—at the heavy-handed irony of some of his earlier efforts. He criticizes the atomic age: Hasselbacher says, "We none of us have a great expectation of life nowadays, so why worry? . . . Push a button—pff bang—where are we?" (3). And again Hasselbacher says, "You should dream more, Mr. Wormold. Reality in our century is not something to be faced" (5). Beatrice, Wormold's secretary says, "The world is modelled after the popular magazines nowadays" (5). So it is no wonder that Wormold models his espionage activities on *The Boy's Own World* as well as on the comic strip adventures of any number of paper heroes. All one need do is turn on a television set to see the truth of Greene's observations. Wormold reasons that if one must play a child's game, he might as well play it all the way.

Wiser than a child, however, Wormold remembers that, when he plays games with Milly, she invariably requires her money back. And, in such seemingly artless comments as these, Greene suggests, haltingly and tentatively, where before he had done so somewhat belligerently and dogmatically, the ultimate responsibilities of the individual. It is the epigraph that gives the reader the clue to the characterization: "And the sad man is cock of all his jests." Melancholy, concerned over his daughter's future, Wormold remains true to an ideal, his feeling for the beautiful child. His secretary Beatrice, who grows to love him, voices the entertainment's theme when she says, "I don't care a damn about men who are loyal to the people who pay them, to organizations. . . . I don't think even my country means that much. There are many countries in our blood—aren't there?—but only one person. Would the world be in the mess it is if we were loyal to love and not to countries?" (209). Butt of all his own jests, Wormold learns that simple loyalty to any one person is not enough, that ultimately loyalty must be given to an ideal stronger than an individual. If *Our Man in Havana* had been a novel rather than an entertainment, it might perhaps have exploited this consideration. And the character of Wormold would have been drawn more from within than from without. But this criticism is unfair; for the reader must concede that *Our Man in Havana* is exactly what Greene intends it to be—an entertainment that is in fact entertaining.

Travels with My Aunt

With *Travels with My Aunt* in 1969 Greene took formal leave of
the category he had devised for financial as well as artistic reasons,
a leavetaking mourned not only by those readers who feel that the
best of Greene is to be discovered in these inventive and suspenseful
works but also by those who find the religious importunities of the
novels burdensome and enervating. Picaresque in form, *Travels with
My Aunt* makes use once again of the motif of flight and pursuit,
portrays the relationship of the older man and the child-woman
that, by the fifties, had become a staple in Greene's works, and
continues the frontier or dividing line as a standard symbol. Unlike
Our Man in Havana which, for all of its comic inventions and witty
dialogue, carefully moderated between farce and seriousness within
the precincts of the thriller, *Travels with My Aunt* succeeds in arous-
ing laughter by evoking character before presenting situation. The
reader becomes immediately aware that the narrator-protagonist
Henry Pulling will somehow succeed in finding his grail once the
irrepressible Augusta appears at her sister's cremation at Golder's
Green. A man-child, made redundant by his banking employers,
content in his bachelor rut while growing dahlias and tentatively
courting a spinster, Pulling is yanked by his aunt into a series of
intrigues which first bewilder, then amuse him as they intrigue the
reader. *Travels with My Aunt* is, along with *Monsignor Quixote* (1982),
one of the, if not the, most optimistic of Greene's works, and
Augusta one of his most successfully drawn women characters.

In his introduction to *In Search of a Character,* the journal of two
of his African voyages, Greene wrote that because the composition
of the novel *A Burnt-Out Case* had proved "recalcitrant" and "de-
pressing" he felt another beyond his powers (ISC, xiii). The depression that he experienced after living for eighteen months with the
character he called Querry was exacerbated, he later explained, by
the pneumonia that he developed in Moscow, a suspicion of lung
cancer, and "a difficult decision in my private life" which caused
him to leave England in 1966 and settle permanently in France.
Greene swung from depression into what he terms a "manic condition" with the composition of the short stories in *May We Borrow
Your Husband?* (1967), a condition that persisted through the composition of *Travels with My Aunt,* "the only book I have written for
the fun of it." Greene identifies the entertainment's theme in *Ways*

of Escape (1980) as "old age and death."[15] The character of Aunt Augusta was based on that of Greene's friend, Dottoressa Moor of Capri, whose memoirs, *An Impossible Woman,* he edited in 1975, and "whose quality of passionate living he discovered in no other woman."[16]

Quoting a Swedish critic who described the novel as "laughter in the shadow of the gallows," Greene claims to have experienced more laughter than shadow during the work's composition, a fact that immediately communicates itself to the reader (*Ways,* 296–97). The entertainment is, as Greene admits, full of private jokes "which no reader would understand," but it is also full of self-referential and literary jokes which any careful reader of his novels would immediately catch. He readily admits, for example, to using the name Visconti after Marjorie Bowen's character in *The Viper of Milan* "which I loved as a boy," and to an innocent pleasure in letting his detective, John Sparrow, describe Visconti as a "viper" (*Ways,* 297). There are scenes set in Brighton reminiscent of *Brighton Rock,* on a speeding train reminiscent of *Stamboul Train,* in a posh hotel reminiscent of *The Comedians.*

To this are added light-hearted, whimsical jokes, new to Greene and a delight to his readers. The search for a father, implicit in such novels as *The Man Within* and *Brighton Rock,* is here counterpointed by Henry Pulling's acceptance of Augusta as his mother. Augusta prods the reader, ever-so-slightly, to think of St. Augustine who prayed that goodness overtake him but not too quickly; and Angelica of the angelic doctor Thomas Aquinas, who constantly refined his moral dicta. There is even a mischievous parodic suggestion of a virgin birth: Angelica suitably pads herself to simulate a nine-months' pregnancy in order to lay full claim to Henry, her sister's son. But Henry is no redeemer, no Christ figure; rather he is Peter Pan, a retarded adolescent on a yearned-for quest, pulled between the two kinds of love symbolized by his mother and his aunt.

What is most remarkable about the entertainment, because of and yet beyond its quixotic adventuring, is its vindication of a loving heart. In *The Comedians* Brown's mother, an "accomplished comedian," had asked her young lover Marcel to pretend to die for love;[17] in *Travels with My Aunt,* Wordsworth, Augusta's young black lover in fact dies for love of her: "I thought," Henry Pulling thinks after discovering Wordsworth's body behind the house he lives in with

Augusta and Visconti, "how his bizarre love for an old woman had taken him . . . to die on the wet grass near the Paraguay, but I knew that if this was the price he had to pay, he would have paid it gladly. He was a romantic, and in the only form of poetry he knew, the poetry he had learned at St. George's Cathedral, Freetown, he would have found the right words to express his love and his death."[18] Soon after this insight he addresses his Aunt Augusta as "Mother," acknowledging what he has learned from Wordsworth and from her.

The references to the "dreadful hollow" behind the "little wood" do more than call forth the reader's memory of the betrayal of love and the madness that the protagonist of Tennyson's *Maud* had discovered there; they in fact tell the reader that Henry Pulling has emerged in middle life from a Dantean wood of error to discover the truth of his emotion for his mother. The reference to Browning's *Pippa Passes,* "God's in his heaven— / All's right with the world!" presented with minimal irony, confirms the validity of the emotion he discovers. Henry is pulled from his English rose garden where he planned to place his "mother's" ashes, suitably urned, into European and South American adventures and intrigues, where his grail is his admission of his love for his mother. He is also rewarded with a marriage to his Dulcinea, Maria, the very young daughter of the chief of customs.

Conclusion

Very often what the novels lose, the entertainments gain: movement and space, a feeling of power and imagination. But as often the novels gain what the entertainments lack: a deep insight into those dark corners of behavior that Greene loves to uncover, even if uncovering involves for many of his readers a questioning of the beliefs of his faith. The strengths as well as the weaknesses of Greene's entertainments and novels can in fact be attributed to the human skepticism he communicates concerning the eschatological core of his Roman Catholicism. In the entertainments this skepticism is largely subsumed by the demands of the form within which it is presented. In the novels it frequently serves as the controlling notion whereby the characterization and action are developed. What in the entertainments is a religious sense becomes in the novels a religious theme.

Ultimately Greene is important for the scope and originality of those novels that have provoked critics and readers alike into philosophical and religious arguments. As has already been pointed out, Greene is primarily a creative writer who happens to be a Catholic, not a Catholic writer. The fact that he uses his Roman Catholicism as background for the action of many of his books is, however, important to an objective appreciation of his artistry. The entertainments are not the thought-provoking documents that the novels are, but they are remarkable in themselves and, in addition, throw light on the meanings and techniques of the more controversial works. Above all, they are first rate in their genre, books that any writer of thrillers or light fiction would be proud to have written. And they demonstrate, above all, the versatility of the writer—his many parts, to use the Elizabethan expression. No wonder then that Greene is thought by many to be one of the greatest writers of our language.

Chapter Three

The Early Work

The Man Within

The Man Within was Greene's third novel, but the first to find a publisher. In his introductory note to the volume in the Collected Edition he says that he should perhaps have suppressed the book, as he later suppressed *The Name of Action* and *Rumour at Nightfall,* "but it would be a little absurd," he continues, "to begin a collected edition with my fourth published novel, *Stamboul Train,* which I hardly rate much higher."[1] The work received the favorable notice of Aldous Huxley, who preferred it to Virginia Woolf's *Orlando,* which was published the same year, and brought him "the rather frightening friendship of Lady Ottoline Morrell"; it was later included by Jacques Maritain in a group of novels along with one of Julien Green's (x).

It is not difficult to understand why *The Man Within* caught Huxley and Lady Ottoline's attention, for it is a far better novel than Greene is willing to admit, indicating in many ways the directions he would take in subsequent works. The divided self, the soured innocence, the device of flight and pursuit, the symbol of the dividing line or boundary, the need to allegorize the gray area between the absolutes of good and evil as a condition of human existence—all the staples of what critics and admirers have come to call Greeneland are apparent in the tale.

Vaguely historical in outline, in some ways reminiscent of Conrad's *The Arrow of Gold* (1919), *The Man Within* portrays the divided psyche of its protagonist, a young and unhappy schoolboy called Andrews. The girl Elizabeth comes to represent idealism in the world and the prostitute Lucy the demands of his animal self. The theme of betrayal, for Andrews betrays both his friend Carolyn and Elizabeth, formulates the design of the novel as the action is presented primarily from the point of view of the fleeing boy. After Elizabeth's death, Andrews changes from pursued to pursuer, reversing the motif of flight and pursuit in what will soon become for Greene a characteristic plot mechanism. Andrews's suicide at the novel's end becomes paradoxically his triumph over the division in his character.

It's a Battlefield

Greene's success with *The Man Within* had brought him to the attention of Ottoline Morell, whom he then used as a model for Lady Caroline Bury in *It's a Battlefield*. Surrogate, the Communist dilettante, was based on his "idea" of John Middleton Murry, "whom I did not personally know," and his uncle Graham Greene "lent a little of his stiff inhibited bachelor integrity to the character of the Assistant Commissioner."[2] The character of the assistant commissioner also demonstrates the influence of Conrad's *The Secret Agent* (1907) whose assistant commissioner has an exotic background not too different from Greene's character. And Conrad Drover, the unhappy lover of his brother Jim's wife Milly, the reader is told, is named Conrad "after a seaman, a merchant officer" who once lodged in his parents' house (128). The city of London, as in Conrad's novel, serves more than the function of setting; it becomes a symbolical terrain upon which the various emotional, political, and ethical skirmishes are fought and, to some extent, serves as an ethical yardstick.

Published in 1934, *It's a Battlefield* is a departure in both mood and purpose from *The Man Within,* but not in theme—betrayal and responsibility. In order to emphasize the spiritual dilemma of the fleeing boy, Greene had kept the backgrounds of *The Man Within* foggy; *It's a Battlefield* is modern in setting and sociological in intention, allowing Greene sufficient latitude to portray ironically and, to a certain extent, satirically twentieth-century institutions and attitudes.

It's a Battlefield has as its central metaphor the battlefield. The epigraph describes an actual battle, "each separate gathering of English soldiery . . . fighting its own little battle in happy and advantageous ignorance of the action; nay, even very often in ignorance of the fact that any great conflict was raging." To Greene the battlefield is the world of human affairs in which God figures very little or not at all. Both Lady Caroline Bury and the assistant commissioner of police dream of the millennium, yet both are too realistic to believe it near at hand. The battlefield is also the world of human emotions where betrayal and greatness are found next to each other. This world is depicted in the reactions of the several characters to the imprisonment and impending execution, or reprieve of that execution, of Jim Drover who, in the heat of a Communist rally, had killed a policeman while protecting his wife, Milly. The action of the novel is presented through the points of view of the characters whose lives are directly and indirectly affected by the question of justice to Drover.

First there is the assistant commissioner, interested only in facts, in this respect anticipating the lieutenant of *The Power and the Glory*. The assistant commissioner believes that justice, morality, and politics are not his concern in the battlefield, in this respect differing from the lieutenant. Asked to investigate public reaction to the execution of Jim Drover, the assistant commissioner concludes that the execution will in no way affect the popularity of the government in power. Opposed to the assistant commissioner, whose very inarticulateness becomes ironically emblematic of his rationalistic attitude, is Lady Caroline Bury, whose interference in the Drover case is prompted as much by humanitarian instincts as by an unwillingness to admit pain and suffering. "I'm frightened of pain," she says. "I've never been able to stand pain" (202–3). Her concern leads her to suggest that the minister who is responsible for Drover might not be above bribery.

Ironically, Lady Caroline and the assistant commissioner are the two spectators who are best equipped to see into the real issues underlying Drover's predicament: social injustice and hypocrisy. In the act of making her will as she speaks to the assistant commissioner on Drover's behalf, she concludes that she cannot leave her considerable wealth to the state "as it's run at the present" (203). Lady Caroline is sustained by a vague faith, as her friend the assistant commissioner is not; ironically, they who represent intelligence and humanitarianism part without warmth.

Those who would be most affected by Drover's execution are his wife and his brother Conrad. Should Drover's death sentence be commuted, he would remain imprisoned for eighteen years. Milly, in love with her husband, would face the impossible task of remaining faithful to him; Conrad, in love with Milly, the impossible task of remaining faithful to both. The triangle relationship that will later inform the action of many of Greene's pieces determines the complexities of the plot.

Like others of Greene's heroines, Milly demonstrates a certain inept malice, her defense against the importunities of the world. She is very close to Rose Cullen of *The Confidential Agent:* "Her happiness had always been shot through with touches of malice. Her husband, contented with his job and his pay, had been the Communist; not Milly, contented with nothing but his love, suspicious of the whole world outside. She had never been able to believe that they would be left alone to enjoy each other. Her malice had been a form of defense, an appeal to other people to 'leave us alone' "(65).

She determines that if she forces the widow of the policeman Jim had killed to sign a petition asking for commutation, she will be doing something useful in her husband's cause. She proves successful, and for a brief hour enjoys the surging emotion of power. But her happiness is cut short by Conrad, Jim's "successful" brother. More out of pity than out of love, he seduces her to shield her from the horrors of life: "He felt no guilt at all; this did not harm his brother, this hopeless attempt to shield her, for she had not even been deceived; she was glad, she was grateful, she was his friend . . ." (133). The love that was to have ennobled him has in effect been prompted by compassion: "They had been driven to it, and holding her body close to him with painful tenderness, it was hate he chiefly felt, hate of Jim, of a director's nephew, of two men laughing in Piccadilly" (133–34). Conrad buys a second-hand pistol and sets about tracking the assistant commissioner. Ironically, the pistol is loaded with blanks, and Conrad is run down by a car after making an abortive attempt at murder. The motif of flight and pursuit thus unifies the actions of those officially and those personally concerned with the execution of Jim Drover.

On the periphery are Kay Rimmer, Milly's sister; her lover Jules, whose overcautiousness keeps him from finding happiness with Kay; Mr. Surrogate, the dilettante political philosopher, whose communism is sham and whose opinion, ironically correct, is that Drover's death will do the party more good than a long imprisonment; and Conder, the newspaperman, who, to relieve the bleakness of his celibacy, invents for himself a family circle of wife, six children, and the concomitant annoyances of domestic bliss. Those who know his many poses—a master spy or, at times, a debonair bachelor— pity him; those who believe his fantasies, envy him. The lives of these bystanders are affected by Jim Drover as they are thrown

together and rally to his cause. They can be compared to the bystanders of *The Power and the Glory* whose lives are changed by the
whiskey priest as he moves toward his salvation.

The activities of the battlefield unify the novel's plot. Milly and
Conrad pursue the battle in their own ways: Milly secures the sig-
nature of the murdered policeman's wife on the petition; Conrad
foolishly buys the pistol and attempts to assassinate the assistant
commissioner. Although Kay resents the fact that her brother-in-
law has got into difficulty, she nevertheless enjoys the notoriety
that her position gives her with Surrogate, who first introduces Lady
Caroline to the problem. Ineffectual Jules enters the lists but simply
forgets to do anything at all; and Conder seeks his facts, while his
imagination works overtime. The essential conflict, however, is
interpreted by the assistant commissioner and Lady Caroline, dis-
passionately by the one, passionately by the other.

The imagery of the novel suggests the prison, while the metaphor
of the battlefield suggests the struggle. The actual prison where
Jim awaits his fate is described early in the action, its cell blocks
full of inmates, some preferred and some not. Kay's factory is described in identical terms; the various parts of the works become
cell blocks, some workers preferred above others, and the girls are
satirically named Greta, Marlene, and Kay—devotees of the cult
of artificial beauty. Surrogate's pink bedroom is his cell, for he
awakens each morning to the scrutiny of his dead wife's eyes in the
portrait that hangs beyond his bed; his jailer is his valet, who knows
him for the lecherous fraud he is. Conrad's office is still another
aspect of the prison; his success has come to him step by step, much
to his surprise, and he has disciplined himself to accept each promotion with humility. And finally Milly's home, the basement flat,
is her cell since her husband's imprisonment. The metaphor of the
battlefield and the image of the prison at the same time lend unity
to a marvelously integrated plot and emphasize the sociological
implications.

The novel also demonstrates, tentatively, Greene's reaching out
to the larger context of religious concern that most characterizes his
work, and the references to prisons and punishment reflect aspects
of a Dantean Inferno. Lady Caroline has a vague faith in moral
progress, yet she is not above using her influence to bring about
her version of justice. She believes that she is on the side of good,
but as the assistant commissioner notes, she has no compunction

about changing sides when she loses conviction (217). Lady Caroline's faith is contrasted to Jules Briton's helpless Roman Catholicism and to the prison chaplain's despondency over his inability to contain his compassion for those who are unfairly dealt with. The assistant commissioner, "like Pilate," washes his hands of the human and political embroilments raised by the commutation of Jim Drover's sentence to eighteen years imprisonment. "I am only a paid servant," he rationalizes, "no more responsible than a clerk is responsible for the methods of a business he serves" (177). At the novel's end he settles down happily to a new clue in another case, which is but another skirmish on the battlefield.

England Made Me

Published in 1935, *England Made Me* is in some ways as sociological in its implications as *It's a Battlefield.* The title indicates, as does its French equivalent, *Mère Angleterre,* the nurturing effect of environment on individuals. The subject matter presents a view of capitalism, "staggering from crisis to crisis," in the economically depressed thirties.[3] The range of characters is sufficiently large to include factory workers as well as captains of industry and government officials who amass fortunes by manipulating events, frequently venturing outside the law to do so, in a system in which power is wealth.

England Made Me is a novel for which Greene confesses a "soft spot," regretting that his readers have not shared his enthusiasm. His assessment is in fact better than that of those readers whose judgment he laments, for the novel is one of his finest. Greene also feels that Kate Farrant is the best drawn of his women characters, with the exception of Sarah Miles of *The End of the Affair,* and he admits to a certain grudging pride in having brought into being Minty, the remittance man who keeps a spider imprisoned in his toothglass in his squalid Stockholm room. "I had no intention," he writes, "of introducing into the story a sly pathetic Anglo-Catholic, a humble follower, perhaps, of Sir John Betjeman, who would steal all the scenes in which he played a part. . . ." Minty belongs to that inimitable gallery of grotesques, sprung, as Greene says, from the "pre-conscious," which includes Acky and Tiny of *A Gun for Sale,* Parkis of *The End of the Affair,* and the dog Buller from *The Human Factor* (vii, x).

Despite its sociological and economic backgrounds, *England Made Me* deals primarily with the affinities of the twins Anthony and Kate Farrant through whose points of view the action is chiefly portrayed. The plot largely concerns their responsibility to and for Eric Krogh, a character modeled on Ivar Kreuger, the Swedish industrialist known in the thirties as the Match King. Again the theme of betrayal is dominant, but to it is closely bonded that of a fraternal love that borders on incest. By being born a few minutes before him, Kate had stolen from her brother the initiative one expects in a man, and Anthony had taken as his share of their joint birthright the charm that would have better served his sister. Of the two Kate seems the more aware, although brother and sister communicate in a telepathic manner from time to time.

The short story "The End of the Party," dated 1929 in *Collected Stories,* deals with the relationship of identical twins and with the idea that one gains initiative at the other's expense. At the conclusion of "The End of the Party," Francis Morton, unable to contain his fear, dies during a game of hide-and-seek when his brother's hand touches his, and Peter inherits his dead brother's fear. In many ways "The End of the Party" looks forward to *England Made Me,* as the novel fragment "The Other Side of the Border," included in *Nineteen Stories* but omitted from *Collected Stories,* reflects upon it. Greene writes in a note to this fragment: "Why did I abandon the book? I think for two main reasons—because another book, *Brighton Rock,* was more insistent to be written, and because I realized that I had already dealt with the main character in a story called *England Made Me.* Hands, I realized, had the same origin as Anthony Farrent [sic] in that novel,"[4] In the introduction to the novel in the Collected Edition he admits that Anthony is an idealized version of someone he knew very well, later admitting that the portrait was based on his brother (ix).

Both Hands, the hero of the fragmentary novel, and Anthony Farrant are made of the same material; they are seedy adventurers who lack even enough courage for jail, and both are at once optimistic and diffident about their charm and their ability to see themselves through. Anthony wears his smile "as a leper carried his bell" (11); as a perpetual warning that he is not to be trusted. Early in the novel he asks Kate to stick by him: " 'Of course,' she said. There was nothing easier to promise. She could not rid herself of him. He was more than her brother; he was the ghost that warned her, look what you have escaped; he was all the experience that she had missed; he was pain, because she had never felt pain except through him; for the same reason he was fear, despair, disgrace. He was everything except success" (11).

The motif of the soured innocence, one that Greene makes capital use of in "The Basement Room" (1935) and in *Brighton Rock,* finds its place within the novel's structure. As children Kate had met her unhappy brother in a barn; she had encouraged Anthony to return to school, and the pattern of his existence had been set—his deceits, his hopeless infantilism, his calculated interests. Kate thinks: "If I could put back time, if I could twist this ring Krogh gave me and abolish all this place . . . it would be dark now and a wind outside and the smell of manure and he with his cap in his hand, and I'd say: 'Don't go back. Never mind what people say. Don't go back,' and nothing would be the same" (23). Kate had sent Anthony back into the world of English conformity and tradition and had made him unfit for the great world of affairs.

The only art that Anthony possesses is that of sharpshooter. At a fair he shoots supremely well and wins for his efforts a vase, which Kate drops and breaks, and a toy tiger. Within the action of the novel both these items assume symbolical proportions. Francis Kunkel in *The Labyrinthine Ways of Graham Greene* points out the symbolical implications of the tiger, "a symbol of Anthony's evasion of responsibility," but he neglects the ironical, almost whimsical, reference to both William Blake and T. S. Eliot.[5] The tiger is a symbol of Anthony's initiative and virility; he promises it to Kate, but it is destined for Lucia Davidge, Loo. The broken vase suggests the impossibility of the brother-sister love relationship. Furthermore, the tiger leads the reader to Loo, and in Anthony's meeting with her on the North Bridge another Eliot note is struck and the ending prepared for:

He thought, one could hardly be more wet if one had been fished up from the lake, and because a thought of that kind was apt to weigh like a cold compress too long on his brain, he laughed it away, "I'm a good swimmer." But it was not true. He had always feared the water: he had been flung into a bath to sink or swim by his father when he was six and he had sunk. For years afterwards he dreamed of death by drowning. But he had outwitted whatever providence it was that plotted always to fit a man with the death he most dreaded. (140)

Similar in structure to *It's a Battlefield* in its manipulation of multiple points of view, its use of irony, and its handling of the theme of betrayal, *England Made Me*'s activities are portrayed primarily through Kate and Anthony's awareness. In Kate's case the emphasis falls on her obsessive love for her brother. She is Krogh's mistress, but her relationship to him is prompted by self-interest and admiration, not by love. Her only agreeable sexual experience with Krogh had been brought on by the stimulus of a visitor who reminded her of Anthony. Anthony's point of view, like Kate's, is controlled by his feeling for his twin. In moments of genuine feeling he admits that he is as bound to her as she is to him. Yet sex is important to him, for it is a large part of love. Love is to Anthony as it is to Ida Arnold, "having a bit of fun"; it is Mabel and Annette and Loo, the hot handclasp in the taxi, the wet mouth, and the tumbled bed.

But Kate's love is for Anthony alone. To have Anthony with her in Stockholm is the full realization of all her plans, what she has plotted and schemed for; yet having Anthony with her brings about his destruction. Her position as Krogh's mistress is to secure Anthony's future as well as her own; when Krogh asks her to marry, she asks for a settlement for Anthony and herself. To deny Anthony is to deny herself; to deny Krogh seems to her at first a betrayal of the future, and the symbol of this future is the modern statue in Krogh's lobby, a form that she admires. Once she realizes that Krogh is not the future but one of "the shipwrecked," to refer to the American title that Greene used to describe the action of the novel, she need no longer dissimulate. But Anthony's betrayal of Krogh is his betrayal of Kate and of himself. Krogh alone is capable of saving himself.

The political and economic aspects of the Judas theme are for the most part described from the point of view of the ruthless and lonely industrialist Erik Krogh. In a scene of hilarious, yet ironic, comic invention—a scene that looks forward to Milly's birthday party in *Our Man in Havana,* the comic involvements of *The Complaisant Lover* (1959), and the comedy of "Under the Garden"—Krogh's character is revealed. Anthony's presence and their escape from the Wagnerian opera prompt in Krogh a memory of happier times before the invention of that vague and undefined "cutter" that brought with it wealth, fame, and responsibility. In a moment of calculated generosity, Krogh agrees to give a newspaperman, Professor Ham-

marsten, the money to produce Shakespeare's *Pericles,* thus adding
a counterpoint to the incest theme.

The action of the novel is further described through the points
of view of Minty, whose life ceased when he left Harrow under a
cloud; by Hall, Krogh's hatchet man who is responsible for Anthony's murder; and by young Andersson, an idealist who is somehow involved in a strike that Krogh is attempting to avert, whom
Krogh and Kate, but not Anthony, are willing to sacrifice.

Point of view is both buttressed and enhanced by a careful use
of stream-of-consciousness, the technique that Greene uses best in
The End of the Affair. A case in point is Kate's reverie in the second
section of part two. She awakens at Krogh's side, thinks of the
impending strike, of Anthony and his job with Krogh's, and of the
toy tiger, the tiger which weaves its way through the entire activity
of the novel. She thinks of her position with Krogh, again of Anthony and of the tiger, and then of Krogh and the only time she
desired him, then of her dying father, and again of Anthony. The
tiger and the blue vase, broken. Then the tiger burning bright, its
sinews of jealousy, of Anthony, of her father. And then the brilliant
foreshadowing passage:

Don't be afraid. Don't hesitate. No cause of fear. No bulls on this exchange.
The tiger bright. The forests. Sleep. Our bond. The new redemption.
And we rise, we rise. And God Who made the lamb made Whitaker,
made Loewenstein. "But you are lucky," Hammond said that day in Leather
Lane, "Krogh's safe. Whatever comes or goes people will always everywhere
have to buy Krogh's." The market steady. The Strand, the water and a
street between us. Sleep. The new redemption. No bulls, the tiger and
the lamb. The bears. The forests. Sleep. The stock is sound. The closing
price. We rise. (77)

The English characters of the novel are contrasted to those of
European or Scandinavian extraction; although a great emphasis is
put on Krogh's internationalism, Kate, Anthony, Minty and, to a
certain extent, the Davidges recognize the advantages and limitations of their British upbringing. Anthony's fate is dictated by the
standards of English society that he is unequipped to contend with,
although he "puts up a good show." Kate's relationship to Krogh
is conditioned by her brother's feeling that one's sister does not ask
her lover to find work for her brother. Minty is content to remember

with nostalgia the delights of Harrow, and he treasures nothing
more than a letter from "the family."

Both *It's a Battlefield* and *England Made Me* are brilliantly planned
and executed novels. The controlling temper of both is secular,
although the religious note is obliquely sounded in the former through
the convictions of Lady Caroline Bury, Jules Briton, and the assistant
commissioner; tentatively in the latter by the toy tiger and the lamb
and the death-by-water references. Both novels indicate enormous
growth in both style and plot construction since *The Man Within,*
and both look forward to the later and more provocative novels
beginning with *Brighton Rock*.

Chapter Four
The Grand Theme

> ". . . to act as the devil's
> advocate, to elicit a measure
> of understanding and
> sympathy. . . ."

Graham Greene replied to Marie-Françoise Allain's question concerning the dichotomy between the entertainments and the novels that *Brighton Rock* started in his mind as a thriller. "From the first sentence," he told her, "my intention was to write a crime novel, but the novel eventually moved in another direction" (140). In his introductory note to the volume in the Collected Edition he points out that although all of his novels and entertainments had been written since 1926, the period of his conversion to Roman Catholicism, he did not feel ready to employ Roman Catholic characters until about 1936. "It takes longer," he writes, "to familiarize oneself with a region of the mind than with a country, but the ideas of my Catholic characters, even their Catholic ideas, were not necessarily mine."[1] Greene's conversion had been intellectually motivated, but not until he fully appreciated Franco's attack on Republican Spain and experienced socialist persecution of religion in Mexico in 1938 did he discover that his belief was more than symbolical: "It was closer to death in the afternoon" (ix).

By 1937, a decade after his conversion, he was "ripe" to develop his themes within a specifically religious framework. He abandoned "The Other Side of the Border" and began work on *Brighton Rock*. The opening pages are all that remain of the originally planned entertainment, and Greene admits that had he not lacked the strength of mind to do so, he would have scrapped them and begun with what is now part two.

The novel as published immediately indicates the confusion Greene admits to as he made his way through the melodrama to the work's essence. The action first focuses on Ida Arnold whose beery humanity is charming and beguiling, then shifts to the more compelling figure of Pinkie Brown. Pinkie then becomes the motivating factor in an action that forces revenge, murder, betrayal, and suicide to yield the distinct possibilities of damnation or salvation within the limits of Roman Catholic conviction. The naturalistic setting of the novel's beginnings inexorably becomes symbolical while, paradoxically, retaining authentic details of time and place. Greene admits that he had every intention of describing the Brighton he knew and loved from boyhood, "but it was as though my characters had taken the Brighton *I* knew into their own consciousness and transformed the whole picture" (xiii). What is apparent now is that *Brighton Rock* was for Greene a necessary exploration of right and wrong and good and evil in the world of ordinary men and women—good-hearted, generous, fine-feeling people like Ida Arnold. One of the most beguiling aspects of the work is the subtle yet relentless manner in which Greene managed to shift his reader's interest away from right and wrong—morally easy Ida—to good and evil—Rose and Pinkie. As the focus shifted, the reader's affection for Ida diminished, and her undeniable humanity, at first so captivating, became tedious and then unreal. What Greene had intended as a simple detective story had become a "discussion, far too obvious and open for a novel, of the distinction between good-and-evil and right-and-wrong," a mystery that would demand first definition—in *Brighton Rock,* then exploration and illustration—in *The Power and the Glory* and *The Heart of the Matter,* and finally confirmation—in *The End of the Affair.* These novels in fact form a coherent tetralogy on a grand theme—"the appalling strangeness of the mercy of God" (x).

Brighton Rock

Moving from the world of *Stamboul Train* and *A Gun for Sale* into that of *Brighton Rock* is much like moving from the square of a medieval village into the dim light of the cathedral to contemplate God under storied capitals where demons and angels battle for the soul of man. Indeed, the morality aspect of the novel makes its kinship to medieval allegory strikingly apparent. Perhaps it is this aspect that induced Sean O'Casey in *Rose and Crown* to criticize the novel so devastatingly:

Never a word, never a public word about the well known and very able catholic writer, Graham Greene's *Brighton Rock,* in which Brighton becomes a city of darkest night and darkest morn, too; in which everything and everyone seems to be on the road of evil. Talk of James Joyce! Joyce had humour, Greene has none; and in the darkest part of Joyce there are always bright flashes of light; here the very light itself is rotten. Even the blessed sun "slid off the sea like cuttlefish shot into the sky with the stain of agonies and endurance." Here the roman catholic girl of sixteen and the boy of seventeen, respectively, are the most stupid and evil mortals a man's mind could imagine.[2]

O'Casey's criticism cannot be put down to his anti-Catholic bias alone, for there is much truth in what he says. Yet it would seem that to understand *Brighton Rock,* it must be read as allegory. The grotesque images of evil are as terrifying as the medieval representations of angels and demons, though, specifically, they owe to Eliot's *The Waste Land:* the broken windows, the ouija board, the gramophone, the Cosmopolitan Hotel, death by water—all have their counterparts in Eliot's poem.

In *Brighton Rock* Greene relates for the first time the themes of corrupted innocence, betrayal, the motif of the chase, and his own images of evil and unhappiness to a specifically religious theme: the Roman Catholicism of the central characters. Good and evil are defined in terms of the religion of the boy Pinkie and the girl Rose. The subject matter is presented in the same melodramatic convention as before: the confrontations and the coincidences still form a portion of the structure, but the chase, the betrayal, and the confession are now determined by a religious cogency.

The plot concerns the racetrack gangs and the razor slashings that accompany the protection rackets. It deals with the bookmakers, the bettors, the gamblers, and the squealers; it makes use of the jargon of the track—"polony," "buer," "carving," "bogies"; and it moves against a background of artificial gaiety—amusement booths and shooting galleries, dance halls and pavilions, piers and pubs. It moves against the sea, the traditional symbol of changeless change, of continuity. In bare outline the novel seems just another thriller: Ida Arnold, the inquisitive person who seeks natural justice; Pinkie Brown, the pursued; Rose, the love element. *Brighton Rock* has all the equipment of the thriller, but the melodramatic contrivances are integrated to give meaning to the religious importunities of the theme. Always there is the felt presence of the Church, urging, defining, commenting, never relenting. And it is this religious frame of reference that gives the novel its coherent allegorical meaning. The central theme is one of justice, of right overcoming wrong.

Pinkie Brown is the seventeen-year-old leader of Kite's mob, the same Kite whose murder was related in *A Gun for Sale.* A publicity man for the *Daily Messenger,* Fred Hale had betrayed Kite to Colleoni (whose name is borrowed from *The Aspern Papers*), a successful racketeer who is friendly with the police. To keep the mob together, Pinkie must exhibit his right of leadership by avenging Kite's murder. Pinkie and the mob apparently start to force stick candy down Fred Hale's throat, even though Ida uses the word "strangled" when she tries to understand how Pinkie killed Hale. The candy that gives the novel its title thus serves as the symbol of Ida's awareness of the sweetness of life and Pinkie's violation of the Eucharist, enhancing his portrayal as a priest of Satan. Later on in the novel, when he and Rose see the broken pieces of rock candy in the confectioner's shops, he feels hubris. Fred Hale in fact dies of heart failure, but as a Catholic Pinkie knows that he has violated one of the commandments of his church.

To escape the vengeance of Pinkie and the mob, Fred, or Kolley Kibber as he is known professionally, attaches himself to Ida Arnold, a good-hearted blonde who frequents the amusement areas. When she leaves him for a few minutes to go to the "Ladies," Hale falls prey to Pinkie and the mob. Back in London, she learns of Fred's death, and, remembering his fear and his desire to live, she discounts the idea of suicide, or death by heart failure. She goes back to Brighton to discover the right and wrong of the matter and becomes involved in the gang war between Pinkie and Colleoni. She bets Fred's horse, Black Boy, and wins enough money to allow her to trap the murderer at her leisure. Greene at first calls Ida "Lily" and presents her singing and humming both popular songs and folk ballads, thereby aligning her with a folk tradition of sadness and loss. The absolutes of good and evil are so commingled in her that she can appreciate only the sadness of Hale's death and the injustice of his having been deprived of existence. She is as bewildered by Rose's goodness as she is by Pinkie's evil, yet she is intrigued by both.

To cover up Hale's murder, Pinkie had sent Spicer, an elderly and timid mobster, to leave Kolley Kibber's identification cards at various places in Brighton so that the time of the murder might not be fixed. At Snow's Restaurant, Rose, a young waitress, finds the card, but she knows that Spicer is not Kolley Kibber. To keep her silent, Pinkie courts her, and she falls in love with him. Ida discovers from Rose that Fred Hale had not left Kibber's card, and she places the guilt of Fred's death on Pinkie. She becomes Fred's avenger.

As her name implies, Ida is described primarily as a mother figure. Fred's pride rebels at the association he makes with her, but all the same she represents the safety and darkness of the womb: "His eyes turned to the big breasts; she was like darkness to him, shelter, knowledge, common sense; his heart ached at the sight; but, in his little inky cynical framework of bone, pride bobbed up again, taunting him 'back to the womb . . . be a mother to you . . . no more standing on your own feet' " (8). The idea of Ida as mother is emphasized constantly throughout the novel, and at one point she even introduces herself to the mob as Rose's mother.

But Ida is much more than a mother figure, for in the pattern of the allegory she represents humanity. She feels that she knows the difference between right and wrong, but she is ill at ease where the issue is one of good and evil. "I'm a sticker where right's concerned," she says (15). She has no religion to speak of, and in this respect she resembles Anne Crowder and looks forward to Richard Smythe in *The End of the Affair*. Ida is vitality and strength; she believes firmly that only what she sees around her is real. She is the humanity of most people, the crowds at Brighton "having a bit of fun." Fred is correct in attaching himself to her, for she is the antithesis of the death that awaits him at Pinkie's hands. Resenting the fact that Fred has been deprived of vital existence, her humanity rushes forth to protest the injustice.

Since Ida discounts the idea of God, preferring to believe in a natural order, it is logical for her to assume the role of avenger: "Somebody had made Fred unhappy, and somebody was going to be made unhappy in return. An eye for an eye. If you believed in God, you might leave vengeance to him, but you couldn't trust the One, the universal spirit. Vengeance was Ida's, just as much as reward was Ida's, the soft gluey mouth affixed in taxis, the warm handclasp in cinemas, the only reward there was. *And vengeance and reward—they were both fun*" [italics mine] (41–42). She consults her ouija board and it given the sanction she needs to set about her mission. The board spells out "FRESUICILLEYE": "Why, it's as clear as clear," she says, "Fre is short for Fred and Suici for Suicide and Eye; that's what I always say—an eye for an eye and a tooth for a tooth." And when she says, "It's going to be exciting . . . , it's going to be a bit of life," she pays the highest praise she can (51). Insofar as Ida believes in the natural world, within the pattern of the allegory her idea of justice is easy to understand. The idea of God's justice, however, is not so facile; right and wrong are consequently seen as aspects of good and evil.

Pinkie Brown believes in right too; but he believes in might controlling right. For he is a Fascist. To coition Pinkie ascribes the ills of the world. Here the reader is reminded of Minty in *England Made Me*. As a child he had rejected his parents after witnessing their Saturday night ritual of sex. In Kite he had found a "father," for Kite had offered him a refuge from sex. The father had died, but Pinkie had prolonged his existence—"not touching liquor, biting his nails in the Kite way . . ." (272–73). Representing life and creation, Ida forces Pinkie to marry the waitress who had seen Spicer leave Kolley Kibber's card in Snow's Restaurant. The natural mother, within the allegory, battles the unnatural father—Ida versus Kite, love and violence opposed. For Kite represents the cult of power as Ida represents the religion of humanity. The strong man in terms of the allegory runs up against the forces of society and is defeated.

The idea of sex is tied in for Pinkie with the notion of purity, a purity conditioned by his Roman Catholic upbringing. His virginity affords him a strength and pride he would not otherwise have. Like Andrews of *The Man Within* and Conrad Drover of *It's a Battlefield,* Pinkie is limited in his knowledge of life; but, unlike them, he has been schooled in the reality of evil by his Roman Catholicism. Pinkie believes in hell and the devil because he knows the exquisite torture of pain; suffering is for him the only reality. When Rose asks him if he believes in hell, he answers: "Of course it's true . . . what else could there be? . . . Why . . . it's the only thing that fits. These atheists, they don't know nothing. Of course there's Hell. Flames and damnation . . . torments" (61–62).

The images of damnation have been constantly with Pinkie and the sex act has become for him the index of the world's evil. Sex had caused Annie Collins to put her head on the railroad lines: "She had to wait ten minutes for the seven-five. Fog made it late from Victoria. Cut off her head. She was fifteen. She was going to have a baby and she knew what it was like. She'd had one two years before, and they could 'ave pinned it on twelve boys" (204). Pinkie knows hell intimately for he sees it in life. When his lawyer Prewitt quotes from Marlowe, "Why, this is Hell, nor are we out of it," Pinkie looks at him with horrified interest, for he thinks that he alone knows the secret (261). The intimations of hell have been constantly around him: the man who collects debris along the Brighton walks, the beggar who has lost the whole of one side of the body, Rose's parents who sell her for fifteen guineas. Life for Pinkie is his parents on Saturday night. Nature that spoke to Wordsworth as "the types and symbols of eternity" speaks to Pinkie of eternity too, but an eternity of pain, "Worms and cataract, cancer . . . children being born . . . dying slowly" (283).

Intimate with evil as he is, Pinkie can recognize its opposite when he sees it. "I'll be seeing you," he says to Rose, "You an' me have things in common" (31). Rose and Pinkie are opposite sides of the same coin; one cannot exist without the other. Yet Pinkie makes the mistake of thinking that goodness and ignorance are one. He fails to perceive that Rose recognizes his evil and nevertheless loves him.

Rose and Pinkie have in common their Roman Catholicism. Coming from Nelson Place, Rose is intimate with the same symbols of evil as Pinkie; but her innocence has not been soured. What is good in her responds to what is evil in Pinkie, and she knows that he can orient himself only in respect to her: "What was most evil in him needed her: it couldn't get along without goodness" (155). Forced to corrupt goodness when he marries Rose to keep her from testifying, Pinkie betrays his virginity, the source of his strength, as he betrays his putative father. Theirs is the marriage of heaven and hell: "She was good, he'd discovered that, and he was damned: they were made for each other" (155).

In terms of the allegory, the chief polarities of good and evil are established by Rose and Pinkie; the middle ground is represented by Ida Arnold. And Ida is able to recognize how alien these two extremes are to her world of man. When she is with Pinkie or Rose, she feels as though she is in a strange country; and she hasn't even a phrase book to help her understand their language. As the representative of human nature, she can distinguish between right and wrong—or so she thinks; but she feels her inadequacy when the issue is one of extreme good or extreme evil. She is indeed an alien in the spiritual drama she precipitates, for the mercy and justice of

God are beyond her comprehension. For her everything is life and vitality; justice to be determined in the world is an eye for an eye, a tooth for a tooth.

Ida has as her allies the forces of continuity, Pinkie the forces of the devil to whom he is dedicated. Time and again he says, *"Credo in unum Satanum."* His energy is as potent as Ida's, but he has chosen to channel it for evil rather than for good. In his limited knowledge of life, in his search for peace—the refrain he constantly sings is *"Dona eis pacem"*—peace and power are synonymous; yet his Catholicism has taught him that each step on the way to power places another nail in the body of Christ. He had thought to channel this energy for good when, as a child, he had wished to be a priest. Celibacy would have been a safeguard against coition, but Kite and the evil he saw dominant in the world about him had won him away from holiness. Ida forces Pinkie to commit himself to the natural world, the world of sex.

If natural justice in the world is to be asserted, Pinkie and his evil must be destroyed. And Ida, humanity, must bring this destruction about. The forces of vitality ally themselves with her when Black Boy wins the race, as Fred Hale had said he would. Pinkie recognizes the moment: "If I was one of those crazy geezers who touch wood, throw salt, go under ladders, I might be scared to—" (127). From the moment of the race his plans are made with extreme care, but his every step is conditioned by a pressure he cannot place. Ida asks questions, she calls Spicer on the phone, she badgers Rose. Pinkie seeks to stem the tide by marrying Rose, by corrupting her to his evil, by asking her to submit to a sham suicide pact. But this is not enough, for Ida is relentless: "Look at me," she says, "I've never changed. It's like those sticks of rock: bite it all the way down, you'll still read Brighton. That's human nature" (247). She rushes to the cliff where Pinkie is forcing damnation on Rose; the policeman with her is bewildered, yet he must do as she commands. She forestalls Rose's suicide and forces Pinkie to his death—and perhaps to his damnation.

When the drama is ended, Rose goes to her confessor and insists that she is unable to repent her failure to damn herself alongside Pinkie. The priest speaks to her of Péguy, the "sinner" who could not accept the thought that God would allow any of his creatures to suffer damnation; he speaks to her of the "appalling . . . strangeness . . . of the mercy of God" (308). His is the voice of the

Church, attempting to reestablish a mean once the passions of men have spent themselves. He intercedes to comfort the living, and he asks Rose to "hope and pray," for the Church does not demand that anyone believe that a soul may be cut off from mercy. He makes the final commentary on the action when he says, ". . . a Catholic is more capable of evil than anyone. I think perhaps—because we believe in Him—we are more in touch with the devil than other people" (309). But Rose remains uncertain, for her knowledge of evil has taught her the reality of damnation. Certain that she carries Pinkie's child within her, she goes home "to the worst horror of all"—the record Pinkie had made for her on which he had told her how much he hated her and what she represented (310). The worst horror of all is that Rose must return to life: life without hope, world without end. Once the drama is ended, evil seems the order of the universe, as continuous as life itself. Pinkie falls into the sea and not even the sound of a splash is heard. The sea absorbs his evil, and it becomes a portion of the natural world. Life for Rose becomes a "horror," for, with the knowledge of Pinkie's hatred, she is denied hope.

So convincing is Greene's portrayal of Pinkie that some readers have wondered about his intention concerning the boy's salvation or damnation, forgetting that the denouement carefully offers a meaningful ambiguity. Greene's action in fact provides both alternatives, in some ways challenging the humanity of his readers. Pinkie is in many ways like Milton's Satan—his mind is its own place and can make a hell of heaven, a heaven of hell. He believes in hell's reality, he deliberately rejects the possibility of God's mercy "between the stirrup and the ground" (110), and he believes, after being carved by Colleoni's mob on the racecourse, that excruciating pain is for him the only truth. Yet he is equally aware of God's grace—the pressure of the great wings that beat relentlessly on the windscreen as he drives Rose to Peacehaven where he intends to trick her into suicide. With the vitriol intended for her blinding him instead he falls into the sea. Whether there is time for repentance or not is the question that is left unanswered. There is the "appalling strangeness of the mercy of God" for readers to accept or reject as they will.

The use of the sensational and the melodramatic in *Brighton Rock* permits Greene to present his theme in terms compatible with his religious thesis. His polarities are sharply defined, and the form of

the novel emphasizes the distinctions while underscoring their cogency. He uses background as symbol and for effect, and the storm
in which Pinkie dies emphasizes the turmoil of the drama. Yet the
storm does not cleanse, except that it exerts its peculiar influence
on the reader. Following upon *A Gun for Sale,* it demonstrates to
what extent the religious note can animate Greene's narrative. No
wonder that Greene thinks that *Brighton Rock* may be his best novel—
for him "a sad thought after more than thirty years" (xiii), but not
for his reader.

The Power and the Glory

In his conversations with Allain, Greene describes *The Power and
the Glory* as "a seventeenth-century play in which the actors sym-
bolize a virtue or a vice, pride, pity, etcetera." Both the lieutenant
and the whiskey priest, he continues, remain themselves to the end:
"The priest, for all his recollection of periods in his life when he
was different, never changed" (129).

The novel grew out of a trip taken through the Mexican provinces
of Tabasco and Chiapas in the winter of 1937–38, in part occasioned
by a libel suit brought against Greene by Shirley Temple, whose
Wee Willie Winkie he had unfavorably reviewed in *Night and Day.*
His publisher sent him sufficient funds to extend his stay inasmuch
as the lord chief justice had taken a severe look at the charge and
Greene might well have been arrested on his return to England.[3]
The novel, as does *Brighton Rock,* makes use of Roman Catholicism
as subject matter, and once again allegory lends the events of the
narrative an excitement above and beyond the melodramatic adventure of flight and pursuit. Greene's protagonist is a reluctant recip-
ient of grace, and to some this fact immediately transforms the work
into a Catholic document of such mysterious overtones that only
the initiated can appreciate it. Yet it remains the favorite of many
of Greene's readers, and he himself prefers only *The Honorary Consul*
to it.

In his essay entitled "The Young Dickens," Greene says of the
world of Charles Dickens, with specific reference to *Oliver Twist,*
that it

is a world without God; and as a substitute for the power and the glory
of the omnipotent and omniscient are a few sentimental references to
heaven, angels, the sweet faces of the dead. . . . In this Manichaean

world we can believe in evil-doing, but goodness wilts into philanthropy, kindness, and those strange vague sicknesses into which Dickens's young women so frequently fall and which seem in his eyes a kind of badge of virtue, as though there were a merit in death.[4]

The Power and the Glory employs ingenious but sometimes heavy-handed satire to portray in the uncommon and startling guise of melodramatic allegory the power and the glory of God through the juxtaposition of two symbolic characters. The whiskey priest, representative of an old, corrupt, and God-ridden world of religion, and the lieutenant of a new political order, representative of the enlightened and philanthropic world of a power cult, are doubles in the Dostoevskian or Conradian sense. The differences that exist in these two symbolic figures are satirically antithetical, each suggesting what the other should be, each accenting the pity that is in the other while denying the evil. Although the immediate implications of the differences in the portrayals of the whiskey priest and the lieutenant are satirical, ultimately, by suggesting the dedication of each to a common cause, they are ironic, for Greene wishes to render the highest justice to both their points of view.

The Power and the Glory portrays Greene's firsthand experience of Mexican politics and religion. In *The Lawless Roads,* published in 1939, he describes his journey of the previous year through Tabasco and Chiapas, Mexican provinces in which the Church was persecuted. Many of the characters and settings that comprise the allegory that is the novel are drawn from life, and their counterparts are to be found in the travel narrative. Dr. Tench, the dentist, grew out of Greene's acquaintance with many dentists, for toothache seems a common ailment in Mexico. The deracinated spirit Greene observed in another dentist, "small bitter exiled widower, caged in his Victorian *sala,* with the vultures routing on his roof" (160). Mr. and Mrs. Lehr, the German brother and sister who befriend the whiskey priest, have their counterparts in Herr R. and his sister who, like the Lehrs of the novel, pacified the terrorists by giving them five hundred acres of worthless land, keeping the productive soil for themselves. Their refuge is the same that Greene had come upon, cross and ill from his wanderings on muleback. The stream where the modest Miss Lehr bathes, the earthenware pitcher on the veranda, all are details drawn from the novelist's experience. The precocious child, Coral Fellows, derives from Fru R.'s daughter, the child who learned her lessons at her mother's knees from a mail-order textbook. And the chief character of the novel, the whiskey priest, is developed from a casual remark made to Greene by his dentist friend, Dr. Fitzpatrick: " 'Oh,' he said, 'he was just what we call a whiskey priest.' He had taken one of his sons to be baptized, but the priest was drunk and would insist on naming him Brigitta. He was little loss, poor man . . . but who can judge what terror and hardship and isolation may have excused him in the eyes of God?" (161).

The hot and humid landscape, presented much like a tapestry in the novel, the huts and the dust, the mules and the flies, the gaseosa stalls, the vultures, the sharks, the carrion—all are contained within the pages of the travel narrative: "It was like the grave, the earth taking over before its time" (208). An atmosphere of death and decay pervades both the travel narrative and the novel, and the image of the carious mouth is constantly juxtaposed with the image of the Eucharist—taking God in the mouth.

What interests Greene in both *The Lawless Roads* and the novel is the attitude of the Mexican state to religion. At the time Greene visited Chiapas and Tabasco, the government was Socialist in intention, but Fascist in method. He quotes in *The Lawless Roads* from Article 3 of the Constitution: "The education imparted by the State shall be a Socialistic one, and in addition to excluding all religious doctrine, shall combat fanaticism and prejudices by organizing its instruction and activities in a way that shall permit the creation in youth of an exact and rational conception of the Universe and of social life" (90). Forced to comply with the tenets of this new order that, indeed, can be defined as a cult of power, many of the priests married, as does Father José in the novel, while many accepted martyrdom. A few preferred to continue their ministry while avoiding arrest at the hands of the police. In outlawing the influence of the Church and in making any practice of its dogma an act of treason, the government under Garrido Cannibal sought to establish a state that would consider the bodily needs of the people and free them from the narrow-mindedness and bigotry of the Roman Catholic Church. It sought to enforce a secular order in place of a religious one. The attempt failed, for the new order could not destroy the forms and symbols of the old. Even the art that sought to exalt the state and edify the populace denied the possibility. In *The Lawless Roads* Greene describes a Rivera mural:

Rivera contributes only one moral with typical grandiloquence—all out-stretched arms and noble faces, white robes and haloes. It is called "Creation": it is full of literary symbols—the Tree of Life, Dionysius, Man, Woman, Music, Comedy, Dance, Tragedy, Science, Temperance, Fortitude. It adapts Christian emblems to a vague political idea, and they become unbearably sentimental in the new setting, far more sentimental than repository art. The pale blue madonna with the seven swords does, however inadequately, represent an exact idea: but the Son in Rivera's "Creation"—what is he but Progress, Human Dignity, great empty Victorian conceptions that life denies at every turn? This is Rivera's way—to try to get the best of both worlds. He is the Leighton or the Watts of the Revolution. (86–87)

In *The Power and the Glory* Greene asserts the vitality of the Roman Catholic Church as he attempts an explanation of the value of its beliefs. For all his weaknesses the whiskey priest becomes the representative not only of his Church but of the cumulative wisdom of the past; in short, of Western humanism. This does not mean, however, that *The Power and the Glory* is either a thesis novel, a saint's life, or a political tract. Rather it is a consistent allegory on the theme of Everyman. For the priest while determining the means of his salvation becomes a man fighting the unifying but degrading urges of a power cult.

The physical structure of the novel is a simple one. The first section deals with the bystanders, those whom the priest touches in his flight. They are Dr. Tench, the dentist; Coral Fellows, the precocious child; Luis, whose mother offers shelter to the fugitive; the chief of police; and the lieutenant, the representative of the power cult. Neither the lieutenant nor the priest is named, so as not to intrude on the allegorical importunities of the dominant theme. The second section deals with the priest's flight from the civil authorities, and it introduces the *mestizo,* the Judas of the allegory. The third section begins with a peaceful interlude, a limbo amidst the melodramatic activities of the novel, during which the priest is in danger of falling back into the complacent ways of his early ministry; and it develops his decision to accept his martyrdom. At this point the motif of flight and pursuit is reversed so that the priest may become the aggressor and the champion of his convictions. Through the priest Greene deploys his major concern: the grace of God exerted on the soul of a man whose weakness is, paradoxically, the symbol of his strength. The figure of the priest allows Greene to work within the anatomy of sainthood.

In *Brighton Rock* Greene defined his religious preoccupations in terms of allegory: he personified good and evil in Rose and Pinkie. Rose was the central character in a symbolic drama, but, more often than not, her goodness was overshadowed by Pinkie's more fascinating evil. Having defined his poles in *Brighton Rock,* he could go on to combine good and evil in a single individual as he does in *The Power and the Glory.* His remark on Frederick Rolfe, Baron Corvo, bears quoting here: "The greatest saints have been men with more than a normal capacity for evil, and the most vicious men have sometimes narrowly escaped sanctity."[5]

In *The Power and the Glory* Greene chose a striking method of presenting his subject matter. On the allegorical level the novel is the whiskey priest's attempt to avoid sainthood. The first American title, *The Labyrinthine Ways*—an allusion to Francis Thompson's "The Hound of Heaven"—indicates that the priest's flight is a flight from God and that the journey he makes is one of self-recognition. Greene makes brilliant use of counterpoint as he describes the priest's flight from the authorities, which is at the same time his evasion of grace. Only after he is betrayed by the half-caste Judas can the priest fully accept his destiny. It is at that moment that the pattern of flight and pursuit is reversed, and the lieutenant becomes the pursued.

Within the frame of the allegory the poles represented by the whiskey priest and the lieutenant are arranged in a satirical fashion; the secular order is represented by the lieutenant, the religious by the priest. The lieutenant's belief is, understandably, the source of his strength; he accepts the violence and brutality that power engenders as necessary and rational concomitants of his faith. He is temperate, completely certain of the value of his creed. He is strong, resolute, and dedicated. He has self-respect. And he is celibate. In short, he is everything that the whiskey priest should be and is not.

At the opposite polarity the priest is a drunkard who periodically seeks to evade his responsibility. There is the smell of decay about him, and the vulture hovers over him as a token of his destiny. When the reader first sees him, he is attempting to flee Mexico; and Dr. Tench, a bystander, is reminded of death: "The man's dark suit and sloping shoulders reminded him uncomfortably of a coffin, and death was in his carious mouth already" (10). He is a coward, and a creature of habit; his great sin is his illegitimate daughter Brigitta, the offspring of his loneliness and pride. Yet the differences between these two men are ultimately points of irony rather than of satire. For Greene, in holding up to contempt the deficiencies of one man, nevertheless caricatures the virtues of the other. Neither is a hero in the traditional sense, yet both portray the force of their convictions.

The destiny of the whiskey priest is implied from the novel's beginning when in the police station the lieutenant places the priest's photograph next to that of the American gangster who assumes the role of Nemesis. The lieutenant says approvingly of the gangster, " 'He is a man at any rate' " (21). The lieutenant looks at the priest's photograph, taken ten years before at a Communion party; and he feels his responsibility keenly as he dedicates himself to his task of ridding his country of the pernicious influence of the priest's Church: "He had the dignity of an idea, standing in the little whitewashed room with his polished boots and his venom. There was something disinterested in his ambition: a kind of virtue in his desire to catch the sleek respected guest of the first communion party" (22).

The lieutenant is described as "a theologian going back over the errors of the past to destroy them again" (23). He is indeed a priest of a political order that promises as its sacraments food, clothing, and security instead of misery, poverty, and superstition. It infuriates him to think that there are people who believe in the myth of a merciful God. The lieutenant's life had begun for him on a day five years before the action of the novel when he had been ordained to destroy the canker of religion. Yet, for all his weaknesses, it is the priest who carries the seeds of redemption and renewal.

The priest comes to an appreciation of God in Man during the night he spends in a crowded prison cell, a microcosm of his world. In the filth and stench he sees human nature at its lowest; and he identifies the evil in the world with that in himself. As a pious woman harangues the priest to hear her confession and two prisoners find comfort in the sexual act, their cries of pleasure reminding him of his weakness and of his daughter Brigitta, the priest sees the people of God, and he understands more clearly than ever before the condition of his kingdom. In the lovers and the other inmates he sees the types and symbols of eternity: "Such a lot of beauty. Saints talk a lot about the beauty of suffering. Well, we are not saints, you and I. Suffering to us is just ugly. Stench and crowding and pain. *That* is beautiful in that corner—to them. It needs a lot of learning to see things with a saint's eye; a saint gets a subtle taste for beauty and can look down on poor ignorant palates like theirs. But we can't afford to" (155–56). Wedged beside an old man who murmurs about an illegitimate daughter, the priest is overcome by an overwhelming pity for suffering and misery. He remembers from experience the beauty of evil: "how much beauty Satan carried down with him when he fell" (156). He sees and feels God in the poor and the helpless; and he finds it possible to pity the half-caste who seeks to betray him.

Having found his own kind, the whiskey priest feels the need of confession. As he tells his fellow prisoners that he is a whiskey priest and the father of a child, he longs for the simplicity of death. He prays for Brigitta, although he knows in his heart that the evil in her is too fixed to be overcome. Yet in his dedication to her, he begins to orient himself into the scheme of God; he opens his heart to grace, and he begins the last phase of his journey of recognition.

The next morning, while still in prison, the priest comes face to face with his antagonist, the lieutenant, for the second time—the first encounter had taken place in the priest's village. The lieutenant does not recognize him either as a priest or as the man he had met in the village, the father of the child Brigitta. Touched by the old man who has no money, the lieutenant gives the priest five pesos, ironically the price of a mass. Astonished, the priest says, "You're a good man" (168).

When he leaves the prison, the priest goes to the home of Coral Fellows, the child who had befriended him earlier and who is, symbolically, his "good" daughter, to discover that she has died. He goes on until he comes upon an Indian mother whose child has been shot three times, perhaps by that same American gangster, James Calver (the name, of course, suggests Calvary), whose photograph had been placed beside his in the police station. The rains come, and the priest is spiritually cleansed. He recognizes the primitive simplicity and the quiet beauty of the Indian mother's belief as she places a lump of hard, brown sugar beside the body of her slaughtered child.

Since his release from prison, the priest has fallen in a state of limbo, his aimless wanderings indicating the searchings of his soul. His experiences in the prison have opened his heart to grace, and the rain symbolizes his soul's state. Delirious, he is found by a peasant who takes him across the border into the province where there is religious tolerance.

Mr. and Miss Lehr nurse him to health. The priest decides that, since he has crossed the border and is no longer subject to the jurisdiction of the lieutenant, he will give up his life of wandering ministrant, go to Las Casas, and secure the formal forgiveness of his Church in confession. But he begins to fall back into the arrogant and slothful ways of his youth, forgetting what he has learned from suffering. Appalled, he welcomes the *mestizo* and the betrayal that awaits him; for after such knowledge as his, the priest knows there can be no forgiveness. The half-caste tells the fugitive that the American gangster has been shot by the police and is asking for a priest. The wounded man had written a note on the back of one of Coral's school exercises—an exercise concerning Hamlet's inability to act once he knows Claudius to be his father's murderer, a counterpoint to the main action of the melodrama. The priest hums the song about a rose in a field that he had first heard while attempting to escape on the *General Obregon* at the novel's beginning.[6] As the priest welcomes his Judas, he becomes the pursuer; and his antagonist, the lieutenant, the pursued.

Over the body of the American gangster, the advocate of the religious order, for the first time in full command of his ministry, opposes the priest of the secular order, in their third encounter. The satirical poles are charged over the body of Nemesis, and a debate ensues. The lieutenant argues that the priest, although himself a good man, is a danger to the well-being of the state and that his destruction is necessary to secure that well-being. He insists that the priest's religion does not free people from want and misery, and that his does. "We'll give people food instead," he says, "teach them to read, give them books. We'll see they don't suffer" (233). To this the priest makes the only answer he can. The poor, he says, are in greatest favor with God, and the kingdom of heaven is theirs. He agrees with the lieutenant that the only certainty of life is death, but he disagrees with him as to what constitutes the essence of living. He points out that he who rules through power and fear is open to the temptations of power and fear; and he insists that unless the minister of the secular order maintain his motives in honesty and truth, nothing but corruption can result from his office: "It's no good your working for your end unless you're a good man yourself. And there won't always be good men in your

party. But it doesn't matter so much my being a coward—and all
the rest. I can put God into a man's mouth just the same—and I can
give him God's pardon. It wouldn't make any difference to that if
every priest in the Church was like me" (234).

The difference in their beliefs comes down to the simple fact that
the priest has perfection as his point of reference. "It's better to
let [the poor] die in dirt and wake in heaven," he says (239). And
here the novel's satire on the political order is made explicit. Once
the lieutenant has clothed and fed the body and pushed the face of
the poor into the dirt to do so—forced them to accept the "sacraments" of political "progress"—what is left but another religion,
one that replaces humility and decency and love with fear and
violence and despair? The priest insists that unless authority begins
from perfection, from God, it will breed corruption. He goes on to
point out that there will not always be good men in the lieutenant's
party. Speaking with the authority of his Church, the priest is
nevertheless aware of his inadequacies as a man; and he has found
the mercy of God incomprehensible: "I don't know a thing about
the mercy of God: I don't know how awful the human heart looks
to him. But I do know this—that if there's ever been a single man
in this state damned, then I'll be damned too. . . . I wouldn't
want it to be any different. I just want justice, that's all" (240).

The notion is again from Péguy;; Greene had used it in the
epilogue scene of *Brighton Rock* when the priest had asked Rose to
hope and pray. Rose's knowledge of the teachings of her religion
had told her that Pinkie was damned, and the lieutenant's intelligence tells him that if there is salvation, the priest is saved. Impressed with the sincerity of the priest, the lieutenant promises to
ask Father José, the conformist, to hear the whiskey priest's confession, even if it means a "triumph for that old corrupt God-ridden
world" (243).

It is their pity for suffering that both the whiskey priest and the
man of power have in common; and they realize too that they will
never be able to agree. This again is an aspect of the novel's satire,
heavy-handed though it may seem. The lieutenant in giving in to
the priest's plea for a confessor feels his weakness, but he refuses to
aknowledge it as an index of his strength. The priest has lived in
the shadow of plenitude, whereas the lieutenant has experienced
vacancy. When Father José refuses to hear the fugitive's confession,
the secular order seems to triumph; but strangely, the lieutenant

experiences the sensation of vacancy as he never has before. The priest has touched the heart of the man; yet in the pursuit of his duty the lieutenant remains inflexible. And indeed he must, or tear the fabric of the allegory; for his capitulation would mean the submission of the power cult to God.

In having submitted to the will of God, the priest has come to an understanding of God in the phenomenal world. Alone in his cell while awaiting execution, he discovers that his love for human beings extends only to Brigitta, his evil daughter. He attempts to bargain with God, offering his damnation for her salvation. He resents the fact that the child who had nothing to do with desiring life is to be damned. He himself is the cause of her evil—he can hate his sin, but he cannot hate the result of it. He thinks of his inability to love all living things, feeling that he has failed God again and that he will approach him empty-handed. He dreams of Coral Fellows, his "good" daughter and sees her as his advocate at the throne of God. In the last moments he realizes the enormity of his human failings, and his tears are those of genuine contrition.

Yet the priest does not go to God empty-handed. Unknown to him he has touched the hearts of three, perhaps four, bystanders: the child Coral; the boy Luis; Mr. Tench, the dentist; and he has made the lieutenant aware of his emptiness. Coral had seen the crosses that the fugitive had left on the wall of the banana barn, and with her first menstrual pain the realization of God in the world had come to her—pain, suffering. Bored by the romanticized saints' lives his mother has been reading him, the boy Luis begins to understand true heroism through the execution of the priest. As the lieutenant walks by, feeling his emptiness, he sees the boy and remembers that just such a one had played with his pistol a few weeks before. Luis spits at him, and the spittle lands on the holster. That night the boy admits another fugitive priest to his mother's house. Dr. Tench watches the execution from the chief of police's window—he has come to remove an infected tooth. As he sees the fugitive die, he determines to leave the country, to return to England, and to set his lands in order. The priest leaves the impression of his heroism on three hearts, and he shows the lieutenant the possibility of salvation.

Perhaps the chief criticism that has been aimed at *The Power and the Glory* is that it is narrowly Roman Catholic. The whiskey priest may be a Roman Catholic, but what he represents transcends the narrow limits of any one religious belief. The fact that he is a Catholic merely intensifies the conflict of the novel and lends dignity to its action. As the fugitive battles the lieutenant and the organized violence that he symbolizes, the Church fades into the background. The priest becomes an individual fighting a guerrilla war for what he believes to be right and true. While finding out, like Everyman, the ways and means of his personal salvation, he succeeds in setting up a reaction as continuous as life itself. Through the character of the priest, Greene approaches the precincts of myth.

The Heart of the Matter

Everyone who has read Graham Greene's *The Heart of the Matter* has in one way or another become aware of the critical furor occasioned by the religious issues arising from the suicide of the protagonist, Major Scobie. Evelyn Waugh wrote in the *Commonweal* upon publication of *The Heart of the Matter:* "To me the idea of willing my own damnation for the love of God is either a very loose poetical expression or a mad blasphemy, for the God who accepted that sacrifice could be neither just nor lovable."[7] It is not the purpose here, however, to paraphrase those critics who for various reasons have accused Greene of being everything from a Manichaean to an existentialist.[8] Yet many readers of *The Heart of the Matter* have made the serious error of attempting to abstract from its pages a personal philosophy or religious belief. Insisting on a prerogative of philosophical and theological speculation, critics and fans alike have failed to recognize that in his serious novels Greene creates an experience of life that is not so much representative of a religious bias as of a human condition. Considering his position as a Catholic writer, Greene's statement to Elizabeth Bowen bears repetition. He says, the reader will remember, that literature has nothing to do with edification, arguing that literature is not amoral but presents a personal moral; and that the morality of an individual is seldom identical with the morality of the group to which he belongs. As novelist, Greene believes that he must be free to write as he wishes, that he must give doubt, and even denial, self-expression. If he cannot do so, he is no freer than a Communist propagandist.[9]

The Heart of the Matter is not one of Greene's favorite works, but only partly because of the arguments in the Catholic journals that it occasioned. In his introductory note to the revised version of the novel he explains that the six years of war that separated it from *The Power and the Glory* had made him "rusty with disuse and misuse." He began work in 1946, "three years after I had closed my small office and burnt my files and code-books."[10] Out of practice and lacking confidence he had trouble getting his character Wilson off the hotel balcony, where he first spies on Scobie, and into a plot. At first Greene vacillated between two books—"one was the novel I wrote; the other was to have been an 'entertainment,' " told from the point of view of the criminal, the detective to be discovered in the final states of the narrative. Wilson, the undercover man sent to West Africa to investigate diamond smuggling and to serve as a thorn in Scobie's side, is all that remains of the discarded entertainment (xiii).

Scobie was primarily conceived as a means of enlarging on the theme of pity, which Greene had outlined in *The Ministry of Fear,* perhaps his most successful entertainment—"the disastrous effect on human beings of pity as distinct from compassion . . . intended to show that pity can be the expression of an almost monstrous pride" (xiii–xiv). The effect on the reader was not what Greene had anticipated; Scobie was perceived as a good man, "haunted to his doom by the hardness of his wife" (xiv).

The problems with the novel, Greene feels, have as much to do with presentation and craft as with subject matter and characterization. In the version he revised for inclusion in the Collected Edition, he restored the sequence he had eliminated in preparing the novel for its original publication in which Louise is sympathetically presented from Wilson's point of view (between chapter one and chapter two of part two). The sequence had seemed at first a breaking of Scobie's point of view and a slackening of narrative tension: "By eliminating it I thought I had gained intensity and impetus, but I had sacrificed tone." The reinstated passage presents the novel as Greene first wrote it, "apart from minor revisions, perhaps more numerous than in any other novel in this edition" (xiv).

Greene admits that he may be unduly harsh in his judgment of the novel, and confesses that he personally has little belief in the doctrine of eternal punishment, the point that continues to perturb readers of the work. He points out that it is Scobie who believes in hell, that suicide is Scobie's solution to save God from himself, "the final twist of the screw of his inordinate pride" (xv).

Pride is without doubt Scobie's great flaw of character, but so commingled with a compassionate awareness of misery and unhappiness, especially in the first half of the novel, that its effects are minimized as he comes inevitably and mistakenly to see suicide as the only useful solution for a problem he thinks he alone has brought into being. Two compelling sequences, among the best that Greene has written, do much to make Scobie one of his most attractive and sympathetic characters.

The first is Scobie's journey to the interior—to his heart of darkness—to investigate the suicide of the boy-man, Dicky Pemberton. First dreams, then hallucination brought on by fever provide premonitions of the novel's denouement while indicating the depth of Scobie's emotional attachment to Louise as well as his love of God. The similarity of names (Louise calls him Ticki to show affection and to taunt him), the symbolism of the hanged-man of the Tarot pack, the suffocating heat, Scobie's awareness of the pathetic debris of young Pemberton's life—all contribute to an unshakeable belief in the essential goodness of the character, a conviction that does not easily fall away. The second such episode is the one that portrays the death of the girl in the sequence that describes the survivors of the torpedoed ship that brings Helen Rolt into Scobie's life. Scobie forms a shadow-rabbit on the wall for the child who calls him "father"; she becomes for him his daughter Caroline, whose death Louise had lived through alone. Then he invents, mercifully, an adventure to amuse the boy who will live. Indeed, the character of Scobie is so well perceived, his humanity so well set forth, that he becomes one of Greene's most challenging and rounded characters. Ironically, it is because his portrait is so convincing that readers become concerned over the religious issues raised by the suicide at the novel's end. Not even the full measure of self-pity that Greene accords Scobie detracts from the characterization. Despite the fact that Greene had intended to separate pity from compassion in Scobie, it is the character's full measure of compassion that distinguishes him.

The point to consider in any discussion of *The Heart of the Matter* is not so much why Greene uses religious subject matter but how; it is important to decide whether or not his use of religious materials invalidates the novel as a work of art. And to do so fairly, Greene must be considered as a novelist who is a Catholic, not as a dilettante of religion and theology, or, to repeat his statement in his essay on the religious aspect of Henry James, "a philosopher or religious teacher of the second rank." The problem then of whether Major Scobie is "saved" or not according to the teachings of the Catholic Church becomes a minor consideration; for the novel presents a personal moral—Scobie's moral—that may not coincide with that of orthodox Catholicism.

Scobie's struggle with himself and with the God of the Catholic Church forms the basis of the conflict: Scobie's pity for suffering humanity forces him to suicide, the sin of despair. And according to the Church, this is damnation. As Kenneth Allott and Miriam Farris point out, "Discussion of the meaning of *The Heart of the Matter* is doomed in advance to sterility if it does not take into account that the words composing the book have been organized primarily with an artistic, rather than a philosophical or theological, intention."[11] Yet it is incorrect to minimize the importance of the religious theme, for it is the frame of reference within which the narrative develops. Neglecting the spiritual conflict within Scobie reduces the novel to a structural tour de force, vitiating the intense spiritual drama that is the novel's reason for being, diminishing the aspect of recognition, and misconstruing the theme of betrayal, interwoven with Scobie's intense love of God, all of which are fundamental to the comprehension of the book. It is more nearly correct to accept Scobie's Catholicism as something akin to the Fatality of Greek drama.

For Major Scobie, as for Arthur Rowe of *The Ministry of Fear,* pity is the keynote of human existence: "What an absurd thing it was to expect happiness in a world so full of misery. . . . If one knew, he wondered, the facts, would one have to feel pity even for the planets? if one reached what they called the heart of the matter?" (139). The imagery of the novel forms an objective correlative for the theme of pity and formulates the mood. References to rusty handcuffs, broken rosaries, swollen pye-dogs, joints of meat, cannon fodder—all eventually resolve themselves into an overwhelming sense of decay. The rosary and the handcuffs as they are woven into the design of the work become symbolic of divine justice opposing human justice. Scobie stands in relationship to his sphere as God does to his. The vulture hovers over him, implying not the terror of death—as it does for the whiskey priest in *The Power and the Glory*—but the terror of life and the remoteness of death: "Couldn't the test of man have been carried out in fewer years? Couldn't we

have committed our first major sin at seven, have ruined ourselves
for love or hate at ten, have clutched at redemption on a fifteen-
year-old death-bed?" (52).

The setting of the novel, West Africa, allows for such imaginative
painting, yet a sense of time and place is fully accommodated. The
rain and the steam, the atabrine-yellow faces, the gangrenous flesh,
all indicate a languor and ennui that allow for an explosion of any
kind. There is an implicit tension created, for the reader is ever
conscious of World War II through the hostility that exists between
the English sector and the Vichy French sector across the river. The
sense of history and the threat of violence are neatly compressed, as
in classical drama, into the relationships that exist among a few
people. The individual struggle is of first importance; the imagery
and the setting form a portion of that Necessity that propels Scobie
on his quest of recognition. The dramatic construction of the plot,
moreover, accommodates the catastrophe.

A middle-aged police officer in British West Africa, Major Scobie,
referred to as "Scobie the Just," a member of Greene's "awkward
squad," one who has had no opportunity to break the more serious
military rules, is passed over for promotion (8). His wife Louise,
for whom he feels only pity and responsibility, urges him to allow
her to go on holiday to South Africa, to escape the malice of her
"friends." To avoid making her unhappy, Scobie borrows from Yusef, a merchant suspected of diamond smuggling by Wilson, the
British agent who fancies himself in love with Louise. Yusef is
presented as the evil aspect of Scobie, and indeed he becomes the
tool of Necessity. The doubling device is of course Conradian.

A torpedoed ship brings Helen Rolt into the pattern of Scobie's
unhappiness. He sees her carried on shore, after forty days in an
open boat, clutching her stamp album like a child. And he falls in
love with her because she is pathetic: "Against the beautiful and
the clever and the successful, one can wage a pitiless war, but not
against the unattractive: then the millstone weighs on the breast"
(49). The situation builds into the eternal triangle; and it is a credit
to Greene's artistry that he is able to pour heady wine into such an
old barrel. Scobie soon realizes that his love for Helen is only another
facet of his pity. He realizes that Helen is Louise and Louise is
Helen, and that he is equally responsible for the happiness of both:
"Pity smouldered like decay at his heart. . . . He knew from experience how passion died away and how love went, but pity always

stayed. Nothing ever diminished pity. The conditions of life nurtured it" (205). After an argument he writes Helen a note: "I love
you more than myself, more than my wife, more than God I think"
(209). The note falls into the hands of Yusef, who blackmails Scobie
into smuggling diamonds for him.

When Louise returns from South Africa, Wilson blurts out that
Scobie and Helen are lovers. To see whether or not Scobie has given
up his mistress, Louise insists that he accompany her to Communion.
How simple it would be, he thinks, to withdraw pity from Helen,
repent his sin in the confessional, and free himself of responsibility.
But he is too honest to pretend a repentance he does not feel. His
confessor, Father Rank, is merely an intermediary; Scobie knows
that the brief rests with God, and he will not add hypocrisy to his
other sins. He knows that he must crucify either God or Louise or
Helen. The suffering of God, however, is unreal, remote; that of
Louise and Helen is nearer—he can feel their pain. He chooses
sacrilege and damnation by taking Communion without having
received absolution at confession: "O, God, I offer my damnation to
you. Take it. Use it for them" (264).

With the sacrilege comes the commissionership that Louise has
so long coveted. Now "of the devil's party," Scobie knows that he
will go from "damned success to damned success" (267); and he
indulges in the bitter jest. With the smuggling of the diamonds
comes his realization that he is "one of those whom people pity"
and the further awareness that his corruption corrupts others (235).
He tacitly agrees to the murder of his boy Ali by one of Yusef's
killers. Understanding that he has destroyed the boy he loves to
keep from bringing hurt to either Helen or Louise, he determines
to set them free of him. He reasons that, if he kills himself, he will
stop crucifying God; and it is God whom he loves above all things:

O God, I am the only guilty one because I've known the answers all the
time. I've preferred to give you pain rather than give pain to Helen or
my wife because I can't observe your suffering. I can only imagine it. But
there are limits to what I can do to you—or them. I can't desert either
of them while I am alive, but I can die and remove myself from their
blood stream. They are ill with me. . . . I can't go on, month after
month, insulting you. I can't face coming up to the altar at Christmas—
your birthday feast—and taking your body and blood for the sake of a

lie. I can't do that. You'll be better off if you lose me once and for all. (304)

He will hurt God once and for all—deprive God of himself as he will deprive himself of God. A voice within tempts him to virtue as to sin: "You say you love me, and yet you'll do this to me—rob me of you forever. I made you with love. . . . And now you push me away, you put me out of your reach." Scobie answers, "No. I don't trust you. I've never trusted you. If you made me, you made this feeling of responsibility that I've carried about like a sack of bricks" (305).

Scobie's sin is that he prefers to trust himself, in his limited knowledge of love, over God. He cannot put his faith in trust of God; for his faith is love and pity its image. Scobie cannot comprehend the "appalling" nature of divine mercy. He knows that the choice for damnation is his alone as he drinks the narcotic. He hears someone calling for him, a cry of distress; automatically he stirs himself to act. Aloud he says, "Dear God, I love . . ." (313).

At the end of the novel Father Rank returns to give comfort to the living, to reestablish the norm of the Church and to give hope for Scobie's soul, even though he committed suicide. "The Church knows all the rules," he says, "But it doesn't know what goes on in a single human heart" (320). He insists that, if Louise has forgiven Scobie, then God can be no less forgiving. Louise remarks that Scobie really loved no one but God, and the reader remembers how often Scobie had been struck by the truth of her perceptions.

The Heart of the Matter takes its epigraph from Péguy: "Le pécheur est au coeur même de chrétienté. . . . Nul n'est aussi compétent que le pécheur en matière de chrétienté. Nul, si ce n'est le saint." Scobie's pity, his love, becomes emblematic of a universal love; it is in matters of trust that he fails. In the process of learning the wherewithal of his religion, he realizes the immensity of human commitment, but he fails to recognize the immensity of the mercy of God. His pride and his humility conspire against him, and, because he cannot trust the God he loves, he commits the sin of despair. In matters of his religion he has become competent, for according to Greene the sinner is very close to God.

In a discerning essay published in *Transformation Three,* Martin C. D'Arcy discusses the anatomy of the hero, albeit somewhat problematically, within a Christian context:

In the Christian scale of values the hero is not easily distinguishable from the saint; it is more a matter of emphasis than of division. The saint cannot be canonized unless he can be shown to have practiced heroic virtues; the man of heroic deeds cannot be called a hero unless there is evidence that his inner spirit corresponds with his deeds, and that his motives are pure. But whereas in using the word saint, the emphasis is on a man's relation to God and his spiritual work for his fellow man, it is prowess and self-sacrifice for others, for friends or a nation, which is uppermost in our thought of the hero.[12]

D'Arcy goes on to point out what C. Day Lewis in *A Hope for Poetry* and Rex Warner in *The Cult of Power* had pointed out before him in the late thirties and early forties. The social organism has grown to such a size that it has complicated man's relationship with the other life, and man has come to associate his limitations with the state. The potentiality of tragic action in either the classical or the Elizabethan sense is limited because the individual no longer finds means to battle so complex and bewildering an organism. The Aristotelian concept of tragic flaw or error in judgment no longer appertains. It is something of this problem that Franz Kafka dramatizes in his works, particularly in *The Trial* and in *The Castle*. Such "heroes" created by Arthur Miller as Willy Loman in *Death of a Salesman* and Joe Keller in *All My Sons* become at best pitiful characters. However, if the frame of reference within which the character moves is defined, if the antagonist is shown to be in some measure a noble one, and if the protagonist has some notion of the force he opposes and why he opposes it, then the possibility for heroism is no longer limited. The error in judgment or the tragic flaw becomes once again a significant consideration. The hero can be as tragic as he was in Greek drama or in Elizabethan tragedy.

This is the case with Scobie. He knows his antagonist, and he recognizes his strength. What he cannot accept is the orthodox Roman Catholic conception of God. For Scobie suffering and love are irreconcilable. He cannot fathom a God who seems not to love those whom he has created, a God who has not the same sense of pity and responsibility as himself. Scobie can love infinite goodness, but he cannot trust it since it allows unreasonable anguish. And in *The Heart of the Matter* Greene's daring is incredible: he pits the individual against God. Scobie becomes at once a traitor, a scapegoat, and a hero; his sense of pity, an image of his love for God, assumes the proportions of a tragic flaw. It is incontestable that he suffers more than he deserves; but whether or not he is damned becomes unimportant in a consideration of his heroism. Yusef becomes Necessity, for he makes the tragedy inevitable; and Catholicism hangs over the novel like the Fatality of Greek drama. Pity and fear are aroused in the reader, and Greene wisely leaves the issue of damnation open at the end. What is important is that Scobie by pleading for humanity opposes God and is defeated, and his excessive pity transforms him into a truly tragic figure.

The references to *Othello* and to *1 Henry IV* appear in the novel for reasons of counterpoint and humanistic extension. When Yusef, the evil that is in Scobie, says, "I am the base Indian," Scobie realizes that his integrity, the pearl worth all his tribe, has been bartered for the happiness of Helen and Louise (233). He has made the mistake of thinking that he can arrange the happiness of others, but he knows in his heart that "no one can arrange another's happiness," for experience has taught him this (93). Like Othello, Scobie loves not wisely but too well. The human entanglement in which he finds himself admits only one solution—suicide. The reference to Hotspur, whose role Scobie had played as a schoolboy, points out, again, that Scobie feels more keenly the loss of his honor, his link to man, than the loss of brittle life. To discuss whether or not Othello is damned and Hotspur saved is absurd, but Greene invites such discussion when he pits Scobie against God. One hopes that Scobie and Othello are, at worst, in a special limbo reserved for literary heroes.

In the light of such conflict with God, it is necessary to accept the religious theme as primary and all other considerations as secondary. It is precisely because Scobie's heroism depends so strongly on a Roman Catholic frame of reference that Father Rank cannot be dismissed as the mere plot contrivance that Allott and Farris consider him. Father Rank must attempt to restore the norm of the Church; its doctrines must be presented as flexible enough to accommodate heroic action: the Church may know all the rules but not what goes on in a human heart. Scobie may have killed himself, but he may have repented in the moment before death. Father Rank's presence is indispensable to the plan of the novel, for Greene's overall dramatic technique in the construction of plot demands, as has been noted, that someone restore balance and order in the world after the passions of men have spent themselves. At the end of *Othello*, Lodovico reestablishes law on the island of Cyprus and returns to

Venice to relate with sorry heart the heavy deed that loads the tragic bed.

But the analogy must not be pressed too far. The contexts within which the two dramas occur are quite alien. Othello is a man of noble deeds because his society has fostered such nobility. Scobie is a simple man who becomes capable of heroism because of a sense of pity. Like Prometheus, he chooses to defy God.

The End of the Affair

In *The Heart of the Matter* Henry Scobie's pride is paradoxically suggested by a readiness to accept the doctrines of the Catholic Church for himself but not for others. He does not so much fear hellfire as he does the permanent sense of loss that the Church describes as one of the consequences of damnation. To be deprived of the God he loves is for Scobie the heart of the matter. Sentimentally he sees himself as Christ committing suicide for mankind (220). Something of this striking notion, dying for love of God, is to be discovered in Greene's next novel, *The End of the Affair,* which concludes the pattern begun in *Brighton Rock* in which the possibilities of damnation and salvation are primary concerns. In *The End of the Affair* the conditions for sainthood are explored and the possibility, to some readers the inevitability, of the heroine's salvation portrayed. In its 29 October 1951 issue, *Time* quoted Greene as saying, "I wrote a novel about a man who goes to hell—*Brighton Rock*—another about a man who goes to heaven—*The Power and the Glory.* Now I've simply written one about a man who goes to purgatory [*The Heart of the Matter*]. I don't know what all the fuss is about." The closures of these novels, however, defy so simplistic a resolution for the situations they present. Yet *The End of the Affair* may well be a novel about a woman who goes to heaven, for Greene is consciously, perhaps even self-consciously, working within the anatomy of sainthood. *The End of the Affair* may in fact be the most Catholic of his novels in the narrowest sense of the definition.

In his introductory note to the revised volume in the Collected Edition, Greene tells his reader that he began the work in December of 1948, that it was in some measure influenced by his reading of the British Catholic theologian Friedrich von Hügel's study of St. Catharine of Genoa. In going over Hügel's life of Catharine, noted in Catholic hagiographies for her ministrations to the sick during the Italian plagues of 1497 and 1501, Greene noted to his surprise that, contrary to custom, he had made no marks about Catharine herself on the pages of the volume. In another of Hügel's essays, however, he discovered that he had marked a passage consistent with the theologian's independent thinking concerning the nature of inner security and moral responsibility: "the purification and slow constitution of the Individual into a Person, by means of the Thing-element, the apparently blind Determinism of Natural Law and Natural happenings. . . . Nothing can be more certain than that we must admit and place this undeniable, increasingly obtrusive, element and power *somewhere* in our lives: if we will not own it as a means, it will grip us as our end."[13] Greene continues that the novel as it developed went astray of the notion he abstracted from his reading of Hügel. *The End of the Affair* was to have been the story of a man "driven and overwhelmed by the accumulation of natural coincidences, until he feared that, with one more, the excuse of coincidence would break" (ix). The mystical element of Catharine's life, noted by Hügel, nevertheless found its way into the character of Sarah Miles as Greene attempted a metaphysical dialectic on the subject of human and divine love.

With the death of Sarah, Greene discovered that he had "no great appetite to continue" the work and that what remained was a "philosophic theme" (ix). In an attempt to reassert something of the original notion, he made minor revisions and changes for the Collected Edition, attempting a more natural explanation of the "miracles" attributed to Sarah in the original version. Smythe's strawberry mark, for example, becomes a "livid spot," Urticaria, which might be explained as having a nervous origin. The book which should have been as long after Sarah's death as it was before, the "coincidences" that should have continued over several years "battering the mind of Bendrix, forcing on him a reluctant doubt of his own atheism" to fulfill Hügel's notion, came to a quick conclusion (x). The last pages, which Greene likes very much, would, however, have remained the same had he gone on to complete the novel as he feels it should have been.

If the notion of doubt yielding inexorably to faith through an appreciation of natural happenings and the mystical element in Sarah's character owe to Hügel, then the imagery and symbolism of *The End of the Affair* owe as much to John of the Cross and T. S. Eliot, for the staircase on which Bendrix dies to be reborn in answer to Sarah's prayer is to be found in both writers, as are the images of aridity and rain. The novel also demonstrates the technical influence of Ford Madox Ford's *The Good Soldier,* a novel that Greene admits to having read many times.

To develop a metaphysical dialogue as an aspect of the novel's thesis, Greene chose, as had Ford in *The Good Soldier,* an unreliable narrator, but he opted for a thoroughly reliable heroine. At one point Bendrix remembers that Sara had once called herself a bitch and a fake, yet there are few elements of either bitchery or fakery in the presentation, for Sarah is consistently honest, always kind and responsive, fully appreciated by the characters she touches on her way to sainthood. Indeed it is Bendrix who is both bitch and fake, for he is jealous, conniving, sadistic, and foolish. One of the flaws of the novel is quite simply the fact, sexual matters excluded, that it is difficult to understand why Sarah loves him. Yet it would be capricious to say that she wills her death merely to be rid of him. Gwen Boardman, on the other hand, finds Bendrix attractive and sees him as an "advance over the previously confused lovers in Greene's work."[14]

Following *The Third Man,* which also employs first-person narration, and *The Heart of the Matter,* in which melodrama yields to tragedy, *The End of the Affair* is for many of his readers a full vindication of Greene as a major artist of the twentieth-century novel. The allegorical and melodramatic contrivances of *Brighton Rock, The Power and the Glory,* and *The Heart of the Matter,* bothersome and repugnant to many, are replaced by devices more consistent with the forms of the modern novel: the emotionally involved and therefore unreliable narrator, stream-of-consciousness, the flashback or time shift, the diary, the letter, the inner reverie, the use of dream for symbolical as well as foreshadowing purposes, and the spiritual debate. In his note to the volume Greene says that his use of first-person narration was suggested by Dickens's use of the device in *Great Expectations.* It is more nearly correct, however, to see it as a confirmation of his awareness of the artistic demands of the novel form and of Henry James, François Mauriac,[15] and Ford Madox Ford on his techniques.

In a number of places Greene has admitted to a reliance on Percy Lubbock's *The Craft of Fiction* for an understanding of the possibilities as well as the limitations of point of view, especially as practiced by James, and in his review of *La Pharisienne* in *The Lost Childhood,* he linked James and Mauriac: "[With] the death of James the religious sense was lost to the English novel, and with the religious sense went the sense of the importance of the human act."[16] To this he added that novelists after James and Flaubert had taken refuge in the subjective novel and that the characters of E. M. Forster and Virginia Woolf "wandered like cardboard symbols through a world that was paper-thin." Greene went on to imply that the novel since the 1930s had restored the religious sense to literature insofar as it had reconsidered the claims of James and Flaubert:

> M. Mauriac's first importance to an English reader, therefore, is that he belongs to the company of the great traditional novelists: he is a writer for whom the visible world has not ceased to exist, whose characters have the solidity and importance of men with souls to save or lose, and a writer who claims the traditional and essential right of a novelist, to comment, to express his views. For how tired we have become of the dogmatically "pure" novel, the tradition founded by Flaubert and reaching its magnificent tortuous climax in England in the works of Henry James. (70)

Greene then proceeded to comment on Mauriac's use of the "I":

> The exclusion of the author can go too far. Even the author, poor devil, has a right to exist, and M. Mauriac reaffirms that right. It is true that the Flaubertian form is not so completely abandoned in this novel [*La Pharisienne*] as in *Le Baiser au Lépreux*; the "I" of the story plays a part in the action; any commentary there is can be attributed by purists to this fictional "I," but the pretence is thin—"I" is dominated by I. (70)

It is through Maurice Bendrix, the "I," that Greene makes the secular commentary on the religious action of his novel. Bendrix, like Charles Ryder in Waugh's *Brideshead Revisited,* is the character on whom the action of the novel leaves the most dominant impression. And like *Brideshead Revisited, The End of the Affair* has adultery for its theme. In Waugh's novel Julia Mottram and Ryder discover that their love is a prelude to a love of God. Ryder's acceptance of the supernatural order in the phenomenal world leads to a religious conversion. The parallel, significant in the light of Greene's overall development, indicates his full awareness of more orthodox approaches to the doctrines of the Church. Waugh, who had severely criticized the theology of *The Heart of the Matter,* applauded Greene's ability to use the religious theme brilliantly and provokingly in *The*

End of the Affair: "Mr. Greene is to be congratulated on a fresh achievement. He shows that in middle life his mind is suppler and his interests wider than in youth; that he is a writer of real stamina. He has triumphantly passed his climacteric where so many talents fail."[17]

Substituting the "advanced" techniques of the contemporary novel for the melodramatic contrivances of the earlier works, Greene attempts to tell the story of a saint. If the reader remembers his assertion that "the greatest saints have been men with more than a normal capacity for evil," the obvious parallels of Mary Magdalene and St. Augustine come to mind. Greene uses polarities, as he had done in *Brighton Rock,* as the means of presenting his theme: Hate and love are different sides of the same coin; and, when the coin is set spinning, the differences are impossible to distinguish. Greene's theme is that adultery—lust—can indicate a love of God. "What do we really know of lust?" writes the saintly priest in Georges Bernanos's *The Diary of a Country Priest,* "Lust is a mysterious wound in the side of humanity; or rather at the very source of its life! . . . God! how is it we fail to realize that the mask of pleasure, stripped of all hypocrisy, is that of anguish?"[18]

A novelist who has not yet committed the crime of becoming popular, Bendrix writes an account of a love affair that began five or six years before his narrative begins. He is uncomfortable in telling his story, and Greene suggests the difficulty of the writer in dealing with materials that are part of his own experience. There are rhetorical questions in profusion, contradictions, and apostrophes—all indicating the spiritual turmoil of the writer, who should be objective, betraying himself into subjective analysis. The reader learns a good deal about Bendrix and feels that he is not the most admirable man in the world. Bendrix's account of the affair is primarily the carnal side, the passionate aspect; Sarah's the spiritual.

After portraying the point of view of his narrator, Greene allows the heroine's diary to fall into the lover's hands. In the diary the reader becomes aware of the spiritual struggle that is the chief concern of the novel. A third perspective, folded into Bendrix's all-encompassing narration, is achieved through Parkis, a detective whom Bendrix hires to spy on Sarah; a fourth through Henry Miles, Sarah's husband, the government functionary whose brain Bendrix has been wanting to pick through Sarah; a fifth through Richard Smythe, a rationalist to whom Sarah goes when she seeks to disbelieve in God. They are, in effect, the bystanders whom the heroine passes on her journey to sanctity. The parallel with the bystanders of *The Power and the Glory* is obvious.

In their study of Greene, Allott and Farris point out that he had toyed with the idea of portraying the action of *The Heart of the Matter* from the point of view of Louise Scobie but had rejected that idea because it would unnecessarily complicate the pattern of the novel. The controlled perspective of *The End of the Affair* allows Greene to develop his principal characters from several viewpoints while, at the same time, concentrating on the monomania of the narrator. The reader is in fact challenged to understand all that the narration implies. The central conflict of the novel is a religious one, yet the reader sees it from various angles. The devices—flashback, diary, reverie, letters—all throw light on a spiritual struggle.

The action of *The End of the Affair* is limited chiefly to an affair between the narrator and the heroine; the bystanders emerge as aspects of the theme only after Sarah's death. Henry Miles, who forms the third corner of one of the two love triangles, is important in the struggle because, as Bendrix observes, he has all the cards stacked in his favor: he is Sarah's husband. Bendrix and Sarah meet at a cocktail party, become lovers, and then separate. She dies; and, because her love for God is stronger than her love for a single man, she becomes a saint. It is God who intervenes to make a saint of Sarah and to put Bendrix on the road to Damascus.

In light of this, it is impossible to agree with those like Norman Shrapnel who, in his review of the novel's first state for the *Manchester Guardian,* insisted that the few "mild miracles" at the end "can be ignored without much loss" (4). These phenomena are the reason for the novel's existence. To deny them is to misunderstand completely Greene's purpose in having written the book, to indicate how carnal love can lead to a recognition and even acceptance of divine love. At the end of the novel, Father Crompton, a more forceful character than either Father Clay or Father Rank of *The Heart of the Matter,* understands Bendrix's pain (196). "There's nothing we can do that the saints haven't done before us" (203), Bendrix tells himself, continuing, "The saints, one would suppose, in a sense create themselves. They come alive. They are capable of the surprising act or word" (203). Because she loves Bendrix too well, Sarah promises God that she will never see him again if only God will restore him to life, for she believes Bendrix to have been killed in a bomb explosion. To make her keep her promise, God sends grace in every conceivable way: an unanswered telephone keeps Sarah from talking to Bendrix; a racking cough prevents her kissing him when she does see him; a husband's early return ties her to her home when she has decided to abandon her promise; and death, at the right moment, keeps her from losing all. Sarah succumbs to the grace of God and becomes a saint.

Bendrix, however, is finally not only doubtful but outraged; and he must be if he is to maintain the balance between the secular and the religious order. Yet, the final impression is made upon him. Because of the flashback technique the last physical occurrence of the novel's action appears on the first page of the book—Bendrix sits down to write his story. He speaks of those early days when "we were lucky enough not to believe" (1). Still the novel is Bendrix's journey of exploration, of recognition; and as he writes his and Sarah's story, he comes to a realization of the place of God in the world. In this manner the motif of flight and pursuit is incorporated into the writer's creative processes: Bendrix attempts to deny God, but God is too persistent a pursuer. The reader learns that Bendrix's spiritual dilemma amounts to an inability "to conceive of any God who is not as simple as a perfect equation, as clear as air" (6), Major Scobie's problem as it had been Péguy's. The convolutions of the novel become the best index to the complexity of the problem of God and grace in the world.

If Greene relied on *The Waste Land* for the imagery of his earlier novels and entertainments, in *The End of the Affair* he relies as heavily on "Ash Wednesday." Greene's interest in St. John of the Cross is patent—later, in *The Living Room,* one of his plays, a character reads from John. Both Sarah and Bendrix, within broad outline, follow the pattern of spiritual awareness described in John's *La Noce Oscura*. Here John describes the individual soul entering into a period of purgation, and he describes the battle between the spirit and the senses. (Eliot's demon of the stair is one of John of the Cross's contributions to "Ash Wednesday.") John describes, as does Eliot, the penitent experiencing despair, rebellion, and drought in his ascent to heaven. He speaks constantly of love, the interceding factor in helping man on his way to God, and John does not minimize the influence of the senses. Like Eliot, Greene makes conscious use of this symbolism, particularly that of the stair. In her journal Sarah describes a dream:

Two days ago I had such a sense of peace and quiet and love. Life was
going to be happy again, but last night I dreamed I was walking up a
long staircase to meet Maurice at the top. I was still happy because when
I reached the top of the staircase we were going to make love. I called to
him that I was coming, but it wasn't Maurice's voice who answered; it
was like a stranger's that boomed like a foghorn warning lost ships, and
scared me. I thought, he's left his flat and gone away and I don't know
where he is, and going down the stairs again the water rose beyond my
waist and the hall was thick with mist. (130)

When Bendrix first meets Sarah, he is not impressed by her
because, paradoxically, she is beautiful. To love, Bendrix must feel
himself superior, chiefly because he has one leg shorter than the
other, a handicap that accounts for a good deal of his cynicism.
Contrary to all his convictions, he falls in love with Sarah, and their
affair progresses. But Bendrix is jealous of Sarah—of her husband
and of her life away from him; he fears that one day she will cease
to love him. There are violent arguments and equally violent
reconciliations.

Sarah refuses to speak of the permanence of their love when
Bendrix encourages her to do so. Yet she often surprises him by
telling him that she loves him more than any man she has ever
known. At this period of her life, there is nothing of the saint in
Sarah; there is no thought of God in her life. There had been men
before Bendrix, and he reasons that there will be others after him.
She finds in him the lover her husband has never been. When she
tells Bendrix that she never loved anybody or anything as she does
him, she does not realize that this "perfect" human relationship is
but a shadow of a greater love. In her complete abandonment to
her lover she reckons at this point only on the gratification of her
physical passions; she does not realize the emptiness of her spiritual
self.

Having once experienced perfect human love with Bendrix, however, Sarah renounces him for God, and nothing short of divine
love will satisfy her. Unconsciously she has made provision for God
in her affair, for she always avoided calling Bendrix by his Christian
name, referring to him as "you." Just as the "I" of Bendrix indicates
the commentary on the physical theme, the "you," in its ambiguity
is expressive of God. It is, therefore, the unseen presence of God
that hovers over them and informs their physical love. Again Greene's
audacity is breathtaking; he succeeds in making his thesis believable

as the unseen "you" makes jealousy and anger the tools of grace. God is the "third man" whom Bendrix engages Parkis to find in the only vestige of melodrama in the novel.

When the novel begins, Bendrix tells his reader how he ran into Henry Miles one rainy night. Henry does not know that Bendrix and Sarah have been lovers; and he, Henry, confides to Bendrix that he thinks that Sarah is unfaithful. Bendrix's hatred and jealousy flare again even though he has had no contact with Sarah for several years. Bendrix agrees with Henry to the advisability of hiring a detective, and he volunteers to relieve Henry of the anxiety by making the arrangements himself. But Henry decides that such a plan is a discredit to him and Sarah. Then acknowledging for the first time Bendrix's obsession, he discovers that Sarah has been his confidant's mistress.

Without Henry's knowledge Bendrix hires Parkis, a good-natured, inept, and humorously conceived detective reminiscent of Jones in *The Ministry of Fear,* to discover Sarah's affair. The pattern of flight and pursuit finds expression on a spiritual level in Sarah's evasion of Bendrix and of God, as well as in Bendrix's evasion. Somehow Parkis manages to secure Sarah's journal—she never suspects that so intimate an account of her life is gone—and Bendrix discovers why she called an end to the affair. He reads her description of that day when, together in bed, the bombs began to fall. Looking to see whether or not the landlady had gone down to the shelter, Bendrix had been knocked unconscious. Finding him in the hall, Sarah believed him dead; she had returned to the bedroom and prayed:

Dear God, I said—why dear, why dear?—make me believe. I can't believe. Make me. I said, I'm a bitch and a fake and I hate myself. I can't do anything of myself. *Make* me believe. I shut my eyes tight, and I pressed my nails into the palms of my hands until I could feel nothing but the pain, and I said, I *will* believe. Give him a chance. Let him have his happiness. Do this, and I'll believe. But that wasn't enough. It doesn't hurt to believe. So I said, I love him and I'll do anything if You'll make him alive. I said very slowly, I'll give him up forever, only let him be alive with a chance, and I pressed and pressed and I could feel the skin break, and I said, People can love without seeing each other, can't they, they love You all their lives without seeing You, and then he came in at the door, and he was alive, and I thought now the agony of being without

him starts, and I wished he was safely back dead again under the door.
(99–100)

Bendrix discovers that the third corner of the spiritual triangle
is God; he had been the silent witness to all their acts of sex and
had intervened to claim Sarah for his own. God had accepted her
promise and had taken Sarah at her word. He *makes* her believe, for
Sarah chooses heaven as surely as Pinkie Brown in *Brighton Rock*
chooses hell. Once Bendrix learns of Sarah's love for God, he transfers
to him the hatred he has felt for Sarah. But he had hated her only
because he loved her. Now, with all the strength of his love, he
hates God, his rival.

Sarah's promise never to see Bendrix again causes her to start on
the long climb to sanctity. Trying to avoid the implications of her
promise, she seeks solace in other men; but all that she experiences
is a sense of dryness. In the early stages of her spiritual awareness
Sarah feels that she doesn't believe in God. But she does believe.
Since physical love no longer affords pleasure, she knows that she
cannot hurt God by being promiscuous. Luckily, she does not think
of suicide as Major Scobie does. Sarah knows that God exists, since
he put the thought of the vow in her mind; and she tries to hate
him. Her hatred is, paradoxically, the statement of her love—she
has yet to learn to put her trust in God. And this she cannot do
until she acknowledges the fact that by betraying her out of physical
life, he has shown her the way to spiritual life. In her early rebellion
Sarah feels that she can leave the desert whenever she wants to: "I
can catch a train home tomorrow and ring him [Bendrix] up on the
telephone . . . and we can spend the night together" (97). But she
knows this is impossible. Sarah has an overwhelming desire to love,
but she doesn't know what to do with it.

The alternating spasms of love and hatred that she feels for both
God and Bendrix eventually bring her to an understanding of spiritual love. She admits that what she had felt for Bendrix was merely
a prelude to the love she feels for God in the novel's crucial passage:

Did I ever love Maurice as much before I loved You? Or was it You I
really loved all the time? Did I touch You when I touched him? Could I
have touched You if I hadn't touched him first, touched him as I never
touched Henry, anybody? And he loved me and touched me as he never
did any other woman. But was it me he loved, or You? For he hated in

me the things You hate. He was on your side all the time without knowing
it. You willed our separation, but he willed it too. He worked for it with
his anger and his jealousy, and he worked for it with his love. For he gave
me so much love and I gave him so much love that soon there wasn't
anything left, when we'd finished, but You. (129–30)

In her love for Bendrix, Sarah finds love for God. And a preparation
is made for Bendrix's orientation into the scheme of God. In learning
to love God, Sarah finds peace, which she leaves to Bendrix as her
legacy. She writes in her journal: "When I ask You for pain, You
give me peace. Give it to him too. Give him my peace—he needs
it more" (130). Again Greene echoes Eliot's "Ash Wednesday" as
Sarah prays for strength and asks for peace.

Sarah's suffering teaches her not only to believe in God, to love
him, but to have faith in him. Her faith is her trust, and it is as
firm as that of the greatest saints. In the letter she writes to Bendrix,
she says: "I believe there's a God—I believe the whole bag of tricks,
there's nothing I don't believe, they could subdivide the Trinity
into a dozen parts and I'd believe. They could dig up records that
Christ had been invented by Pilate to get himself promoted and I'd
believe just the same. I've caught belief like a disease. I've fallen
into belief like I fell in love. . . . I fought belief for longer than
I fought love, but I haven't any fight left" (159).

In her flight from Bendrix and from God, Sarah had stumbled
into a Catholic Church and she had determined to become a member
of it. Henry and Bendrix, who find a common bond in their love
for Sarah, decide against a Catholic burial. There is no record of
Sarah's ever having been baptized, and Bendrix refuses to permit
Henry to make the arrangements that would have pleased Sarah
most. For Bendrix is determined to hate Sarah's God for having
deprived him of her. One remembers how bitterly he had hated
Sarah only a few weeks before. The pattern begins anew: Sarah hated
God for making her keep her vow; now Bendrix hates because he
must. The Catholic priest who enters into the action of the novel
at the last minute, in a manner more forceful than is usual with
Greene's priests, sets about his job of asserting the norm of the
Church. He argues against cremation at Golder's Green, but Bendrix, in his hatred, is firm in wanting to inflict a secular burial on
Sarah. "I wanted her burned up," he writes, "I wanted to be able
to say, Resurrect that body if you can. My jealousy has not finished,

like Henry's, with her death. It was as if she were alive still, in the company of a lover she had preferred to me" (148).

The day of the funeral Bendrix meets by appointment a writer of reviews named Waterbury. Instantly disliking the young man, he takes his girl away from him. Bendrix knows that he cannot love the girl, but he insists on proving his masculine superiority to the reviewer. What Bendrix really wants is to show Sarah that he can get along without her, but he immediately realizes the futility of his gesture. He implores Sarah in prayer to get him out of his predicament, not for his sake but for the girl's. Conveniently, Sarah's mother comes on the scene, and Bendrix wonders whether it is coincidence or an answer to his prayer that has brought Mrs. Bertram along. From her he learns that Sarah has been a Roman Catholic all her life, that she had been baptized at the age of two. The sainthood of Sarah becomes surer and surer, and the Roman Catholicism of the heroine becomes, indeed, much like the Fatality that hangs over Major Scobie, the referent that gives meaning to the narrative.

The "miracles," or the "blind determinism of natural law," begin to accrue. Lance, Parkis's son, ill with appendicitis, asks his father for the gift that Sarah had promised him. Parkis secures an old child's book from Henry, and Lance dreams that night that Sarah touches him on the side and cures him of his pain. Bendrix thinks about the coincidence, but he dismisses the idea of miracle. As the representative of the secular order, he is well within his rights to do so. Nevertheless, he cannot help but remember the priest's comment to Henry: "It only goes to show what a good woman your wife was" (197).

In her flight from grace Sarah had gone to Richard Smythe, a rationalist, who in true nineteenth-century fashion preached of the impossibility of belief in God. Smythe spoke to Sarah of the confusion implicit in the gospel texts, of Christ's never claiming to be God, and of chaos in the world. To keep from believing in God, Sarah had sought the proofs that would deny his existence; but each "proof" had made her feel more strongly within herself the truth of God's reality. Smythe's face, marred by "livid spots," had touched her pity. She had loved Smythe because of his unhappiness, understanding that his rebellion against God was induced by the physical defect. Here the theme of pity is brilliantly aligned with a sense of God and the humility of the saint. When Bendrix runs into Smythe several days after the funeral, he discovers that the discoloration has disappeared from his face. Smythe first tells Bendrix that he has been treated electrically; later, over the telephone, he admits that the mark had disappeared of itself, and Bendrix remembers that Sarah had recorded in her journal how she had kissed it. He knows that such disfigurements are often hysterical in origin and that they can be reasoned away by psychiatric treatment; but this time he cannot dismiss the idea of a miracle so easily.

As far as the structure of the novel is concerned, these "occurrences" or "coincidences" at the end cannot summarily be put aside. Inasmuch as Greene works consciously with the anatomy of saint-hood and the precedent of sinners being the preferred of God has been set by such luminaries as St. Augustine and Mary Magdalene, the reader accepts the fact that Greene wishes the coincidences to be considered as physical proofs of a divine purpose. To all intents and purposes, Sarah Miles becomes a saint, and the next steps in her spiritual recognition are beatification and canonization. Yet it will never come to this because Bendrix, in his hatred, refuses to allow the facts of Sarah's life to be "vulgarized." As the representative of the world in general, Bendrix's "rational" approach to the dilemma seems viable, but it is at odds with his emotional perceptions.

The novel ostensibly ends on a note of perplexity. Bendrix finds himself in the center of indifference, on the rim of the everlasting yes. He is dominated by hatred, which Father Crompton correctly diagnoses as pain, but he knows that hate is the opposite side of love's coin: "I said to Sarah, all right, have it your way. I believe you live and that He exists, but it will take more than your prayers to turn this hatred of Him into love. He robbed me, and . . . I'll rob Him of what He wants in me. Hatred is in my brain, not in my stomach or my skin. It can't be removed like a rash or an ache. Didn't I hate you as well as love you? And don't I hate myself?" (210). Capable of great hatred, Bendrix is equally capable of great love; and the reader cannot believe that he is too old to learn. Somehow, the Blessed Damozel is leaning over the golden bar of heaven yearning for him, and he has just begun to love.

Technically *The End of the Affair* is brilliant. Greene's use of the diary and of the journal allows him not only to characterize his people but also to portray the various levels of meaning of the spiritual drama enacted. Bendrix looks at Sarah; Sarah looks at herself as she looks at God. The bystanders look at Sarah, and she leaves her mark on them. The dream sequences allow Greene to describe in symbolic terms the conflict within her, and the debates allow him to give concrete expression to her struggle and to fulfill the demands of the metaphysical dialogue. The time shifts permit him to show the reader the various phases of the development of the action and to portray the state of Bendrix's mind as he describes the affair.

The End of the Affair is, perhaps, the most Catholic of Greene's novels. Even Waugh complains that the novel is too sectarian in that it implies that the Church is like a secret society. Many of Greene's previous works had ended with the death of the central characters and had permitted a priest to reestablish the norm of the Church after men had finished wrestling with their souls. In The End of the Affair, however, the theme of sainthood is so obviously Roman Catholic in its development that the importance of the priest as spokesman is negligible, consequently permitting a more fully developed characterization of him as a person. Furthermore, the role is minimized by the fact that the melodramatic framework has disappeared, and an epilogue consequently unnecessary.

Melodrama had afforded Greene the best opportunity to portray a spiritual theme allegorically in Brighton Rock. In The End of the Affair, however, there is no need to allegorize. In The Heart of the Matter the Roman Catholicism of Major Scobie had hung over the British sector of Africa like fatality. The reader had appreciated the dramatic structure of the novel and had been able to sympathize with a protagonist whose damnation had wisely been left undetermined. In The End of the Affair, however, Greene moves away from melodrama into the broader dimensions of impressionism and psychological realism, as he comes closer to the novel that both Ford and Mauriac define in their works. Mauriac makes use of the modern devices of novel writing, and Greene tries his hand at these before going on to create characters who approximate in their own idiom the complex individuals that dominate Mauriac's Bordeaux country. As a result, Greene's technique becomes more realistic, his characters more believable, his artistry finer.

Since Brighton Rock, Greene has developed the scope of the novel in England; he has devoted more and more energy to characterization and less and less to the contrivances of plot. The religious theme has been more and more artistically integrated into the over-all pattern of the novels until, in those novels that follow The End of *the Affair,* it becomes one with the plot. By using devices such as the diary, the dream, the reverie, the time shift, and the debate, Greene gives symbolic unity to *The End of the Affair* while characterizing his people. The spiritual dryness and the symbol of the stair that Sarah describes in her journal are expressive of this ability. Nevertheless, in *The End of the Affair*—as in *The Power and the Glory*—Greene reasserts the value of love. Perhaps the greatest miracle of all is that he brings Henry Miles and Bendrix, the chief bystanders, to a closer understanding of one another.

Chapter Five

Transition

> "Only God and the author
> are omniscient, not the one
> who says 'I'"

The Quiet American

The Quiet American grew out of Greene's first-hand experience of Indochina. In the early fifties he had covered the guerilla war in Malaya for *Life,* savoring the "sense of insecurity, the danger of ambush on the roads, the early morning inspections of the rubber plantation, tommy-gun in lap."[1] Pleased with the article, *Life* had commissioned him to cover the campaign of General de Lattre in Vietnam. That piece, however, failed to please *Life*'s editors and was later published in *Paris Match.* "I suspect my ambivalent attitude to the war was already perceptible—my admiration of the French Army, my admiration for their enemies, and my doubt of any final value in the war," he writes in the introductory note to the volume in the Collected Edition. The character of Alden Pyle, the quiet American, was suggested by an American attached to an economic aid mission, whom the French suspected as a member of the C.I.A., "a man of greater intelligence and of less innocence," who lectured Greene on the need of finding a "third force" in Vietnam, "the great American dream which was to bedevil affairs in the East as later it was to do in North Africa" (xvii).

The End of the Affair had all but eliminated the melodrama that characterizes so much of Greene's work. So interiorized was the action that Greene from time to time, to give his characters something to do, had sent them on walks, many of them in the rain, through, in, and around the common they lived by. So frequent were these walks that the common becomes symbolic of the reconciliation portrayed at the novel's conclusion in Bendrix and Henry's friendship. Yet violence was implicit outside the immediate setting of the novel in the constant threats of the German rockets falling on the city of London, and violence catalyzes the crucial scene of Bendrix's death and rebirth on the staircase.

The Quiet American, like *The End of the Affair,* also presents an interiorized drama, one not so noticeable, perhaps, because of the many scenes of carnage graphically and journalistically presented. It is, nevertheless, the protagonist's emotional and intellectual acceptance of the source of this violence that gives the novel its meaning. Like *The End of the Affair, The Quiet American* makes use of an unreliable narrator whose motives must be fully appreciated if the novel's theme is to develop cogently through the action. Greene also employs other aspects of the so-called impressionist form, as he had done in the preceding novel: time shifts, dreams, and what Ford Madox Ford calls a *"progression d'effet,"* that is, a gradual and inexorable unfolding of an action whose full meaning is discerned in the final or penultimate sentence of the artifact. The novel's ostensible theme is revealed toward the novel's end when Captain Trouin says to Fowler, who professes to remain uninvolved in the politics of real and ideological warfare, "It's not a matter of reason or justice. We all get involved in a moment of emotion and then we cannot get out" (170). The ultimate theme is revealed by Fowler's concluding remark, "Everything had gone right with me since he [Pyle] had died, but how I wished there existed someone to whom I could say that I was sorry" (211).

For Fowler the moment of emotion occurs not so much as an electrifying epiphany, as it does for Sarah Miles, but as the last impression of a cumulative series of images of senseless bloodshed— the sight of the woman covering the mutilated body of the child on her lap with her hat. The Pieta image becomes a comment on the existentialist notion of engagement or detachment that animates the characterization as it adds to the dialectic of belief and nonbelief in God, the ultimate theme of all of Greene's works. Alden Pyle, who also sees the carnage brought on by the diolacton bombs that he has made accessible to General Thé and the Third Force, looks at the blood on his shoes and thinks, automatically, that he will have to have them cleaned before he can report the "incident" to his superior. That Fowler and Pyle are conceived as Conradian doubles adds to the dialectical aspects of both the internal and external themes.

Although *The Quiet American* does much more than pay lip service to the philosophy of existentialism, the novel is in reality a further

elaboration of the same theme that informs *The Ministry of Fear* and
The Heart of the Matter. *The Quiet American*—like *The Heart of the
Matter* before it—compresses the political issues into the differences
that exist among human beings. The ideologies of Alden Pyle, the
quiet American; of General Thé, the exponent and head of the cult
of power mysteriously referred to as the Third Force; of Vigot, the
disinterested French administrator of justice who reads Pascal; of
Heng, the Communist, who forces Fowler to "engage" or to take
sides if only "to remain human"—all these are dramatized in the
relationships that ultimately form the meaning of the novel. For,
although the background is political and although the existentialist
philosophy goes a long way toward explaining the anti-Americanism
of the book, *The Quiet American* is primarily about human beings
involved in a political and ethical dilemma. In his study of the
existential premise in the novel Gangeshwar Rai posits that Greene's
attitude towards communism as well as to the United States reflects
a "hatred for Communism which is hostile to individual freedom
and his antipathy towards America . . . stands for present indus-
trialized civilization in which the individual has no place."[2] Be that
as it may, Fowler aligns himself with the Communists, for their
faces are more human to him than Pyle's.

Existentialism insists on the cult of the individual—on what
Sartre calls "le culte du moi." One branch of existentialism, Sartre's,
denies God and makes atheism the reigning philosophy governing
individual conduct. Under the branch of Catholic existentialism, as
defined by the philosopher Gabriel Marcel, God is somehow, and
for many rather mysteriously, accepted and what amounts to free
will accommodated. Strangely, it is Sartrian existentialism that best
defines Greene's approach to Fowler in *The Quiet American* rather
than its Roman Catholic counterpart.

At the heart of Sartrian existentialism lies the point that may
have attracted Greene, who is always the champion of the individual:
the individual's freedom of choice, or his "engagement." The most
compelling aspect of Sartre's existentialism is that it demonstrates
the essential and indefinable character of man, a process of definition
that often produces anguish, "angoisse." For Sartre only a dead man
(and here Pyle might be considered) can be judged, for he alone is
"defined"; he alone has finished forming himself. Only the dead
man has achieved totalization of experience and existence. The living
man may evade responsibility, paradoxically "creating" himself as

he exercises this freedom. The moment of choice, of engagement, must at last come if the individual is to achieve essence; and the moment of choice, of engagement, may, and in Sartre's novels frequently does, bring death.[3]

In *The Quiet American,* as in classical drama, the sense of history is dynamically superimposed on the actions of those who go about the business of life. The city of Saigon becomes a microcosm that reflects much of twentieth-century political thinking. *The Quiet American* is, consequently and not surprisingly, one of the few major novels that does not directly make use of a Roman Catholic background, although Fowler's estranged wife and Vigot, the inspector of police, are both Catholics. Fowler, a middle-aged newspaper reporter—he resents the term "journalist" because it implies a commitment to the world that he feels he cannot make—is nominally an atheist, although several times he addresses himself to a God in whom he does not believe. Aided in his occupation by Dominguez, an enigmatic Christian-Moslem who has the ability to discern the germ of truth in the mystifying reports of offensives and counter-offensives that inundate the city, Fowler lives with Phuong, his beautiful mistress, enjoying his opium pipe and placidly but cynically an uncomplicated existence. Into the "uncommitted" pattern of his life comes Alden Pyle—American, aged thirty-two, Harvard-nurtured, innocent, and full of intellectual idealism and enthusiasm learned from the texts of York Harding, an American economist. Fowler and Pyle respect and discover a reciprocal understanding of each other's basic integrity and goodness, but neither can be referred to as sinless. They come to an appreciation of one another as good men in the scene in which they are attacked by guerrillas as they shelter in a sentry hut on the outskirts of Phat-Diem. Fowler is wounded in the skirmish and Pyle saves his life, for which Fowler is by no means grateful.

Criticized by American reviewers for its anti-Americanism, *The Quiet American* has been misunderstood because of and in spite of the ironic commentary Fowler makes concerning Pyle's commitment to democracy and to action: "He was young and ignorant and silly and he got involved. He had no more of a notion than any of you what the whole affair's about. . . . He never saw anything he hadn't heard in a lecture-hall, and his writers and his lecturers made a fool of him. When he saw a dead body he couldn't even see the wounds. A Red menace, a soldier of democracy" (26).

The point that has been neglected is essentially the core of the novel's meaning. What Greene intends to depict in the course of the novel's activity is that idealism, when uninformed by experience, is a dangerous weapon in a world coerced by the cult of power, symbolized by General Thé and his mysterious Third Force. Greene wishes, moreover, to satirize the belief that money alone can secure peace and understanding. The poem from which Fowler reads as he betrays Pyle is Arthur Clough's "Dipsychus," the twin-souled; and its satiric refrain, the reader will remember, is "So pleasant it is to have money, heigh ho!" (197). Equally important, Greene wishes to describe in Fowler the cowardice implicit in living an "uncommitted" life in a world on the brink of destruction.

To fulfill his thematic intent, Greene employs the innocent abroad, Alden Pyle, who is symbolically the opposite of Henry James's innocent, the American sent to a decadent Europe to reestablish the importance of the human act. Greene's innocent becomes a leaven that brings about bloodshed and tragedy, for his limited understanding of good is inadequate in a world corrupted by the experience of evil. Pyle is compared to a "dumb leper who has lost his bell, wandering the world, meaning no harm" (33), and as a hero in a boy's adventure story who is impregnably armored by good intentions and ignorance; indeed he derives from Anthony Farrant of *England Made Me*. To Fowler, Pyle is like his country. "I wish sometimes you had a few bad motives," Fowler says to him, "you might understand a little more about human beings. And that applies to your country too . . ." (148). However, Fowler comments as ironically on his own position as he does on Pyle's. Both men are in fact aspects of goodness, and much of the novel's meaning centers on the genuine friendship that develops between the two. "You cannot love without intuition" (10), says Fowler; and later he asks: "Am I the only one who really cared for Pyle?" (15). Fowler's repressed idealism is informed by experience; Pyle's abstract idealism by inexperience.

The pawn in this game of experience versus innocence is Phuong, whose name means phoenix. In the plot she represents both the enigma of the East and the desire of Vietnam for political status. Her allegiance to Fowler is neither romantic nor materialistic; she is not, however, incapable of loyalty. She leaves Fowler and attaches herself to Pyle—"youth and hope and seriousness"—who promises her the status she seeks. Ironically this to him is Boston—conformity to American social patterns—and he fails her more than "age and despair" (11). What Fowler offers her is the understanding of experience and the tenderness of his kindly cynicism. At the novel's end, after his betrayal of Pyle to the Communists, Fowler is able to offer her the marriage she desires, for his wife agrees in a moment of generosity to give him a divorce despite her Anglo-Catholic scruples.

Although *The Quiet American* fulfills the existentialist pattern, the philosophy that animates the character of Fowler is the same as that which decides the activities of Arthur Rowe in *The Ministry of Fear* and of Major Scobie in *The Heart of the Matter.* Stripped of Rowe's sentimentalism and of Scobie's religious preoccupations, Fowler seems less noble than his predecessors; but he is, nevertheless, propelled by the same compassion. Again this pity is visualized as a form of egotism when Fowler says: "I know myself and I know the depth of my selfishness. I cannot be at ease (and to be at ease is my chief wish) if someone else is in pain, visibly or audibly or tactually. Sometimes this is mistaken by the innocent for unselfishness, when all I am doing is sacrificing a small good . . . for the sake of a far greater good, a peace of mind, when I need think only of myself" (124). When he can no longer deny the images of suffering that "impinge" on his consciousness, to use Ford Madox Ford's term, he acts to forestall Pyle's blundering attempts to bring about a better world as approved by the American ideology he has abstracted from the textbooks of his mentor York Harding. Fowler's action involves betrayal of the man he has learned to understand and, in his own way, to love, and the reader is asked to remember the point that Greene has made in other works—that Christ was more beloved of Judas than he was of his other followers. The Christ-Judas parallel cannot be pressed too far, however, for the novel's predominant tone is secular and controlled by Fowler's all-encompassing narration, which examines critically commitments of all sorts.

Fowler is, furthermore, the most Conradian of Greene's heroes, and there is a curious parallel to *Victory* to be seen in the novel. Although Fowler and Heyst are separated by years of political and social change, they are both fundamentally unengaged souls whose detachment is challenged by emotion. Each avoids entrapments and each egotistically shuns commitment—Heyst because of early training, and Fowler because of the disappointments of experience. And yet both are made aware of the importance of the human act, and each makes a choice—Heyst for life which, ironically, commits him to death. Fowler is trapped by his pity for suffering, first when he sees the dead guard at the outpost, then when he sees the dead child on his mother's knees after Pyle's diolacton bomb explodes in the square. Fowler realizes that uninformed innocence in a ravaged world amounts to pain and suffering that can be counted as dead bodies and mutilated children. After the crucial meeting with Granger, an incident that has been much admired but little understood, Fowler realizes his affinity to Pyle; and he asks, "Must I too have my foot thrust in the mess of life before I saw the pain?" (208). He goes into the street, without hope, to find Phuong, who waits vainly for the dead Pyle. Fowler has taken sides to remain human, and the realization of his compassionate spirit overwhelms him. The novel ends with the sentence, "Everything had gone right with me since he had died, but how I wished there existed someone to whom I could say that I was sorry" (211). And the irony needs no comment.

Although *The Quiet American* makes only casual mention of religious matters, there is in its shadows the same religious feeling that infiltrates the entertainments and justifies their ethics. Although Fowler does not believe in God, he nevertheless addresses him. He leaves Pyle's death not to chance, or to Fate, but to God when, at the novel's end, he wishes there were someone to whom he could say that he was sorry. The statement is tentative, and the reader interprets it as Greene would have him do. What Fowler is searching for is permanence. "From childhood I had never believed in permanence," he says, "and yet I had longed for it. Always I was afraid of losing happiness" (42). The religious sense is also reinforced by the nature of Pyle's death. He does not die from the knife wounds that the Communists inflict upon him; instead, he drowns. The scapegoat and the drowned man and the Judas motif add the religious note that helps explain Greene's ultimate meaning.

A Burnt-Out Case

Something of the annoyance that Greene felt as a result of the celebrity and notoriety he achieved because of the popular success of *The Heart of the Matter* and *The End of the Affair* is reflected in the characterizations of *A Burnt-Out Case*. André Rycker, the dilettante-theologian married to an ingenuous wife young enough to be his daughter, is one of Greene's most unsympathetic characters and perhaps his only despicable Roman Catholic. The same annoyance, but in lesser degree, is reflected in the character of Father Thomas, who twists facts to justify his vocation, and Greene's indignation over his treatment by the press in the figure of the obese Parkinson, whose grotesqueness almost rescues him as a character. Yet Dr. Colin, who quietly and heroically treats the lepers, and the Father Superior, who runs the hospital where Greene's protagonist Querry seeks asylum, are well and sympathetically portrayed as are Fathers John and Philippe, who are too busy doing the work of the leprosarium to worry about moral or theological problems.

Greene's annoyance, obviously, had little to do with the generally favorable critical reception of *The Heart of the Matter* and *The End of the Affair* but, rather, with the appeals made to him as a "Catholic novelist" by lay readers and clerics alike. In his introduction to *A Burnt-Out Case* he indicates something of the beleaguering that he was subjected to. Some of his readers, furthermore, detected in his protagonist's loss of faith a lapse of belief in his own Catholicism. In response to a letter written to him by Evelyn Waugh, he wrote that there were aspects of Querry in his own character as there had been in Fowler's. He added that his plan for the novel was "to give expression to various states or moods of belief and unbelief. The doctor, whom I like best as a realized character, represents a settled and easy atheism; the Father Superior a settled and easy belief . . . Father Thomas an unsettled form of belief and Querry an unsettled form of disbelief. One could probably dig a little of the author out of the doctor and Father Thomas."[4] In the dedication to Dr. Michel Lechat, on whom Dr. Colin is partly based, Greene describes the Congo setting of the novel as a region of the mind and the novel's thematic purpose as "an attempt to give dramatic expression to various types of belief, half-belief, and non-belief, in the kind of setting, removed from world-politics and household-preoccupations, where such differences are felt acutely and find expression" (vii). The task of writing *A Burnt-Out Case* proved so difficult that at the time Greene felt another full-length novel to be beyond his capacity.

There is in fact a feeling of enervation about *A Burnt-Out Case,* although its craftsmanship is superb. The plot builds convincingly, the central character possesses sufficient mystery, the Conradian element emerges clearly and forcefully, sometimes humorously. Yet the dilemma seems contrived, and the denouement unconvincing. Perhaps, as Joseph Kurismmotil has observed, the religious impulse had spent itself with *The End of the Affair,* and the novel "is more in the nature of an afterword" (151).[5]

In the journal that Greene kept while traveling in the Belgian Congo, he records how in January 1959, he began his journey "with a novel already beginning to form in my head by way of a situation— a stranger who turns up in a remote leper-colony" (*ISC,* xiii). *In Search of a Character* indicates Greene's approach to the problems of novel writing while making the point that his characters shape themselves within the situation to emerge from the pages as unique and sometimes terrifying individuals. In other words, *In Search of a Character* is another proof that Greene does not approach his craft from the point of view of the dilettante Christian theologist. Indeed, for the dilettante theologian Greene has little more than contempt, and Rycker is the best example of this attitude.

The journal includes Greene's notes on the incidence and the varieties of leprosy; it records his observations on leprophobes and leprophiles, and it suggests his compassion for the lepers themselves, their social and domestic difficulties. The journal also records his genuine admiration for the nuns and priests who care for the ills of the body before worrying about the nature of sin and grace among the lepers; it suggests Greene's affection for those who dedicate their lives to the care of the afflicted. It is no wonder then that Dr. Colin in *A Burnt-Out Case* refused to take shape as Greene had at first anticipated. So strong is Greene's feeling for Colin that the doctor at the novel's end assumes the responsibility that Father Rank in *The Heart of the Matter* and the priest in *Brighton Rock* are accorded— he makes the final, choric commentary on the story's action; he restores, therefore, a sane and normal perspective to the little world of the leper colony.

The journal further describes—perhaps this is its chief interest— the emergence of the character who came to be called Querry, his name suggestive of his search and longing. It records the character's transition from an Englishman who knew no French to a half-Englishman with a thorough competence in French because of his Belgian parent, his occupation as an architect, and his vocational and amatory successes. As pointed out above, the journal also tes-tifies to Greene's concern with his craft—his nervousness over a correct beginning; his fear that he might over-plot, tell a "good" story; his worry over the credibility of the situations; and his concern over transitions. In short, the journal defines the numerous observations, hesitations, starts, and stops that go into the composition of a novel. Although not so detailed as *The Lawless Roads, In Search of a Character* is indispensable in a consideration of Greene's artistry, not only because it points out that Greene is not a dogmatist, but rather that he is a writer of great talent whose Catholicism may not be conveniently overlooked like a bad case of psoriasis.

Published in 1961, *A Burnt-Out Case* reflects the same serious tone that characterizes *The Power and the Glory, The Heart of the Matter,* and *The End of the Affair.* And like these novels, *A Burnt-Out Case,* a return to third-person narration, makes use of background for effect and for symbolic value; but the emphasis falls— as it does in all of Greene's major works—on the relationship between character and event.

An architect of international reputation as well as a notorious lover, Querry makes his way hundreds of miles up one of the Congo's tributaries to a leprosarium. "Are you stopping here?" asks Colin, the physician who treats the lepers. To which Querry replies, "The boat goes no further" (14). The resemblance to Conrad's *Heart of Darkness* is apparent, but the mysteries are indeed different. In *In Search of a Character* Greene says of Conrad's story, "It is as if Conrad had taken an episode in his own life and tried to lend it, for the sake of 'literature,' a greater significance than it will hold" (33). In *A Burnt-Out Case* Greene also grapples with this problem, as he struggles to keep the "episode" from assuming greater significance than it will hold.

Querry is a Roman Catholic who has gone beyond feeling. He does not know what he is looking for; nor, he says, does he care. Long before his journey to Africa he had come to the limit of his emotional and spiritual resources. A man to whom success as an ecclesiastical architect had come too easily, he had grown dissatisfied, his art frivolous; ironically the decline had been noticed by none but himself. The world had gone on acclaiming him until his head "callused with pride and success" admitted that his faith, his vocation, even his love-making, were sham. In the fable he invents for Marie Rycker, he assumes the disguise of a jeweler who had loved God: "He had believed quite sincerely that when he loved his work he was loving the King and that when he made love to a woman he was at least imitating in a faulty way the King's love for his people" (186).

With the discovery that he could no longer believe in God, whose existence he had once proved by "historical, logical, philosophical, and etymological methods," the jeweler of Querry's fable had accepted the fact that his work had been done for love of himself (181). Nevertheless, and this is the novel's point—"types of belief, half-belief, and non-belief"—Querry is not willing to concede that his own nonbelief may be after all a final and conclusive proof of God's existence. At the novel's end Dr. Colin says in a choric comment, "You're too troubled by your lack of faith, Querry. You keep on fingering it like a sore you want to get rid of" (228).

Perhaps what Querry is seeking is a return to usefulness and integrity. The doctor and the priests teach him much about genuine compassion and understanding; the lepers teach him much about suffering and unhappiness. Deo Gratias, Querry's servant is a burnt-out case—one in whom the disease has run its course, having eroded in this instance all the fingers and toes. He and Querry come to parallel one another: Querry's spiritual mutilation matches Deo Gratias's physical handicap. Querry's search for usefulness is symbolized by Pendélé, a place of contentment that Deo Gratias remembers from childhood. Pendélé, neither the Christian heaven nor a pagan sanctuary, becomes for Querry a reason for living—usefulness, innocence perhaps, an escape from success and the demands of the ego. Paradoxically, it is Querry's reawakening interest in human suffering, the rebirth perhaps of compassion, that keeps him from finding Pendélé and ultimately brings about his death. By the novel's end Querry is pronounced cured of the disease that has left him symbolically a burnt-out case; Dr. Colin says: "He'd learned to serve other people, you see, and to laugh. An odd laugh, but it was a laugh all the same" (236). The reader remembers how often Querry had accepted Colin's prognoses.

The key to Querry's character is ambiguity: the mystery that Querry arouses as he moves among the lepers, the priests, the French and Belgian colonials, the government officials. Greene says in his notes for the novel, "I feel that X must die because an element of insoluble mystery . . . has to remain" (*ISC,* 38). The means that Greene chooses to dispatch Querry is one that he used many times before, the triangle. Querry becomes innocently involved with Rycker and his childlike wife, and is killed by the jealous husband. But despite the triangle relationship, *A Burnt-Out Case* does not record—as Orville Prescott insisted upon the novel's publication in his review in *The New York Times*—Greene's "curious conviction that sexual guilt is the beginning of wisdom and that adultery is one of the better paths toward grace."[6] Indeed Querry feels no guilt for his sexual promiscuity. Prescott, it seems, is reading *A Burnt-Out Case* in the light of *The End of the Affair* and *The Heart of the Matter,* novels in which the problem of adultery is indeed important. For Prescott goes on to say, "The subtleties of religious dogmas have never been very tractable for fiction. Novels steeped in eroticism and largely preoccupied with sins of the flesh are a poor media for the dramatization of problems of faith."[7]

"Eroticism" and "dogma" hardly seem suitable equivalents for *A Burnt-Out Case.* Rather it is what Querry represents to others that forms the heart of the novel and lends it its "mystery." To Rycker, the *colon,* he is the Catholic architect, versed in dogma and knowledgeable in theological matters. Rycker seeks consolation for lechery and pride, but Querry is too shrewd to allow himself to be persuaded that Rycker's squalid egotism is anything more. To Father Thomas, Querry is a living hero, perhaps an embryonic saint. ". . . Don't let's recognize them before the Church does. We shall be saved a lot of disappointment that way," says the Superior (98). To the majority of the priests and to Dr. Colin, Querry is a man seeking a place for himself in the world of men and, to some, in the eyes of God. To Parkinson, the journalist, he is "good copy." Querry recognizes in him, just as Scobie recognizes in Yusef, the degradation and decay that is in himself. Parkinson is to Querry as Gentleman Brown is to Lord Jim.

To Maria Rycker, Querry is escape from the tedium of African plantation life and the intolerable concupiscence of her marriage. It is her naïveté—Querry spends an innocent night with her in a hotel—that leads to the denouement of the novel and to Querry's death. The situation is, however, difficult to credit; it occasions, therefore, the chief shortcoming of the novel. The fact that the irony is so apparent—Querry's affair, no affair at all—makes the scene, despite its comic and ironic overtones, difficult to accept. Querry, who seeks above all to safeguard the precarious peace that he is slowly finding at the leprosarium, is too old a hand to be caught by such a feminine wile.

A Burnt-Out Case is not Greene's best novel, but it is a fine piece of writing and a meaningful exploration of various shades of belief. It indicates, as do the other novels, that Greene is a novelist who does not take just one religious stance but a variety of stances; and that these are dictated not by dogma but by what the novelist has chosen to face in "this" novel. His works contrast greatly with the dogmatic Marxian novel—as he himself has pointed out in the exchange of letters, cited earlier in this study, with Elizabeth Bowen and V. S. Pritchett. The Marxian novel offers judgments that are much more in the cards at the outset. In the final analysis, what Greene does is to make a case for Christianity, not just Roman Catholic dogma, on aesthetic grounds. To insist on his Roman Catholicism as do those about whom he complains in the novel's introduction is to misunderstand his Christian humanism and to lose sight of his artistry.

Chapter Six
A New Beginning

"I believe, rather, in a sort
of purgatory"

In his introduction to *A Burnt-Out Case,* Greene quotes from his correspondence with Evelyn Waugh who had detected in Querry's unsought-for fame as a Roman Catholic artist a wavering of belief in Greene himself. "With a writer of your genius and insight," he answered Waugh, "I certainly would not attempt to hide behind the time-old gag that an author can never be identified with his characters. . . . I suppose the points where an author is in agreement with his character lend what force or warmth there is to the expression" (xii). For Greene Querry "was a victim of disbelief," but not so himself. For him faith and disbelief remained, he insisted, as always the alternate black and white squares of Bishop Blougram's chess board, and Cardinal Newman's dictum that "it is a contradiction in terms to attempt the sinless Literature of sinful man" a rationale for his explorations of human character. What Greene found useful to himself as an artist after the physical and psychic energy that he had expended on *A Burnt-Out Case* was not so much a reaffirmation of his Catholicism as the discovery of comedy in what was for him "the blackest book I have written." As a result of that book he discovered the tragicomic region of La Mancha, where "I expect to stay" (xvi).

This is not, however, to say that there had been no comic lightness in the works before *A Burnt-Out Case.* A humorous bent is easily detected in several of his earliest short stories, most notably "When Greek Meets Greek" and "Alas, Poor Maling." Certainly one of the funniest scenes in all of Greene's novels occurs in the heroically conceived *The Heart of the Matter* when a bewildered Scobie returns home to find his wife Louise's suitor Wilson stretched on the floor suffering from nosebleed. In *Our Man in Havana* Greene had been wryly diverting as he conducted his sad hero Wormold through his escapades as a spy. But there he had not so much discovered comedy

121

as he had farce, and the frivolity of that novel had, as farce had done in most of his earlier work, underscored the sadness of life. The epigraph from Dante that precedes the narrative of *A Burnt-Out Case,* "I did not die, yet nothing of life remained," however, implied a need to understand the comic form, one that involved definition within a consideration of Dante's infernal as well as sublime attributions of comedy. He would, perhaps, have to populate his own Inferno and Paradiso before undertaking the Purgatorio of the here and now.

Unlike Waugh's fictional modern waste land, Greene's had in his own words been peopled by "pious 'suburbans' . . . the educated, the established, who seem to own their Roman Catholic image of God, who have ceased to look for Him because they consider they have found Him" (xiv–xv). He would not find the protagonist of *A Burnt-Out Case* in such a landscape; he would look for him, and as it now appears, for any characters that might follow him, among those described by Unamuno: "in whom reason is stronger than will," characters who "feel themselves caught in the grip of reason and hailed along in their own despite, and they fall into despair, and because of their despair they deny, and God reveals Himself in them, affirming Himself by their very denial of Him" (xv). And in his conversations with Allain, Greene admits that for him *A Burnt-Out Case* "represents a breaking away from my other books" insofar as its conflict reflects an inward journey" (96).

It would be a mistake, however, to regard *A Burnt-Out Case* as a watershed in Greene's artistic development. To admit consciously a preference for comedy, a form comparatively new to him, and to portray a search for meaning within a new breed of character necessitated, it now seems, not only definition but also reorientation. Such changes would suggest a searching backward look, a revisiting of former landscapes. This may have been facilitated by the preparations he began making for his new Collected Edition, the first volumes of which began appearing about 1970, the introductions of which, in fact, reflect a growing awareness of the possibilities of tragicomedy. To a certain extent, Greene would be pouring old wine into new barrels, and this, perhaps, explains the revisiting of certain characters and incidents that readers have noted in these later novels, and accounts, possibly, for the element of self-parody found in several of the books, a luxury easily affordable to one who had sufficiently mastered his subject matter and craft. The psychological preoccupations accounting for his themes, as Greene had indicated in "The Lost Childhood," had been irrevocably set by his earliest experiences; and these "obsessions," to use Allott and Farris's term, had explained and justified a consistent and peculiarly affective set of symbols that evoked not only his characters' spiritual yearnings but also the modern waste land in which they carried on their search. Perhaps only by defining comedy in its extremest manifestations and yet in a characteristic dialectical manner—which explains the darkness of *The Comedians* and the brightness of *Travels with My Aunt*—the inferno of a loveless heart to the triumph of a loving one—could Greene go on to create Plarr and Castle, who are Querry's logical descendants. The early novels had refined the ambiance of Eliot's *The Waste Land;* those following *A Burnt-Out Case* would move into the milieux of *Ash Wednesday* and the *Quartets*. But first *The Comedians*.

The Comedians

Set in Haiti, *The Comedians,* a first-person narrative, appeared in 1966, its darkness more terrifying and menacing than that of *A Burnt-Out Case,* with at least its possibility of redemption. The antiheroic protagonist of *The Comedians,* a man simply named Brown, defines his concept of comedy when he says of himself and, as it turns out, mistakenly of his mistress Martha, "Neither of us would ever die for love. We would grieve and separate and find another. We belong to the world of comedy and not of tragedy" (198). Brown's reliability as a credible narrator can of course be challenged, but only if the self-indicting nature of his irony is misunderstood. Michael Routh explains Brown's presentation of himself as a "laughingstock," his "self-ridicule of traits in need of correction" as "unintentional parody," for Brown, he continues, "is hiding his true self from both his own conscious mind and from ourselves as audience."[2] Gangeshwar Rai, on the other hand, contends that Brown as an existentialist is fully aware of his attitude to events as that of a "happy-go-lucky comedian" who assumes the comic stance as the only possible one in an absurd world."[2] And Alan Kennedy puts down what he calls the "narrative inconsistencies" of the novel to an inability on Greene's part to come to terms with a consistent notion of comedy: "one is forced to conclude that confusion and not ambiguity underlies the use of metaphors of drama in this novel."[3]

Kennedy's concerns can, however, be explained by Brown's attempts to understand the disparities between the divine attributes of comedy and their more human derivations. Brown is, in fact, one of Greene's most credible narrators, for his indictment of flaws in others becomes indictments of flaws in self. Nevertheless, the mode of presentation presents certain difficulties that are not easily explained.

Brown's training as a Roman Catholic by the Jesuits, to whom he had been abandoned by his mother, his early passion for theological study, his admission that he had once thought to become a priest, fully equip him in fact to see into the heart of the matter. His references to a Manichean God "as an authoritative practical joker" (30), to the roulette wheel as a talisman of fate and chance, and his consistent view of himself as a role-player who performs his parts with style and elegance transform Brown into one of Greene's most self-aware characters. He is, despite his sophistication and cynicism, not far removed from Pinkie Brown who, as schooled in his Catholicism as Brown is, knows that after such knowledge as his there is little chance for forgiveness between the stirrup and the ground. The Conradian doubling of Brown and Jones as the former's dislike for and jealousy of the latter fade, allows Brown, furthermore, to see Jones as a brother, a "semblable," and himself clearly as one of the "tarts" and not the respectable "toff" he pretends to be throughout a greater part of the narrative.

If *The Comedians* is a comedy then, it is not one in the generally accepted meaning of the term, for it does not define a movement from despair to happiness, as Dante's *Divine Comedy* does, but one from horror to despair. Rather the novel is Greene's version of contemporary dark comedy, employing farce and sensationalism as aspects of its method. In his attempt to portray the reluctance of contemporary man to accept divine affiliation, Greene examines, problematically to be sure, human commitment and political engagement in a world menaced by the fear and confusion emanating from a power cult.

Within the parameters of the narrator's peculiar irony, which makes Brown covet a paperweight shaped like a coffin on which are inscribed the letters RIP, the novel presents the contemporary world as an Inferno from which only the power of love can rescue the individual; in this respect it is Greene's version of Dante's hell. The problem posed by the novel resides in the difficulty of recognizing the comedians, for their elegance and style easily deceive. Occa-

sionally those who appear least qualified to play their roles as comedians reach a point where the part overwhelms them—reality
and pretense coalesce, or, to employ Yeats's phrase, the dancer
becomes indistinguishable from the dance. In the novel Jones becomes the role he plays, yet the face he presents to the narrator and,
as a result, to the reader reveals comic eccentricity and grotesqueness.
Brown is aware of the irony of the "modest stone" placed by the
immigrants at the border to commemorate Jones's exploit, but the
truth within the irony is the simple fact that Jones for a moment
became the character he pretended to be and deserves to be
remembered.

Greene would have his reader believe that the comedians of the
novel are in some measure worthwhile, that they represent a band
of initiates in an absurd and meaningless world. But he wants his
reader to be equally aware of the ludicrousness of thinking of Jones
as a tragic figure, for the world of *The Comedians* cannot accept
tragedy. At the novel's end the Haitian insurgents who had used
Jones to advance their dream of freedom are symbolically housed in
an abandoned insane asylum in Santo Domingo.

The comedians in the novel are consequently and for the most
part presented as pretenders, neither good enough nor grand enough
for tragic emotion. Martha's husband, the ambassador of an unnamed
South American country, amplifies the definition when he refers to
comedians as members of an honorable profession. "If we could be
good ones the world might gain at least a sense of style" (163).
Comedy, then, is to an extent dependent on the manner with which
one conducts his life, and in this novel style is allied with mimesis.
A postcard from his mother had brought Brown to Haiti, and her
last question to him had been, "What part are you playing now?"
(73). After her death he had discovered a note she had written to
her young lover, "Marcel, I know I'm an old woman and as you
say a bit of an actress. But please go on pretending. As long as we
pretend we escape. Pretend that I love you like a mistress. Pretend
that you love me like a lover. Pretend that I would die for you and
you would die for me" (312). But Marcel, had, in fact, died for
love, proving himself no actor. Brown's love affair with Martha
Pineda is just such role playing. For several years he has pretended
and prospered, achieving a false sense of security; but Papa Doc
Duvalier and the Tontons Macoute now threaten not only his equanimity but also his ability to play the part of lover and nonpolitical

adventurer. His early Roman Catholic training has, however, made him fully aware of the implications of the parts he plays.

In his dedicatory note to his publisher Frere, Greene writes of his setting, Haiti under the dictatorship of Dr. Duvalier, "Papa Doc":

Poor Haiti itself and the character of Doctor Duvalier's rule are not invented, the latter not even blackened for dramatic effect. Impossible to deepen the night. The Tontons Macoute are full of men more evil than Concasseur; the interrupted funeral is drawn from fact; many a Joseph limps the streets of Port-au-Prince after his spell of torture, and, though I have never met the young Philipot, I have met guerrillas as courageous and as ill-trained in that former lunatic asylum near Santo Domingo.

Like a Kafka enigma, Papa Doc remains mysteriously within his palace, his laws enforced by the Tontons Macoute, bogeymen whose insignia are the slouched hats and sunglasses behind which they hide their uncertainties. The Voodoo element comes into play in the course of the novel's action, and an equation is drawn between Papa Doc and Baron Samedi, the prince of the dead of Voodoo belief. The Tontons approximate a mysterious fraternity of terror infinitely more menacing than that of the cultists. The chief representative of the power cult in the novel is Captain Concasseur, who is responsible for the mutilation and emasculation of Joseph, Brown's servant in the hotel Trianon.

Brown, Smith, and Jones arrive in Port-au-Prince on a Dutch vessel ominously called the *Medea,* Brown to return to his luxury hotel which he has been unsuccessfully trying to sell in the United States; Smith, a former presidential candidate who ran against Truman on a vegetarian ticket in 1948, together with his wife, to set up a vegetarian center; and Jones, an inept adventurer who calls himself "Major," to engage in a military maneuver of dubious nature. The purpose behind the names is, perhaps, to lend an Everyman aspect to the narrative, and one is tempted to see even the name Greene as a satirical aspect of the comedy.

Brown has been conducting a love affair with Martha Pineda, the wife of a South American diplomat. She is the mother of a five-year-old child, Angel, whose claims keep her from abandoning her family for Brown, whom she says she loves. The affair, bittersweet and reminiscent of many love triangles in Greene's fiction, is resumed the night Brown returns to Haiti. Brown admits several times that what he seeks in a love affair is not so much happiness as defeat; and ironically there is a sort of success at the novel's end— Brown and Martha both realize once they are safely over the border in Santo Domingo that their love affair belongs peculiarly to Port-au-Prince, that it was but the reflection of the horror and terror of the times.

Brown has been brought up a Catholic, but he is unlike the Catholics Greene has previously portrayed. The passionate pity of Scobie has given way to a tragicomic irony, which is also the chief mood of the novel; Brown is much more tolerant of success than any of Greene's other heroes, but he is infinitely less compassionate. His Catholicism is not the leper's bell that it is to the whiskey priest and Sarah Miles; it is instead a cloak of indifference, a means whereby the stupidities and the atrocities of the world can be warded off, and perhaps explained. Yet Brown's rejected Catholicism remains for him a standard of measurement, in Haiti a valid one, for Catholicism liberally sprinkled with Voodooism is the religion of the majority.

Through the Smiths, or perhaps because of the Smiths, Greene expresses a certain amount of anti-American sentiment reminiscent of that in *The Quiet American.* Dr. Magiot remarks at one point, commenting on the naïveté of the United States' belief in Duvalier as a bulwark against communism:

We are an evil scum floating a few miles from Florida, and no American will help us with arms or money or counsel. We learned a few years back what their counsel meant. There was a resistance group here who were in touch with a sympathizer in the American Embassy: they were promised all kinds of moral support, but the information went straight back to the C.I.A. and from the C.I.A. by a very direct route to Papa Doc. You can imagine what happened to the group. The state department didn't want any disturbance in the Caribbean. (285)

Although he bears much in common with Alden Pyle of *The Quiet American,* the good vegetarian Mr. Smith is by no means the same sort of deluded innocent. He is capable of appreciating the opportunism and graft-seeking of the corrupt Tontons Macoute; and he even has the courage to admit that his vision of setting up an American Vegetarian Center in either Port-au-Prince or the new city, Duvalierville, is impractical. Despite their being vehicles for

satire, Mr. and Mrs. Smith emerge as the two strongest characters
in the novel; they are saved by their humanity, by their certainty
that there is goodness in the world. Ultimately, it is their dedication
to their cause, as Brown comes to understand, their sincere and
straightforward desire to better the human situation—by reducing
acidity in the human body—that makes them heroic in Brown's
view.

It is also through the Smiths that the theme of commitment to
an ideology enters the novel, again satirically. As in *The Quiet
American,* existentialism can be accepted as a philosophical deter-
minant. Its jargon is kept to a minimum, yet the theme of engagement emerges cogently, demonstrated in the action of the
comedians who make up the drama.

"Major" Jones, who at first appears to be the biggest fraud of
all, a "tart," as he calls himself, is a committed man by the novel's
end; but his commitment is farcically handled. He passes himself
off as an organizer of military affairs, but he fools only those who
wish to be fooled. He dreams, he invents, and he deludes, at times
even himself. But there is something about the man that endears
him to others. Tin Tin, the girl at Mère Catherine's bordello, likes
him because he makes her laugh; and Brown's mistress Martha, in
whose embassy Jones takes shelter when his bogus papers are discovered by Captain Concasseur, likes him too, and for the same
reason—he makes her laugh. Brown knows that he himself has
never learned the trick of laughter.

Together with Dr. Magiot, the intellectual Communist, Brown
arranges for Jones to escape the Tontons and to join the partisans,
who under young Philipot, a one-time Baudelairean poet, are attempting to unseat Papa Doc in their bumbling and ineffectual
ways. However, Brown's decision to help the partisans is motivated
not by a feeling for the rightness of their cause, or by the danger
and the excitement, or by his awareness of the childlike innocence
of their exploit, but by the unreasoning jealousy that he feels toward
Jones. Again, the reader is reminded of Fowler. Jones is a comedian
within the broadest meaning of the term; but unlike Brown, who
cannot—perhaps because of his early Roman Catholic training—,
he follows the gleam, and there comes a point where the dream and
reality coalesce. In a last glimpse of Jones, the reader sees him
limping along, unable to keep up with the partisans because of his
flat feet. He remains behind, a comical version of Hemingway's

Robert Jordan, to fire upon the Tontons in order to make it possible for those he has pledged to support to survive, if only temporarily.

Of all the comedians, Brown alone remains unengaged. He is a con man grown old whose most successful venture has been peddling bad paintings to the nouveaux riches. His mother's postcard had brought him to the Trianon, and her last question had been a challenge, "What part are you playing now?" Brown's love affair with Martha, however, has been something more than just pretending; it is a desperate attempt to capture stability in a fear-menaced world, and it is compounded as much of the desire to inflict pain as it is of a desire to dominate. For several years Brown has prospered in Haiti, achieving a false sense of security; but the coming of Papa Doc and the Tontons has destroyed not only his business but his sense of belonging as well. He finds himself involved with innocence, with the Smiths and with Jones, who, thematically, serve to set off and to illustrate his failure.

The problem of Brown's Roman Catholicism is crucial to an understanding of both the characterization and the theme of the novel; it is indeed the chief challenge of the book. The Voodoo black mass in which Brown's servant Joseph participates makes a sensational counterpoint to the religious promptings of the novel; the figure of Baron Samedi is associated with Papa Doc, the personification of evil. But the black mass does not necessarily suggest a breakdown of religion. At the novel's end, it is contrasted with the mass the priest reads over the body of Joseph in the insane asylum in Santo Domingo where the insurgents are cared for. Brown's failure, then, does not illustrate a religious breakdown; his is a failure of character.

Brown's failure is his inability to accept reality, and it can best be explained in existential terms. He can detect innocence, appreciate goodness, admire courage, and—even if for the wrong motives—help the cause of right. But he is so practiced a comedian that he cannot transcend the limitations imposed by the role. All his religious explanations seem like so many rationalizations, and he fools neither himself nor the reader. Brown can appreciate commitment: to retain his self-esteem, to support his ego, he is forced into action. Although his sympathies are with Dr. Magiot, Philipot, and the insurgent cause, Brown makes no real commitment to anything, not to love, not to religion, not to God, not to innocence. It is only right that at the novel's end he becomes a partner in an undertaking business. In his black suit and black hat he appears a comic Baron Samedi. He no longer belongs to the world of the living; symbolically and literally he serves the dead.

Since the appearance of *The Man Within* critics have accused Greene of being pessimistic. The truth of the matter is that he is not the most cheerful of writers, but *The Comedians,* tragicomic though it is, full of farcical touches and humor of a macabre and grotesque nature, is the gloomiest as well as the most challenging of his works. At least Major Scobie loves God, in his own mistaken way; at least the whiskey priest finds honor, albeit unwillingly; and Sarah Miles achieves a sort of gratuitous sainthood. Querry in *A Burnt-Out Case* finds the hint of an explanation; he glimpses Pendélé. But there is only a pathetic part left for Brown to play in *The Comedians*. There is not even the saving factor of remorse as in *The Quiet American,* although the notion of confession is introduced in the final stages of the action; Fowler wishes at the end of *The Quiet American* that there were someone to whom he could say he is sorry for his participation in Pyle's death. Fowler at least is spurred to action after witnessing the carnage caused by Pyle's plastic explosives. But there is no emotion in Brown, only ego. Jones and Smith may indeed illustrate contrasting aspects of the theme of innocence, but within the pattern of the novel they serve merely as foils to set off the failure of the individual.

The Honorary Consul

The Honorary Consul is Greene's first novel to profit from the extremes of definition that he had portrayed in *The Comedians* and *Travels with My Aunt,* which he describes as the happiest book he has written. The horror of the former gave way to gaiety and laughter in the last of Greene's entertainments as Henry Pulling discovered a vita nuova in his admission of love for his mother Augusta. Published in 1973 *The Honorary Consul* portrays in realistic tragicomic terms a quest for meaning. Its epigraph is taken from Thomas Hardy, "All things merge in one another—good into evil, generosity into justice, religion into politics . . . ," underscoring the ambiguity that is an aspect of tragicomedy.

Written between 1970 and 1973, the period when Greene was rereading and writing the introductions to the first volumes of the Collected Works, which to some extent may explain its self-referential nature, *The Honorary Consul* grew from a dream he had about an American ambassador who as the work took shape was later "quietly liquidated" by Charlie Fortnum and Dr. Plarr. The events of the plot, the kidnapping of a consul and the turning out of a priest from the barrio of the poor, were echoed by real life events in Paraguay, and Greene was for a time inclined to give up a story so closely anticipated by reality. It was, he says in *Ways of Escape,* a difficult book to write, yet it remains the favorite of his novels (301–6). In his conversation with Allain he gives as his reason his success in showing the evolution of his principal character (129).

In *A Burnt-Out Case* Querry had been left on the verge of admitting love; Plarr in *The Honorary Consul* finds his grail as Henry Pulling does in *Travels with My Aunt.* The novel allows, as neither of these novels had, for that self-assertion and self-transcendence that motivates the emergence and appreciation of tragicomedy, as Paul Hernadi has observed.[4]

Ostensibly a novel concerned with the consequences on those both directly and indirectly involved in political kidnapping, *The Honorary Consul* is in many ways a continuation of one of Greene's major preoccupations since the publication of *The Man Within* in 1927— the anatomy of love. The theme is spoken at the novel's end by Charley Fortnum, the honorary British consul, "pitiably small beer,"[5] who is mistakenly apprehended by Paraguayan guerrillas for the American ambassador, "People do get caught up by love. . . . Sooner or later" (309).

Set in a riverport town on the Paraná River, a boundary between Paraguay and Argentina, the novel introduces Dr. Eduardo Plarr, "like a watchman waiting for a signal" (18), as its antiheroic protagonist. Born of an English father and a South American mother who resides comfortably in Buenos Aires eating sweets, Plarr lives in an "adopted" country (15), within sight of the land that his father chose to fight for and perhaps die in for idealistic reasons which remain undeveloped within the novel. Plarr recognizes, as his father had before him, that he is an "exile" in a continent of exiles, and that as such he is denied the "simplicity" that belongs "to those who were native-born, those who could take the conditions of life, however bizarre, for granted" (16), a simplicity nevertheless confused by the concept of machismo in a country more under the influence of Rousseau and Chateaubriand than of Freud (20). For machismo Plarr seems to have a mild contempt, nurtured perhaps by his scientific training as a physician; it is a concept of human action from which he mistakenly exempts himself.

Plarr's exile and the border he looks at become a means of introducing the motif of unplaced loyalties, ambiguous motivations, half-understood ideologies, and seemingly unfathomable spiritual yearnings that the novel explores. The Paraná serves the same funtion as the baize door in "The Basement Room" and the Tabasco-Chiapas border in *The Power and the Glory;* it is the line between the light and the dark, the spurious and the real, the heart and the mind. The light and dark imagery suggests the religious element of the novel, and serves the theme of commitment which comes to exemplify a search for meaning in a confused and bewildering universe. As he had done in *The Heart of the Matter* and *The Quiet American,* Greene yokes religious importunities to ideological meaning so that the religious and the political are shown to be essential aspects of the human capacity for love, tolerance, and understanding. The burden of the novel becomes, consequently, the possibility of the assimilation of Plarr into the country of the spirit. There are no certainties whatsoever in *The Honorary Consul.*

Reared a Roman Catholic by Jesuit priests, the young Eduardo had lost his father to a political cause, a wound from which he still aches as the novel's action begins. Plarr, who wonders if his father has been killed by the extremists or whether he is alive and rotting in some derelict prison, has lost faith in the Roman Catholic God of his youth, believing instead that "Nothing is ineluctable. Life has surprises. Life is absurd. Because it's absurd there is always hope" (23), a belief that aligns him to a degree with contemporary existential thinkers. Yet the novel is by no means an attempt to expound philosophical or theological tenets, for Greene is in the *The Honorary Consul* as he has always been in his fiction, neither a theologian nor a philosopher but a novelist whose creations exemplify the living thought of the times. It is not so much Plarr's Catholicism or existentialism as his search for a father that animates the characterization and gives resonance to the complexities of human and divine love.

Plarr's search, presupposing a quest for meaning in an absurd universe, allows Greene to initiate and then exploit an intricate pattern of Conradian doublings that not only amplify the theme but also add to the suspense and excitement of the fable. The bungled attempt by the guerrillas to first kidnap and then hold for ransom the American ambassador not only forms the basis of the plot but justifies the tragicomic form that the novel defines.

Plarr, who is having an affair with the honorary British consul's wife Clara, who is pregnant with his child, is asked by an old schoolfriend, Leon Rivas, to aid the guerrillas in their attempt to free political prisoners from the other side of the border. Rivas tells him that his father may be one of the prisoners. Plarr reluctantly secures the information about the visiting ambassador's visit from the honorary consul, Charley Fortnum, who has been asked by the authorities to serve as interpreter during the official visit. The guerrillas unwittingly capture Fortnum instead of the ambassador, and Plarr is summoned to the barrio of the poor where the kidnappers hold their victim for the ransom they expect to negotiate with the Argentinian government. Fortnum, an alcoholic, has been given a drug that affects him in combination with the Scotch he constantly drinks. When Plarr sees Fortnum, he tells Rivas and the other kidnappers that they have kidnapped the wrong man, and that there is nothing physically the matter with him. Fortnum, however, recognizes Plarr, who returns to the city to find himself suspected of complicity by the police. What follows is a dissection of Plarr's motives in further involving himself with Fortnum's plight.

Leon Rivas, the reader is told, had first wanted to be a lawyer-champion of the poor, but he had become instead a priest. When he joined the fight for freedom, he left the priesthood and married a peasant woman called Marta. His affiliation with the leader of the insurgents, El Tigre, had been as much a search for a father as a belief in the inherent goodness of the poor and the inability of the traditional god to make life meaningful. "In a wrong society," says Rivas to Plarr, "the criminals are the honest men" (126), adding to this a further observation, "South America is our country, Eduardo. Not Paraguay. Not Argentina. You know what Che said, 'The whole continent is my country' " (127–28). Rivas appears, at first, a modern-day Manichaean, believing that the wrong god is temporarily in power of the secular and theological orders. If he kills, Rivas believes, the murder will be as much this gangster-god's fault as his own: "He made me what I am now. He will have loaded the gun and steadied my hand" (262). But beyond this concept, Rivas still maintains a belief in the power of light: "I think sometimes the memory of that man, that carpenter, can lift a few people out of the temporary Church of these terrible years, when

the Archbishop sits down to dinner with the General, into the great
Church beyond our time and place, and then . . . those lucky ones
. . . they have no words to describe the beauty of that Church"
(261).

Plarr insists that he does not understand Rivas's remarks, yet he
is impressed by the reverence that his boyhood friend is held in by
the guerrillas he leads, the reverence, Plarr knows, that is given to
the priest as a father figure. The fact that Rivas claims to pity his
God further bewilders Plarr, for he has yet to understand that he
too may be motivated by desires and promptings beyond the rational. He is, nevertheless, aware of his inability to love Clara or
to commit himself to the guerrilla cause, perhaps because he feels
subconsciously betrayed by the father who preferred to remain behind rather than accompany his wife and son to the comparative
safety of Argentina:

There were no sentimental relics in his apartment—not even a photograph.
It was bare and truthful—almost—as a police station cell. Even during
his affairs with women he had always tried to avoid that phrase of the
theater, "I love you." He had been accused often enough of cruelty, though
he preferred to think of himself as a painstaking and accurate diagnostician.
If for once he had been aware of a sickness he could describe in no other
terms, he would have unhesitatingly used the phrase "I love," but he had
always been able to attribute the emotion he felt to quite a different
malady—to loneliness, pride, physical desire, or even a simple sense of
curiosity. (171)

When he leaves Clara to rejoin Rivas and the guerrillas, who call
him to help Charley Fortnum who has been shot in the foot while
making a feeble attempt to escape, Plarr does not answer her question: "What do you want, Eduardo? Tell me. Please. What do you
want? I want to know what you want, but how can I know if I do
not understand?" (205). The fact that he leaves her question unanswered, an indication of the ambiguous aspect of his spiritual
yearning, perplexes him until the novel's end when he goes to Perez,
the police officer, to negotiate for the guerrillas. It is love, commitment, and allegiance that ultimately align Plarr and Rivas, for
each serves in a Conradian manner to illuminate the other, the
emptiness of the "uncommitted" as opposed to the perplexity of the
"committed."

The doubling device extends beyond the coupling of Plarr and Rivas into the relationship drawn between the three principal father figures: Charley Fortnum, who sometimes facetiously calls himself Mason; the novelist Jorge Julio de Saavedra, whose novels deal with South American national pride and machismo and whose best known work is significantly entitled *The Taciturn Heart;* and Plarr's true father. Plarr thinks that it is only a romantic quirk that has led him to align himself with Rivas and the guerrillas in the vain hope of securing his father's release. When he learns that his father has been killed while attempting to escape his prison of fifteen years, he is, however, not surprised. He has rejected Saavedra's concept of machismo, although he has learned to feel compassion for the novelist who jealously guards his appearance of success; but he has not been able to deny the appeal made to him by drunken, loving Charley Fortnum.

For in Fortnum, Plarr discerns that which is lacking in himself, an ability to respond to another. Before he goes to Perez, Plarr confesses to Rivas, in the novel's crucial scene, his lack of human feeling. He ironically insists that he does not suffer from machismo, but that he is only jealous of Fortnum's love for Clara: "I'm jealous because he loves her. That stupid banal word love. It's never meant anything to me. Like the word God. I know how to fuck—I don't know how to love. Poor drunken Charley Fortnum wins the game" (295). Both Plarr and Rivas are shot by the police, Rivas first confessing to Plarr that he was never intended to be a killer, Plarr jokingly assuming the role of priest by absolving his friend of his sins.

In the novel's concluding chapter, an epilogue following the melodrama of the deaths of Plarr and Rivas, it is Fortnum who performs the function of chorus, underscoring the ambiguity of the novel's action. Having waited with Plarr and Rivas and the other kidnappers in a sort of limbo, "the anteroom of death" (315), Fortnum has learned to appreciate the true heroism, not the machismo, of Plarr's gesture. The anteroom of death suggests the here and the now as a purgatory, a preparation. Fortnum finds hope in Clara and Plarr's unborn child, telling Clara that they will name the child Eduardo. He rejects Clara's pitiful lie that she had never loved Plarr, discarding too her statement that Plarr never loved her. Perhaps what Fortnum understands is that Plarr did come to experience a form of love, for in being jealous of the consul he found himself on the periphery of feeling, in the shadow of commitment. Unlike Othello who loved first and was then jealous, Plarr must experience jealousy before he can love. His jealousy, awakening his humanity, becomes in fact the indication of his ability to be.

The Honorary Consul is a rueful comedy. In *The Comedians* the adventurers considered themselves not good enough for tragedy; at best they saw themselves as actors who performed the absurd activities of life with style and grace. Here Plarr refers to his obsession for Clara, his involvement with Rivas and the guerrillas, as the stuff of comedy. "For heaven's sake," he says, "let this comedy end in comedy. None of us are suited to tragedy" (277). But the novel ends in hopeful ambiguity, suggesting that only the good, the strong, and the kind are capable of straightforward tragic action, that although the world no longer allows for the clearcut dignity of ennobling tragedy, it can provide, albeit tentatively, a muted heroism.

The Human Factor

In *Our Man in Havana,* Greene's farce of 1958, Henry Wormold's secretary Beatrice says, "I don't care a damn about men who are loyal to the people who pay them, to organizations. . . . I don't think even my country means that much. There are many countries in our blood—aren't there?—but only one person. Would the world be in the mess it is if we were loyal to love and not to countries?" (209). The problem of loyalty, both to God and man, is one with which Greene has always grappled, and it is the chief concern of *The Human Factor* (1978). In a world in which convictions are relative and allegiance frequently a matter of employment and the skill necessary to keep that employment, loyalty and treason become private considerations. The individual who knows his beliefs and is willing to act upon them becomes doubly dangerous; for his convictions not only confound the politics of government but threaten the status quo.

The protagonist of *The Human Factor* is Maurice Castle, assigned after field service in Africa to Section 6 of British Intelligence. In his early sixties, Castle patiently bides his time until his retirement, living in suburban Berkhamsted with his black wife Sarah and his stepson Sam. Seemingly a solid and respectable member of the service which he hopes has forgotten him, Castle is considered safe by his superiors because of his innocuousness: "Dullish man, first-class, of course, with files—it's generally the brilliant and the ambitious who are dangerous," says Daintry, the investigator assigned by Sir John Hargreaves to locate the leak in Section 6 of the "firm."[6] But Castle is in fact a double agent who has preserved his cover by the same clever dissimulation that has become part of his life: he drinks J and B, for example, because its pale color allows him to drink doubles with no one the wiser. It is only Sarah who appreciates the care with which Castle preserves his appearance of stolidity. Yet she does not know that because of his love for her Castle has for several years been leaking official secrets to the Communists.

In South Africa, fearful for the life of his wife, whom he had used as an agent, Castle had accepted the help of a Communist agent named Carson in freeing Sarah from an apartheid prison. Through Carson, Castle had glimpsed a meaning of love that religion had not been able to give him since childhood. "I left God behind in the school chapel, but there were priests in Africa who made me believe again—for a moment—over a drink," he says to Sarah, and continues: "Perhaps I was born a half believer. When people talk about Prague and Budapest and how you can't find a human face in Communism I stay silent. Because I've seen—once—the human face. I say to myself that if it hadn't been for Carson Sam would have been born in a prison and you would probably have died in one. One kind of Communism—or Communist—saved you and Sam. I don't have any trust in Marx or Lenin any more than I have in Saint Paul, but haven't I the right to be grateful?" (94). Castle, according to his mother, has "always had an exaggerated sense of gratitude for the least kindness" (98); and what he seeks is a "permanent home," a place where he can be accepted as a citizen "without any pledge of faith, not the City of God or Marx, but the city called Peace of Mind" (94). In this respect he is like Querry who in the heart of darkness seeks for Pendélé. To find that peace of mind Castle must play a game of intrigue and deceit while remaining true to his commitment to Sarah.

A representative of the apartheid agency referred to as BOSS, Cornelius Muller comes to London to first threaten and then destroy Castle's precarious serenity. Described as a man without prejudice because he is without an ideal, Muller is sent by MI 5 to Section 6 to uncover the defector in an assignment given the schoolroom code name of Uncle Remus. The leaks from Castle's department, insignificant though Castle knows them to be, are nevertheless of interest to the Americans and the C.I.A. inasmuch as they threaten the relationship of certain African nations and the free world with respect to the gold, diamonds, and uranium upon which a world balance of trade depends. Muller is surprised to find his old adversary Castle in Section 6 and later even more surprised to learn that Castle has married Sarah. He quickly discerns that Sam is too dark to have been fathered by Castle, and inadvertently passes important information about Uncle Remus to Castle, who feels that he must turn this information over to the Communists, even though he has warned them that he can no longer continue as a double agent.

Assigned by Sir James Hargreaves to find and stop the leaks coming from Castle's department, Captain Daintry and Dr. Emmanuel Percival first suspect Davis, Castle's colleague and friend in the department. "We aren't the stuff of double agents, you and me," ironically says Davis to Castle (59). Davis is poisoned by Percival, his death made to seem cirrhosis of the liver brought on by too much drink. Castle, however, feels little responsibility in having brought about the death of his friend.

At this point in the novel the chessboard imagery that has served to suggest the nature of espionage becomes structural, and the theme of flight and pursuit of which it is an aspect dominates the action. In his correspondence with Elizabeth Bowen and V. S. Pritchett, Greene had referred to Browning's "Bishop Blougram's Apology," pointing to the use of the white and black squares of the chessboard as aspects of his convictions concerning the relative power of good and evil. In *The Human Factor* chess is used to emphasize the relationship between the players in the espionage game as well as the moral and ethical obliquity required by the game itself.[7] Dr. Emmanuel Percival, who becomes Castle's chief adversary within the intrigue of the novel, echoes Castle's words when he says to his superior Hargreaves, "Enjoy, only enjoy. I don't pretend to be an enthusiast for God or Marx. Beware of people who believe. They aren't reliable players. All the same one grows to like a good player on the other side of the board—it increases the fun" (147). Perhaps for this reason Castle feels little remorse for Davis's death, for Davis is an expendable pawn.

Within the chess pattern, which serves primarily as a device to lend suspense to the flight and pursuit pattern, Sarah is the black Queen, and Castle functions as the piece whose name he bears, for what he most desires is security for Sarah and Sam. Carson can be seen as a Pawn sacrificed for the Queen's safety. The boy Sam becomes the all-important Pawn, for it is he at the novel's end who keeps Castle and Sarah apart. The black Knights can be seen as Halladay, the contact, and Boris, Castle's control. Dr. Percival, because of his ability to jump from healing to death, can be viewed as a white Knight, or Knave; and Hargreaves, who does not overly insist on fair play and ethical action, can be seen as his counterpart. Curiously the Bishops are either powerless or absent in the match. In the novel's crucial scene, which recalls the prison scene in *The Power and the Glory,* the priest to whom Castle goes for comfort only proves to him that he is "another victim of loneliness and silence like himself" (167). Even Buller the dog, surprisingly one of the novel's most successfully drawn characters, can be seen as a Pawn foolishly sacrificed to catalyze the action. The final result of the match is stalemate, however, for although Castle escapes from England, and the Communists have promised to send Sarah and Sam after him, he is deprived of his Queen by Sam who has no passport. Sarah's commitment to her son takes precedence over her love for her husband.

In the brilliantly managed sequence in which the disguised Castle escapes from England, the question of assumed identity intensifies the ambiguity of motivation that propels the players of the espionage game while, at the same time, moving the action across the frontiers that separate the so-called free world from the Communist world. For in *The Human Factor* the border, as it does in *The Honorary Consul,* counterpoints the relationship between the subconscious and the conscious, between ideology and action, thought and commitment. Safe in Moscow, with no knowledge of the language, the red star over the University replacing the castle looming over the Berkhamsted common, Castle, like Plarr, finds himself in a world both bewildering and inimical to him. When he finally speaks to Sarah on the telephone, he appreciates that although he has crossed the frontier to personal safety, isolation and loneliness are the price that he must pay for having served his Queen. There are at least two countries in Sarah's blood, and Sam's has the better claim. As George Steiner has aptly observed, Castle comes, like Kierkegaard, to understand that the loneliest man is the one who has no secret, "or, more exactly, who has no one to whom to betray a secret."[8]

Anyone familiar with Greene's novels will from the very first page of the narrative find himself in the familiar environs of Greeneland. *The Human Factor*'s ambiance may appear gray, yet disenchantment and sterility are not significant aspects of the terrain. *The Human Factor,* like *The Honorary Consul,* is a revisiting of familiar themes and situations, and the reader will find himself beguiled by the wit and dexterity with which Greene comments on his previous works while at the same time telling a suspenseful tale. The action is set partly in Berkhamsted, Greene's birthplace, where the common and the castle that towers above it come to represent British tradition. Maurice Castle and his wife Sarah are intentionally given the same names of two of Greene's best-known characters, Maurice Bendrix and Sarah Miles of *The End of the Affair;* and the same passion that inspires the former is given, although muted, to the later lovers. Certain patterns and motifs, as well as characters, hearken back to many of Greene's earlier works, and it becomes another aspect of the game patterns of the novel to pinpoint similarities and variations. The divided self; the call of pity; betrayal, commitment and responsibility; the chase and the border—all are motifs both familiar and haunting. And the references to Uncle Remus and Tinker Bell remind the reader of the innocence of childhood soured by the experience of maturity.

But *The Human Factor* is not so much a nostalgic revisiting of familiar places, or an exercise in self-indulgence, as it is, as are all of Greene's novels, a work that reflects the psychology of the times, in this case the psychology of defection. Modeled loosely upon the careers of the English public servants who defected to Moscow—Guy Burgess, Kim Philby, and Donald Maclean—*The Human Factor* probes the forces that produced the British character and rendered it vulnerable. In his introductory note to *The Confidential Agent* Greene writes: "A writer who is a Catholic cannot help having a certain sympathy for any faith which is sincerely held and I was glad when more than twenty years later Kim Philby quoted this novel in explaining his attitude to Stalinism. It seemed to indicate that I had not been far wrong, although at the period I wrote I knew nothing of intelligence work" (xi).

Hargreaves and Daintry and Percival represent the Establishment, as Castle supposedly does; they protect the white Queen who remains aloof. But Castle is motivated by his love for Sarah, the black Queen, whereas the motivation of his antagonists remains abstract. The snobbery of caste is hinted at, but more importantly, through the character of Dr. Percival, the sterility of an ideology, perhaps its death, is approached. For Emmanuel Percival, portrayed as a Knight within the chess pattern, also refers to the quester of medieval legend and to the Fisher King. Given to fishing, and described as having a taste for smoked fish and fine wine, the doctor, supposedly a healer, is instead a dealer in death. He feels no remorse for mistakenly killing Davis. At the funeral he reflects that Davis's coffin does not contain a fish, and then on the pity of the fact that one could not throw a man back into the river of life as one could a fish. He responds "Q. E. D.," instead of Amen when the minister says, fatuously, at the end of the service, "The sting of death is sin, and the strength of sin is the law" (145). Ironically, Castle too is sterile, and though his love for Sarah, although courtly, is made to seem a bit ridiculous, it is, nonetheless, a potent force. For Castle, as for Hamlet, the time is out of joint; but unlike Hamlet, Castle is powerless to set it right, although he does try. References to Trollope's novel of a swindler's courage, *The Way We Live Now,* as well as references to *War and Peace* and *Robinson Crusoe,* emphasize the relative certainties of earlier times, as the references to Tennyson and Browning do in *Travels with My Aunt,* while commenting on the ethical impoverishment of an atomic age. Castle, who like Major Scobie cannot resist a call of distress "however it was encoded" (113), knows that hate is an automatic response to fear, and that fear is the order of the times. His challenge to fear is his love for Sarah.

The Human Factor is, furthermore, homage to Greene's chief mentor, Joseph Conrad, and especially to Conrad's novel of espionage and counterespionage, *The Secret Agent.* In Conrad's novel the secret agent, Verloc, is lulled into complacency by the seeming equanimity of his wife, Winnie. He fails to understand Winnie's obsessive love for her dim-witted brother, Stevie, whom she resembles in moments of intense preoccupation. Conrad dramatizes the ambiguous and multifaceted motivations of the doubled characters, Ossipon and the professor, the assistant commissioner and the Great Personage, Verloc and Chief Inspector Heat, who are involved in the game of espionage. The use of doubles, furthermore, allows Conrad, as it does Greene, the opportunity not only to dramatize the involvement of his characters but also to move satirically through all levels of government, from the most important members of Parliament to the most insignificant emigré whose presence is sanctioned by the nation. Indeed, the relationship between the police and the anarchists is shown to be one of mutual dependence as is the interdependency of the espionage agents in *The Human Factor*. Greene takes his epigraph from Conrad, "I only know that he who forms a tie is lost. The germ of corruption has entered his soul," and thereby emphasizes the theme of loyalty to individuals over causes that Beatrice refers to in *Our Man in Havana*. To press indebtedness further is to misunderstand the intention of Greene's novel, which is quite simply to deal convincingly in a modern context with loyalty to love and its counterpart, in this case, betrayal of country and tradition. That Greene succeeds in making his protagonist not only believable but sympathetic is sufficient testimony of his achievement.

The Human Factor may not be Greene's greatest accomplishment in the art of the novel. Castle is by no means the haunting figure that either Scobie or Bendrix is, nor is the theme of betrayal rendered as poignantly as it is in *The Heart of the Matter* and *The Quiet American*. In the novels of the thirties through those of the sixties a soaring imagination and intense conviction are at work, evidenced on every page of narrative, despite occasional flaws of presentation and seeming inaccuracies of characterization. But *The Human Factor* is, nevertheless, a novel that stands alongside the best of Greene's works in that it reveals Greene as an immaculate craftsman. The narrative is fast paced, witty; the style is impeccable, dry; and the meaning brilliantly deployed through character and event. It may not be his best novel but it is certainly a good one.

Doctor Fischer of Geneva and *Monsignor Quixote*

The Human Factor was followed by two very different but equally successful novellas, *Doctor Fischer of Geneva or The Bomb Party* (1980) and *Monsignor Quixote* (1982), the former a cautionary tale on the subject of power and greed, the latter Greene's homage to Cervantes. *Doctor Fischer of Geneva* can be most profitably read as a fantasy that depends for its success on the logical working out of a macabre jest, referred to by the alternate title. As such it is a jeu d'esprit. *Monsignor Quixote* on the other hand, is a parable which centers on the triumph of the loving heart.

In *Doctor Fischer of Geneva* a fairly reliable narrator reconstructs the events of the previous few months in an attempt to assess and understand the emotions that had led him to the crucial bomb party that he had not only witnessed but had participated in. A middle-aged translator who works for a chocolate factory in Geneva, Alfred Jones recounts his meeting with Anna-Luise, Dr. Fischer's young and beautiful daughter, his surprise and joy in the love that they shared, his delight in their marriage. Because of Anna-Luise, and despite her warnings, Jones is drawn into Fischer's orbit. Portrayed as a "Jehovah and Satan" figure, Fischer is notorious for the expensive gifts he presents his sycophantic and greedy guests after humiliating them at his lavish dinner parties (153). Although reminiscent of the GOM, the god-figure of *Loser Takes All,* Fischer is better read as a modern Manichaean gangster-god who enslaves others by using his immense wealth as bribes. Anna-Luise's death in a skiing accident draws Jones into Fischer's net, but armed with "memories of love," Jones defeats Fischer's attempt to suborn him with the promises of power and wealth.[9] All Jones and Fischer's other guests have to do at his final and most elaborate party is choose from a bran tub a firecracker that may or may not propel him into the next world. By renouncing power and wealth, Jones, who prefers death to life, defeats Fischer, who is in a sense hoist with his own petard. His suicide at his last supper suggests the despair of Judas, the death of the heart that has drawn inward. Implicit in Fischer's action is the biblical adage of winning the world and losing the soul. If the novel ends without the threatened bang, the reader is not fully certain that Fischer's death is a whimper. What he does understand is that Fischer plays his game according to his own rules.

Monsignor Quixote presents from its very outset two fully realized characters whose profoundest beliefs, simply held and emotionally tested, not only portray their essences but convince the reader of their authenticity. They are characters conceived with warmth and presented with affection who exist in their own right, not as spokespersons of religious or political assertion. Through his innocence and dignity, Father Quixote, the descendant of a fictional character, portrays the best elements of religious faith, and his traveling companion, Sancho, former Communist mayor of Toboso, a fervor for and dedication to the cause of human justice. Their adventures, ranging from the purchase of purple socks and a cross suitable for a monsignor to the viewing of a pornographic film called "A Maiden's Prayer," delight, amuse, and edify. Never before has there been so cloudless an horizon in Greene's fictional sky.

In these later novels Greene seems in some ways to be emulating Shakespeare who, after the strenuous exertions of the great tragedies, turned to a less heroic form, one that allowed him to examine more problematical aspects of human maturation. The principal characters in *The Honorary Consul* and *The Human Factor* may seem to express more doubt than they do certainty, but those of *Travels with My Aunt* and, given the nature of the jest, those of *Doctor Fischer of Geneva* express more certainty than despair. The principal characters of *Monsignor Quixote,* however, approach the sublime. In all of these novels, all's well that ends well, more or less.

Greene has, in fact, moved in these later books from the more dogmatic implications of Roman Catholic belief that characterize his novels from the thirties through the sixties into a broader kind of Christian humanism. What his personal convictions are vis à vis his Roman Catholicism are matters of private conscience; the characters he presents to his public, however, are another matter. Julian Symons is essentially correct when he writes that "the human being lives, the novelist writes about the lives of others. Graham Greene the novelist has found strength in his later work through a Manichaeism that balances faith and works, passivity against action, pleasure against goodness, detachment against involvement. Sometimes the balance tips one way, sometimes the other" (1089). But he is less perceptive in his evaluation of *Monsignor Quixote* which, he says, "will not weigh heavily on the scale of Greene's achievement" (1089). The characters of the novella are conceived with warmth and affection; they exist not only on the pages in which they appear, but beyond them as well. They are characters who, like Hamlet, are felt rather than perceived, and what remains with the reader long after he has put down the book is what remains with him long after he has witnessed the tragic events of Shakespeare's play: the knowledge that goodness and truth and beauty exist and ultimately give life whatever meaning it has. In *Doctor Fischer of Geneva,* Jones concludes in the epilogue that "Death was no longer an answer—it was an irrelevance" (155). The Monsignor's life of faith, in quite another manner, testifies to the truth of this observation.

To those who have read his words with an enthusiasm and an eagerness not unmixed with anxiety and sometimes bewilderment, whether these words appeared in fictional, dramatic, autobiographical, or journalistic form, Greene seems to be saying in *Monsignor*

Quixote, as does Shakespeare in *The Tempest,* "Look. I have come through."

The Tenth Man

In 1983 Greene learned that a story he had written while under contract to MGM in 1948, while he was working on *The Third Man* for Carol Reed, was being offered for sale by the studio. Anthony Blond, who had recently purchased the publication rights, sent the manuscript to Greene, who remembered the piece as a two-page outline. What the author discovered instead was a complete short novel, which he must have written as a preliminary to a screenplay, perhaps as he had done with *The Third Man.* He found the work not only readable, but in many ways preferable to *The Third Man.* With Blond's acquiescence *The Tenth Man* was published by the Bodley Head, the author's share of the royalties going to MGM.[10]

Rereading the novel prompted Greene to look through his own archives, where he discovered the original treatment, done for Alberto Cavalcanti, of *Our Man in Havana.* This, along with another projected screen treatment entitled "Jim Braddon and the War Criminal," he included in the volume along with *The Tenth Man.* The satire on the secret service, entitled "Nobody to Blame," indicates the changes necessitated by the Cuban locale of the final version of *Our Man in Havana,* and most notable besides the general simplification of the plot is the fact that Richard Tripp, who became Wormold, is more or less happily married. The "Jim Braddon" sketch offers further evidence of Greene's prescient ability to anticipate political and social events, here in connection with Israeli attempts to find and bring to justice the criminals of the Holocaust. The international searches for both Klaus Barbie and Josef Mengele are anticipated by the strange events of Jim Braddon's life, who after an air crash awakens without a memory to conclude that because he looks like a notorious war criminal he is in fact the man who is being hunted throughout the world.

Because of its tautness, economy, and melodrama, *The Tenth Man* at first reading appears to belong to the entertainments, a category that Greene still maintained at the time of the work's composition. Subsequent readings, however, reveal the fact that the work more nearly fulfills the requirements for the definition of the novel already cited in this study: it presents characterization of depth and motivation that is both complex and ambiguous. Reading the novel presents much the same satisfaction that one gets in drinking a forgotten bottle of vintage wine. That Greene published *The Tenth Man* as a novel, while comparing it favorably to *The Third Man,* seems apposite as well as appropriate, especially since the central character, who suggests not only by his name but also in his appearance and demeanor Charlie Chaplin's Little Tramp, is fully drawn, his religious attachment an integral aspect of the total characterization.

In some ways proleptic of Arthur Miller's *Incident at Vichy* (1964), *The Tenth Man* begins, as do the best of Greene's fables, with immediacy and purpose, the initial emphasis placed on the reckoning of clock time. A group of Nazi-held hostages jealously measure time as a relief from the tedium of internment. The prison setting, purposefully left vague, enhances the notion of a limbo from which the hostages will move into the world of the living or the dead. The conditions of imprisonment anticipate those that Greene will present in *The Honorary Consul* years later. Time in the prison limbo is guarded by the mayor of Bourges and by an engine driver named Pierre, each insisting that his own timepiece provides the more accurate reading. Time functions, then, on both a physical and a metaphysical level to lend impetus to what becomes a morality play on the subject of survival and belonging.

Jean-Louis Chavel, "a lonely fellow who made awkward attempts from time to time to prove himself human" (41), is one of three hostages chosen by lot from thirty to be executed in reprisal for the killing of "the aide-de-camp of the military governor, a sergeant and a girl on a bicycle" (48). Like Conrad's Lord Jim, Chavel is unprepared for the event; he panics when he draws his lot, then offers to exchange his fortune of 300,000 francs and his family home at St. Jean de Brinac for his life. A young hostage called Janvier strikes the bargain, and Chavel is left without the identity he had never truly possessed. He tries once, the narrator tells the reader much later in the novel, to call back the bargain; but he is refused. Like Jim, who immediately understands his missed opportunity for heroism after he has jumped from the *Patna,* Chavel is thrown into the destructive element; and like Conrad's antiheroic protagonist he must keep himself afloat with minimum effort to discover his dream of selfhood. Given 300 francs when he is released from imprisonment and calling himself Charlot, he revisits the Paris he had inhabited as a prosperous lawyer before his imprisonment by the Nazis, to discover what he has suspected—that he no longer belongs.

Outside a urinal Chavel, now Charlot, is mistaken by an actor named Carosse for Pidot, adding a fillip to the lost identity theme. A collaborator fleeing from the Resistance, Carosse gives Charlot another 300 francs, this and the 300,000 of Chavel's fortune suggesting in multiples of ten the number 3 of Christian story, as well as the indulgences of Catholic belief. With nowhere else to go Charlot makes his way to his former home at St. Jean de Brinac, now inhabited by Janvier's mother and his sister Thérèse. Like many other of Greene's heroines Thérèse is attractive in her bitterness, her gamin knowledge, and her recklessness of spirit. She accepts Charlot as one who had known her brother in prison, telling him that she lives only to revenge herself on Chavel for having tricked her brother into death. She offers him work as a handyman, employment he is glad to take, for it allows him to live in the home of his ancestors. Attracted by her mournfulness, her monomania, and her ability to hate, Charlot soon learns to love Thérèse. He meets again his boyhood friend Roche, disfigured because of an accident, who fails to recognize him. Roche speaks to Charlot of the Chavel who was, accusing him of an unloving heart.

The coming of the actor Carosse, who has added murder to his crime of collaboration, challenges Charlot's precarious equanimity and catalyzes the novel's denouement. Carosse is to Chavel what Gentleman Brown is to Conrad's Jim, an alter ego, but one possessed of the charm and audacity that the original lacks. When Carosse tells Thérèse that he is Chavel, she spits on him. Carosse soon discerns that Charlot loves Thérèse, but he knows that he, an actor, can convince Thérèse that he cares for her despite her believing him to be the man who had beguiled her brother to his death. When Thérèse's mother dies, Charlot goes into the town to fetch the priest, a young man without sentiment or emotion whose function is simply to administer the sacraments, a far cry from Father Rank and Father Crompton. The priest advises Charlot that, unless the girl hires a woman to live with her, he must leave to avoid gossip. To protect her not only from Carosse and the town, but from himself as well, Charlot challenges the actor, identifying himself as Chavel, but Carosse shoots him. Charlot, now Chavel, in effect accomplishes what Henry Scobie does in *The Heart of the Matter* when he commits suicide to save Helen and Louise from the pain that he brings them.

Having sacrificed himself for her, thus repaying the life he had bargained from her brother, Chavel dies. His final act, in accordance with his lawyer's training, is to guarantee by legal deed—or so he believes—for Thérèse's mundane future.

The religious aspect of the novel, neither belligerently nor dogmatically presented, becomes one of the novel's chief merits. "When he dies," Thérèse says prophetically to Charlot of Chavel, "you can take your oath it will be in a state of grace with the sacrament in his mouth, forgiving all his enemies. He won't die before he can cheat the Devil." Of herself she says, "I'll be the one who is damned. Because I shan't forgive. I shan't die in a state of grace" (87). That Chavel dies to protect Thérèse and that Thérèse discovers her need of love suggests a grimly optimistic conclusion to the story of Chavel's search for self. What Chavel discovers is that the "simple track" of love is "infinitely more desirable" than the obscure route that "one failure of nerve" had forced him to wander as the tramp Charlot (61, 70).

The Tenth Man is one of Greene's most remarkable fictions, in large measure because of the manner in which the religious element is portrayed—without apology, integral to character, setting, theme. Although its brevity and spareness suggest that it be placed in the same category with *The Third Man*, it more rightly deserves to be considered alongside the novels of Greene's maturity.

Chapter Seven
The Drama

Much critical attention has been given to Greene as a novelist who deals with religious themes in his major works, and novels such as *Brighton Rock, The Heart of the Matter, The Power and the Glory,* and *The End of the Affair* have gained for him a sizable literary reputation. Nevertheless, a great many of Greene's admirers cling to the belief that the best of Greene is still to be found in his early thrillers: *A Gun For Sale, The Confidential Agent,* and *The Ministry of Fear.* Add to this that all save one or two of his works have been translated into motion pictures, *The Third Man* gaining immense popular success, and one finds a writer of "many parts." Comparatively little critical attention, however, has been given to Greene the dramatist, despite the fact that he has written several plays that have received critical and sometimes popular acclaim in both the United States and England.

These ventures into drama are not surprising when one remembers that Greene had been much preoccupied with dramatic presentations in several of his novels, especially in *The Power and the Glory* and *The Quiet American.* In his introduction to *A Gun for Sale,* he comments on his early passion for drama: "In those days I thought in terms of a key scene—I would even chart its position on a sheet of paper before I began to write. . . . It was as though I wanted to escape the vast liquidity of the novel and to play out the most important situation on a narrow stage where I could direct every movement of my characters (viii).

Perhaps it needs to be pointed out once more that Greene's apprenticeship as film critic for *Night and Day* and the *Spectator* and his knowledge of cinematographic techniques and tricks of suspense contributed to the sense of melodrama apparent in his early novels and entertainments. In the later novels, however, his themes were developed with a careful eye for dramatic possibilities engendered in and by the action: in *The Power and the Glory,* for example, the main theme—the power of God versus the power of a godless state—is developed in the dramatic debate between the whiskey priest and

149

the lieutenant of the new order. In the introduction to *A Gun for Sale*, Greene says that he reached the logical climax of this method of presentation in *The Honorary Consul*, where the entire meaning of the novel is revealed in the dialogue between Plarr and Rivas in the hut scene at the novel's end.

Today Greene's plays are usually read because of the light they throw on the novels and entertainments; they reveal nevertheless a thorough knowledge of dramatic forms and an ability to impress upon these forms an idiosyncratic view of man, nature, and divinity. *The Great Jowett*, a radio play first aired by the BBC in 1939 but not published until 1981 by the Bodley Head, indicates Greene's fundamental interest in human character. Benjamin Jowett, known as Jowler, the legendary head of Balliol College, Oxford, in the later nineteenth century, is presented as a series of seeming contradictions. His predilection for the aristocracy is countered by his desire to provide education for the poor, his capitulation to the Establishment in signing his allegiance to the Thirty-Nine Articles by his readiness to support the poet Swinburne against the college authorities and by his humility in not even questioning Swinburne's emendation of his translation of a passage from Plato. The more traditional plays, *The Living Room* (1953) and *The Potting Shed* (1957), not only present believable characters while recapitulating favorite themes but also add a dimension to the theater that might be called religio-philosophical dilemma. *The Complaisant Lover* (1959), a farce with a serious edge, stands in relation to *The Living Room* and *The Potting Shed* much as *Our Man in Havana* relates to the novels and its predecessor entertainments. *Carving a Statue* (1964) throws light on the energy and frustration expended in the creation of art, and *The Return of A. J. Raffles* (1975), a comedy of manners, indicates Greene's abiding interest in adventurers who live on the perimeters of danger. *Yes and No* (1983), a one-act play, reveals Greene in a satirical mood, and *For Whom the Bell Chimes* (1983) his predilection for the grotesque.

The Living Room

The Living Room uses for its situation the triangle relationship that has characterized the novels since *The Heart of the Matter*. As in that novel, the religious theme of the play insists on a character's inability to conceive of a kind and understanding God. The major conflict becomes that of the individual against the orthodox religious conception of a just and merciful God. In the second scene of Act I Michael Dennis, pulled between his pity for his neurotic wife and his passion for Rose Pemberton, asks James Browne if he believes in justice. James replies, stating the theme: "It's a mathematical term. We talk of a just line, don't we? God's exact, that's all. He's not a judge. An absolute knowledge of every factor—the conscious and the unconscious—yes, even heredity, all your Freudian urges. That's why He's merciful."[1] But once again Greene is not so much interested in questioning the beliefs of his Church, as in presenting a dilemma in which human beings are forced into an emotional cul de sac. To ask of either *The Living Room* or *The Potting Shed* an answer to the religious problems posed by the plays is, once again, to misunderstand his intention. In his novels and plays Greene is above all concerned with individuals who make a place for themselves in an experience of life that, ultimately, they control.

Peter Glenville, the British producer of *The Living Room,* points out in the introduction to the 1957 William Heinemann edition that the play was difficult and unexpected both in theme and manner. He goes on to characterize it as a drama full of mood and challenge, elusive and yet passionate with conviction; as a drama that borrows nothing from stock theatrical convention, and one whose meaning is to be discovered through style, rhythm, and imaginative concentration on the essentials of character:

The majority of English plays are romantically conceived, and their absence of intellectual vitality is compensated for by a warm optimism in the emotional pattern. In this play there is a firm and masculine optimism in the matter of intellectual conviction, combined with a searing pessimism that concerns the question of immediate satisfaction of emotional needs. Moreover it is written within the framework and premise of Catholic belief. This play is no apologia for Catholicism. . . . The play is not for or against Catholics, it is about them—or rather about certain individual Catholics who find themselves (through their own fault) in a terrible dilemma. . . .[2]

In other words, the reader need not concern himself with the tenets of Catholicism except as they reflect upon the actions of the characters who find themselves involved in an experience of life that seems to admit no earthly solution.

The Living Room concerns Rose Pemberton's coming to live with
her great aunts after the death of her mother. The aunts, Teresa
and Helen Browne (their names perhaps allusions to Teresa, the
Little Flower, and to Helena, the determined mother of Constantine)
are intensely and narrowly Roman Catholic. Although she has been
brought up a Roman Catholic, Rose is not fanatical in her devotion;
her father was, after all, not a Catholic. Teresa and Helen care for
their brother James, a priest unable to continue in his office because
of an accident to his legs. Like Father Rank in *The Heart of the
Matter,* James feels keenly his limitations when called upon to assist
the suffering. Although she is the younger of the two sisters, Helen
is the stronger willed. And when she discovers that Rose is having
an affair with Michael Dennis, the middle-aged executor of her
estate, she cruelly induces Teresa to fall ill, thereby making an
appeal to Rose's pity and keeping her from running off with Michael.
Helen reasons that it is better for Rose to conduct an affair and
remain within the Church and the framework of its forgiveness than
to cut herself off from repentance by living an adulterous life as
Michael's common-law wife.

Michael Dennis is committed to a neurotic wife who resembles
Mrs. Fellows, Coral's mother, in *The Power and the Glory* and Louise
Scobie in *The Heart of the Matter.* The three women have in common
the early deaths of their innocent daughters. Dennis is bound to his
wife by pity, as Scobie was to his; but, unlike Scobie, he is willing
to cast off his responsibility to his wife in the hope that he will
find happiness with Rose. Helen invites Mrs. Dennis to her home,
and the unhappy wife asks her husband's mistress to pity her. In a
tense and brilliant scene Greene brings all the issues in the drama
into focus. Michael runs after his wife, for he cannot disallow the
passionate pity that he feels for her. Bewildered, Rose turns to the
priest, but the best he can say to her is, "You've got a lifetime to
fool yourself in. It's a long time, to keep forgetting that poor
hysterical woman who has a right to need him" (58). Overcome
with pity and grief, Rose says:

You tell me if I go off with him he'll be unhappy for a lifetime. If I stay
here, I'll have nothing but that closet and this—this living room. And
you tell me there's hope and I can pray. Who to? Don't talk to me about
God and the saints. I don't believe in your God who took away your legs

and wants to take away Michael. I don't believe in your Church and your Holy Mother of God. I don't believe. (59)

Rose can find no other solution for her grief but suicide; like Scobie in *The Heart of the Matter,* she dies uttering a prayer: "Our Father who art . . . who art. . . . Bless Mother, Nanny and Sister Marie-Louise, and please God don't let school start again ever" (60). Rose reverts to the innocence of her childhood as she takes her life. But her death is not completely futile: Teresa defies Helen. No longer will Teresa fear death; symbolically she makes her bed in the living room, the room in which Rose has died; thus she denies Helen's fear of death and exhibits her faith in a forgiving God.

The Living Room ends on a note of perplexity, as it asks the audience if God is as simple as an equation, as clear as air? Will he damn for all eternity a creature whose dilemma seems insoluble by human standards?—in essence the problem of *The Heart of the Matter. The Living Room* deals with Roman Catholicism as a factor that emphasizes the individual's responsibility to self and to a code. In Rose, the futility of life without love is described. The conception of her death may perhaps be better understood in the light of Scobie's suicide and of Sarah Miles's dedication to God in *The End of the Affair,* for Greene seems again in the play to question an orthodox Roman Catholic attitude toward suicide and salvation. Rose's suicide need not be viewed, however, in the same perspective with Scobie's death and Sarah Miles's physical decline. The play presents its issue clearly, dramatically, and economically, and the knowledge of Greene's preoccupation with this theme merely enhances.

Through Father Browne, as with Father Rank, Greene reasserts a favorite motif, the "appalling" nature of the mercy of God. Father Browne insists that no one knows what Rose was thinking at the precise moment of her death and that God can be no less forgiving than a woman—a line that comes almost verbatim from *The Heart of the Matter.* The fact that James cannot give Rose the help she needs at the moment she needs it contributes to the tragedy. In *The Heart of the Matter,* Father Rank is more convincing as a priest than as a character involved in precipitating the tragedy, while in the drama Father Browne contributes to the dilemma and hastens the tragedy. His words at the end of the play recover the general order of the Church. Again, as in Elizabethan drama, the person of greatest authority reasserts a general order before releasing the audience.

Perhaps the most interesting aspect of the play, aside from the dilemma, is Greene's use of the principal symbol of the living room, the room inhabited by the elderly sisters and the only one in a large house in which there has been no death. The room is, on a literal level, the expression of their fear of death; yet it is symbolic too of the narrowing of human experience into a restricted sphere that seems somehow, and perhaps paradoxically, to be Hope. This hope is a reaffirmation, and through Teresa Greene exploits a belief in the mercy of God and in a life after death. The eccentricity of the room, its furniture, the lavatory opening off it, the fact that it is on the third floor of an old house indicate the limited and thwarted perspective of the human being seeking understanding of God's justice in the world. The living room is life; hence Rose's suicide in it derives greater meaning, and the "hint of an explanation," to use Greene's own term, is more readily appreciated.

The character who is best drawn and who demonstrates most ably Greene's ability in the sphere of the drama is Helen Browne, a "good" woman. The catastrophe revolves upon her meddling; but whether this meddling is divinely inspired or not is a consideration that, although provocative, does not add to the tragic inevitability of the dilemma. Helen meddles. Her reasons are to her clear and cogent, but whether they are right or not is moot; it is sufficient to know that these reasons help to bring about the suicide. It is through Helen Browne, as well as through Rose Pemberton, that Greene advances the secondary theme of the play: Which is the greater sin? To cut oneself off from grace, as Rose would do in living with Michael outside the "living room"? Or to sin and remain near the source of grace and the possibility of salvation?

To repeat, Helen Browne is a good woman, in the bosom of the Church. Yet she is scheming, calculating, cruel, and insensitive. She is a self-willed despot who insists on controlling the destiny of her niece, proclaiming her right to care for the girl's position as a Roman Catholic. In conception, Helen Browne is close to François Mauriac's Brigitte Pian of *La Pharisienne* who, as does Helen, insists on dominating the spirit of her husband and her stepchildren. Helen is a hypocrite, but she is not evil. Men may hate such people—but not God. The point is that through Helen's meddling, others are made aware of the reality of God. But at what cost? Helen makes her influence felt upon her brother James and upon her sister Teresa; and as she succeeds in contributing to Rose's suicide, she succeeds in keeping her within the Church. After Rose's death, when Helen attempts to keep Teresa from sleeping in the living room, she is, in a real sense, denying the teaching of her Church that the dead do not die. If the living room is symbolic of hope, then Helen denies hope. She judges and arranges life, for she fears death. "Stop it," says her brother James. "We've had enough of this foolishness. God isn't unmerciful the way a woman can be. You've been afraid too long. It's time for you to rest, my darling. It's time for you to rest" (67).

The Living Room ends on the same note of ambiguity as *The Heart of the Matter.* James Browne reestablishes, as best he can, the norm of the Church; he insists that the living are not forced to believe, as Helen does, that Rose is damned. He insists that, although Rose had spit at the word "prayer" and had hated God in the minutes before she died, God alone can judge her motives, for hate and love are often one. "If He exists, He loved her too," he says to Michael Dennis, "And you don't know and I don't know the amount of love and pity He's spending on her now" (65). Teresa affirms this statement when she turns to Helen and says, "Why shouldn't I sleep here? We're not afraid of the child. And there'd be no better room for me to fall asleep in forever than the room where Rose died" (67).

The Potting Shed

The Potting Shed makes use of the Lazarus theme, one that Greene had earlier employed in a short story called "The Second Death." The story, dated 1929 in *Collected Stories,* describes the life of a man who had once been given up for dead. "Suppose I had been dead," he says to a dying friend who, one learns later, had himself profited from a miracle. "I believed it then, you know, and so did my mother. . . . I went straight for a couple of years. I thought it might be a sort of second chance. Then things got fogged and somehow. . . ."[3] As the dying man prepares for his second death, he begs his friend to reassure him that the first death had been nothing but a dream. "It would be so dreadful . . . if it had been true, and I'd got to go through all that again. You don't know what things were going to happen to me in that dream. And they'd be worse now. . . . When one's dead there's no unconsciousness any more forever" (549–50). One will remember too that Greene's novel *The End of the Affair* employs "miracle" as part of the thematic material.

The Potting Shed also makes use of the detective story framework that Greene utilizes in many of his entertainments and novels, and this dimension adds to its suspense and action. As the play opens, the audience is confronted by a mystery. The Callifers are gathered at "Wild Grove" for the impending demise of old Callifer, the head of the family, who in his youth and vigorous middle age had preached an extreme rationalist belief. The mystery develops through Anne, the granddaughter, who assumes a symbolic position in the drama akin to that of Ida Arnold in *Brighton Rock,* since it is she who precipitates the denouement. Neither James, old Callifer's younger son, nor his Uncle William Callifer has been summoned to "Wild Grove," once a great country seat but now an old house encroached upon by the chimneys and the mill towers of an industrial neighborhood.

Anne, however, has sent James a telegram, and he has come to his father's deathbed hoping to learn what in his life makes him incapable of experiencing any deep-felt emotion. "Sara, what's wrong with me?" he asks his divorced wife. "You're not alive," she says. "Sometimes I wanted to make you angry or sorry, to hurt you. But you never felt pain."[4] His inability to participate in the human community gives James the only pain that he understands, and this is more an absence of feeling than anything else. He has no memory beyond waking up in a sick bed in his fourteenth year and wondering what accident or circumstance had turned his parents against him. The mystery is somehow connected with the potting shed at the bottom of the garden, amongst the laurels; and James fears the place.

In the second act it is discovered that, at the age of fourteen, the boy had hanged himself in the shed. He had fallen under the influence of his Uncle William, a Roman Catholic convert who had become a priest. The boy's father had rudely disillusioned his beliefs in the "Mysteries" of the Church; as a result of his rational "awakening," James had attempted suicide. The body had been discovered by the gardener, Potter, who, on trying to revive the boy, had assured himself that he was dead. William had come into the potting shed and promised God his only valuable possession—his faith— to spare the boy he loved. And God had struck the bargain.

James, who had come back to life with no memory of his innocence or of his love, is a living dead man. Fearing the revelation of the "miracle" and what it would do to the reputation of the rationalist Callifer, his parents had withdrawn from James. To affirm the miracle would be to affirm the existence of God. Mrs. Callifer says, "Oh, the Callifers knew everything. It was all right to doubt the existence of God as your grandfather did in the time of Darwin. Doubt—that was human liberty. But my generation, we didn't doubt, we knew" (73). And Mrs. Callifer says of her husband, "All his life he'd written on the necessity of proof. Proof. And then a proof was pushed under his nose, at the bottom of his own garden, in the potting shed. . . . I could hear him saying to himself, 'Must I recall all those books and start again?' " (64–65).

James's meeting with his uncle in Nottingham affords him the knowledge he needs to understand himself, and it provides him with the information about his past that allows him to exist in the present and for the future. When he tells his wife that he can now love her because he acknowledges God, she is as frightened by his belief as before she had been frightened by his lack of conviction or, as she phrases it, his love of Nothing. What convinces James of the reality of God is his understanding of Uncle William's life without faith, once God had heard his prayer. A room without faith, his uncle's presbytery in Nottingham—in some ways reminiscent of the "living" room of the earlier play—is, James says, like a marriage without love. God is in the world and to deny God is to deny life: "Something happened to me, that's all, like a street accident. I don't want God. But He's there—it's no good pretending. He's in my lungs like air" (71). The play ends on a symbolic note of optimism. Discovered asleep on the window seat, Anne tells of her dream—she had found a lion asleep in the potting shed; on awakening, it had licked her hand.

The Potting Shed is a better play than its predecessor, for it deals more economically and more dramatically with human motives—especially with fear—despite the fact that at times the action is static. As Jacob Adler has aptly observed, the play's third act suffers from too much talk following the successive revelations of its second—James's death and rebirth as recounted by Mrs. Potter, the knowledge of Uncle William's recovery of his belief in the God who had answered his prayer thirty years earlier. "One cannot help feeling," Adler writes, "that the third act exists for the sake of providing

an explicit happy ending . . . for the sake of expounding a philosophy which the effect of the miracle demonstrates."[5]

The added dimension of mystery, however, introduced through
the innocent character Anne, contributes to the effectiveness of the
whole. As does Ida Arnold in *Brighton Rock,* Anne emphasizes the
necessity of admitting the truth, of bringing into the light the
actions of the past so that they may lend meaning to the present
and to the future. In this sense she is humanity, bright and alert.
And the potting shed that James and his parents have feared for so
long is, as was the living room, the place of hope, the place of life;
it is not to be feared and shunned, but to be acknowledged and
accepted. Once its importance in the life of the Callifers has been
admitted, it becomes a tool shed for gardening equipment. Those
who had feared it had feared the truth of the miracle that took place
within it thirty years before the action of the play. It is, consequently, a more effective symbol than the living room had been.

What lends the play its atmosphere and contributes to its effectiveness is Greene's handling of the Lazarus theme. In allowing
James to admit his death and accept his return to life as a miracle—
the result of his uncle's bargain with God—Greene manages to
establish clearly the major notion of the drama. Only upon the death
of H. C. Callifer, who hypocritically guarded the rationalist values
upon which the family prestige depended, can the truth be revealed.
The number thirty is, of course, used to suggest the Christian idea
of betrayal, and James's role as scapegoat becomes more readily
understandable. There are other symbols used in the play, some of
which perhaps again derive from T. S. Eliot. The polluted river,
the encroaching industrial city, the harmony of the garden, the
baying dog, the hanged man all have their echoes in *The Waste Land*
and in "Ash Wednesday." But these symbols are so integrated into
the fabric of the play that an understanding of the theme does not
depend on their explication.

The Potting Shed was written with two third acts, one for the
American production in 1957 and another for the British production
in 1958. There are minor textual changes in the first two acts that
add little if anything to the general development of the play's action.
But the American version lists the time of the play as autumn, and
the final scene takes place during the Christmas season, thus allowing Greene to capitalize on the symbolism of the Nativity. The
British version sets the play in the spring, and the implication is

that the action culminates around Easter, although nothing is specifically mentioned. This setting in time, it seems, is surer symbolism; for the idea of rebirth is the one that sustains the activity
of the drama. The potting shed and the garden become more
meaningful.

The third act in the American production has James explain his
new-found faith to his wife Sara, capitalizing on the broken-marriage
theme. In the American version Sara is softer, more willing to
understand her husband's new belief. The British version, however,
has James explain his new-found belief to his mother who is, after
all, of greater importance in the overall meaning of the play, for
she has for thirty years protected her husband from the implications
of the "miracle." In the British production Sara is less agreeable
about accepting James's new faith. She had been frightened by his
belief in Nothing, and she is now equally alarmed by his belief in
God. Whether he will succeed in remarrying her is left tentative.
Both third acts end with the optimistic telling of Anne's dream of
the lion licking her hand.

The miracle in *The Potting Shed* is strongly reminiscent of the
central occurrence of *The End of the Affair.* Sarah Miles asks God to
spare Bendrix's life, offering to stop seeing him. After God answers
her prayer, she proceeds to greater and greater awareness of his
existence. Unlike Sarah, William Callifer goes on in his existence
without faith until he is given the proof of the miracle. Again the
question of grace is left in abeyance, adding a provocative titillation
for the reader who is more interested in religious controversy than
in drama.

The Complaisant Lover

"It's unfair," says Victor Rhodes, the cuckolded husband to Mary,
his wife, ". . . that we're only dressed for a domestic comedy."[6]
Earlier in *The Complaisant Lover,* he had said, before the knowledge
of his wife's unfaithfulness was known to him, "I can assure you
there are very few situations in life that a joke won't ease" (2).
Although *The Complaisant Lover* adds enormously to Greene's stature
as a playwright and to his popularity as an entertainer, it is by no
means the provocative study of human entanglements that his previous plays are. *The Complaisant Lover,* furthermore, makes no specific
reference to religious matters; the only commentary made on the

moral appropriateness of the chief actors' complaisance is oblique at best. But certain ambiguities of speech and humor may be construed to suggest a subterranean religious feeling.

In the characterization of Mary, Greene draws against a background of literary "emancipated" women. There are echoes of Ibsen's Nora and Hedda and of Shaw's Candida, but the play is uniquely "Greenien" in the mixture of sadness and sweetness that describes the predicament of the lover who seeks in his affairs a knowledge of experience, not a return to innocence. Clive Root has always loved married women; and, when Ann Howard offers him her innocent love on whatever terms he desires, he is forced to refuse her, for as he says: ". . . Perhaps I fall in love with experience. . . . Perhaps I don't care for innocence. . . . Perhaps it's envy of other men, and I want to prove myself better than they are" (12). There is a dramatic counterpoint developed through Anne's infatuation for Clive, for Mary's adolescent son is smitten with Ann, giving her such tokens of esteem as a badly stuffed mouse and an electric eye that doesn't work.

The climax of the play develops in a hotel room in Amsterdam where Mary and Clive have gone for a holiday, Mary having invented a friend called Jane Crane to put her husband Victor off the scent. Victor arrives a day before he is expected; he finds Mary in her hotel room, the mythical Jane gone, and Clive close by. He suspects nothing, but Clive, to precipitate the action, pays a bellboy 100 guilders to pen a poisonous note informing the husband of his wife's infidelity. When the note arrives in London, Victor, annoyed at his failure to understand the situation, confronts Mary with the facts. She begs him not to force her to a decision, for the habit of marriage is sixteen years strong in her. Like Henry and Sarah Miles in *The End of the Affair,* they have grown used to one another's company, and the habits of domestic life are too strong to be easily broken. Clive Root is no Maurice Bendrix, however, nor could he be in the farcical context of the play. Root's jealousy and his mania for possession are equally as strong as Bendrix's; but he has his knowledge of past love affairs to sustain him. He realizes that he will accept Rhodes's terms and remain Mary's lover, until one day he will find it no longer possible to be complaisant. And then the end of the affair.

The moral commentary is, of course, obliquely made in the final moments of the play. The long years of married habit, of domestic comfort, and of children's teeth and shoes and holidays will indeed intrude upon and disillusion the lovers. In the final analysis, the husband and wife relationship will prove vital, and the family will be preserved. The domestic comedy will have run its course, and the routine blessings of home comfort and everyday morality will be reasserted.

The Complaisant Lover represents Greene asserting his command over a comic form, just as he had in *Our Man in Havana*. That once again he chooses a cliché situation and then invests it with a charm and grace peculiarly his own offers further testimony of his consummate artistry. The cuckolded husband—asserting his prerogative as husband, understanding his wife's yearning for romance and her need to be protected—emerges as one of Greene's strongest and most sensible heroes, despite his penchant for grotesque tricks and schoolboy humor. The amoral rationale of the play is sustained by the charm and wit of the lines and by Greene's remarkable sense of the ridiculous. The introduction of Dr. Van Droog in the Amsterdam hotel room is little more than farcical invention; but, in the general handling of the climactic scene, it is sheer brilliance, punctuating as it does the ridiculousness of the situation and accentuating at the same time the moral obliquity that on the surface characterizes the play.

The fact that Victor is a dentist is significant too. One remembers Dr. Tench of *The Power and the Glory,* and Greene's reference to the carious mouth, the symbol borrowed from *The Waste Land.* The carious mouth is gone; for it does not belong in a domestic farce. Yet the reference to teeth, the fact that the lover has a badly filled upper canine, adds to the sense of the ridiculous and the absurd. All in all, *The Complaisant Lover* is brilliant invention, Graham Greene at his entertaining best. Like every other piece that he has done, it emphasizes his ability to adapt to new conditions, to new forms.

Carving a Statue

Produced in 1964 *Carving a Statue* suffers from a confusion of dramatic forms, for it is neither comedy, nor farce, nor tragedy, nor symbolical or absurdist drama, yet it demonstrates aspects of all of these. Nevertheless, by the play's end its central meaning emerges cogently and forcefully: man creates his own god as he struggles through time and matter toward reconciliation with the urge that lies behind all things.

Greene complains in what he has ruefully entitled "Epitaph for a Play" that the critics hastened the play's demise, for which, iron- ically, he was grateful inasmuch as *Carving a Statue* was difficult to write and evidently even more difficult to produce. But he adds that the critics' contention that the play was symbolical and theo- logical went wide of the mark, for they had mistaken "an association of ideas" for symbolism and theology.[7]

Be that as it may, it is difficult not to read the play as conventional allegory, and the carving of the statue, which is the play's unifying action, as structuring symbolism. Furthermore, the characters of the drama are named the Father, the Son, First Girl, and Second Girl; and the Statue of the Father, which the Father-sculptor is carving, has knees that seem to possess no knowledge of the act of kneeling. The character of the Father-sculptor is, in some ways, reminiscent of Joyce Cary's Gulley Jimson of *The Horse's Mouth,* but in that novel Cary insists on the joy of the creative experience, whereas Greene's artist insists on its pain. Greene tells his reader that the character of the Father was based on Benjamin Robert Haydon, "who was obsessed—to the sacrifice of any personal life— by the desire to do great Biblical subjects, already, even in his day, out of fashion . . . surely a farcical character, though he came to a tragic end" (12). There is, perhaps, also a hint of Browning's Grammarian in the characterization of the Father who seeks to discover the truth of experience in his dedication to an art that is by and large beyond his capacities of expression.

The play contrasts the concept of a loving God with that of an unheeding or detached deity who has forgotten that creation for which he is responsible. The eyes of the statue upon which the Father-sculptor works either squint or look askew upon the world of the studio and its occupants below. At one point the Father- sculptor says to the Girl his son has brought to the studio as he looks at the figure's head: "Now I can see Him properly again with his head in the clouds. Tomorrow I'll get back to work on that left eye. Like it was when He looked at the world and loved what He'd made. At the end of the sixth day. Gentle, mild, satisfied, loving" (52). Later, he asks Dr. Parker, who has come to examine him: "Do you think even He kept up with His creation? Before He could turn round beautiful Adam became the unbearable Israelite Abraham"

(65). As he worships his creation, the Father-sculptor ironically emulates his God, viewing his only Son from the distance of his pride in self as a Maker. The sacrifice of the deaf and dumb girl the Son has learned to love—she dies in a street accident—seems to make no point except to serve as another example of the workings of a capricious deity.

Carving a Statue is not Greene's best play. Its chief interest, perhaps, is the light it throws on his continuing dialogue with the deity as the force within all things; on the obsessive nature of the creative agony through which the artist challenges while at the same time pays homage to this force through the action of emulation. The Father says at the play's conclusion: "I hate Him and yet He's all I have. If I haven't worked at Him enough during the day I can't sleep, and when I've worked I wake in the morning and know that what I've done is wrong. He owns my sleep, and He poisons it with dreams. He gives me ideas and when I follow them He gives me a sneer of stone . . ." (71).

The Return of A. J. Raffles

A witty backward look to the fin de siècle when breeding, manners, and tact meant more than wealth and ambition, *The Return of A. J. Raffles* was produced in 1975. Greene's attempt at comedy of manners is ahead of its time in its handling of a homosexual theme, one which he had hinted at in his entertainment, *The Third Man,* and fully exploited in the short story "May We Borrow Your Husband?"

In his author's note Greene playfully defends his assertion that the legendary Raffles had died in Africa, the report of which, he writes, originated with his friend Bunny who "had every reason for falsifying history to disguise the fact that, far from being in South Africa, he was, at the date of Spion Kop, incarcerated in Reading Gaol, where he had the good fortune to meet Oscar Wilde."[8] But Greene does admit to deviating from historical fact by extending the life of the Marquess of Queensbury for several months and by suggesting a rather improbable friendship between him and the Prince of Wales. The gold box, as important a prop to *Raffles* as the handbag to *The Importance of Being Earnest,* and the Prince of Wales's difficulties with "uniforms" are, Greene writes, "in no way fictitious." The play is, in other words, a fantasy that succeeds for those who are willing to accept frivolity and insouciance as ends in themselves.

The first act presents Bunny and Lord Alfred Douglas preparing for a night on the town. They are interrupted by the appearance of Inspector Mackenzie, the sleuth who had pursued Raffles before the report of his death had called quits to his investigations. Mackenzie turns out to be a disguised Raffles, returned from the dead to reclaim his chambers in Albany and his lover Bunny. Douglas, or Bosie, presented more benevolently than is usual in his relationship with Oscar Wilde, cajoles Raffles and Bunny into burglarizing his father's safe as a means of revenging himself on Queensbury for withholding his allowance since the Wilde trial. Raffles accepts the challenge.

The second act begins with Bunny breaking into the bedroom of the country house that Queensbury has lent to a Mr. Portland and his mistress Alice. Portland is the Prince of Wales, his incognito loosely worn. Raffles enters, carrying champagne. The Prince and Raffles, disguised as a waiter and calling himself Mr. Jones, immediately establish a rapport, each appreciating the taste, humor, and discernment of the other. The Prince fully credits Raffles's account of his experiences in the Boer rebellion and becomes his ally when the real Inspector Mackenzie and Queensbury interrupt them. Bunny escapes.

Looking for the German agent who, according to intelligence reports, is attempting to steal the Prince's love letters to Alice, to be used by the Kaiser to defame his cousin, Mackenzie recognizes Raffles and arrests him. The German agent, also disguised as a waiter, had entered the room before Raffles, but carrying a bottle of champagne of inferior vintage. Raffles had carried in a bottle of Mumm '84, a fact that has helped endear him to the Prince. Queensbury is indignant that his safe has been robbed, and Mackenzie, although pleased by his arrest of Raffles, is disconcerted by the escape of the disguised German spy in a sufficiently thickened plot.

The third act unravels the complications engendered in the second. The waiter with the inferior champagne is revealed as Captain von Blixen, the German agent. Queensbury, who had fallen off the roof of the Burlington Arcade in pursuit of Raffles in an attempt to recover his stolen money, is carried into Albany chambers on a ladder. Like Raffles before him, he is supposedly dead, and Bosie prematurely rejoices in his father's demise. Raffles and Bunny return the letters and the gold box to the Prince, who in turn convinces

Mackenzie that no crime has been committed. The gold box becomes a gift from Mr. Portland to the waiter who had called himself Mr. Jones. The Prince extracts a promise from Raffles that he will give up burglary in England and concentrate on cricket. Captain von Blixen will be given diplomatic immunity and more than likely make his way to Africa. Queensbury, frustrating his son Bosie, rises from the dead. The play's theme is spoken by the Prince once all the complications have been smoothed away: "We seem at last to be reaching what I have always desired in politics, a peaceful understanding" (87).

Not favorably reviewed when it was performed at the Aldwych by the Royal Shakespeare Company, *The Return of A. J. Raffles* is both curious and challenging, provided one approaches it with an open mind. Only Martin Esslin, with his customary understanding of the differences between theater and drama, saw to the play's center:

By lovingly reconstructing the late Victorian milieu . . . Graham Greene is enabled to say a great deal, indirectly, about his own time by contrast as well as tragic irony. In the figure of the ageing Prince of Wales on the eve of becoming Edward VII he finds a brilliant spokesman for much that needs to be said about the virtues of *his* society and, by implication, the barbarisms of ours. And at the same time he enables us, enlightened, liberated denizens of a 'permissive' age to laugh about the barbarisms of that period, its naive patriotism, imperialism, love and sport and stuffiness.[9]

The disrobing of the Prince's mistress Alice in the play's second act becomes, in the overall context of the play, more than the sensational striptease it at first appears to be: as Alice's skirts and corsets fall to the floor, she is revealed in all her flesh and frailty; as her Victorian costume falls away, her unaccommodated humanity speaks to our times as eloquently as it did to hers.

As a writer of detective stories, novels, entertainments, movie scripts, and stage plays, Graham Greene has managed to create one of the most significant bodies of literature in the twentieth century. His first two plays are first-rate drama. They are not "religious" plays, although they do attest the existence of God and make capital use of a religious theme. They are primarily strong and realistic portrayals of human beings caught in emotional difficulties. *The Complaisant Lover* may be better theater than its predecessors, but it is not as good drama. *Carving a Statue* and *The Return of A. J.*

Raffles, not as successful as their predecessors, nevertheless indicate in Greene's enlargement of his own sense of dramatic form, a full awareness of those risks that redeem life. Greene is better, in the final analysis, when he deals with human beings caught up in a tragic human condition of their own devising than when he treats a farcically contrived plot, no matter how funny.

Yes and No: A Play in One Act and *For Whom the Bell Chimes*

Published in 1983, *Yes and No: A Play in One Act* reveals Greene's penchant for the satirical at its best. In the two character play, a director is ostensibly coaching an actor to speak his lines, "Yes" or "No," in a play by a Frederick Privett whose pauses are significantly different from those of Harold Pinter. The chief actors in Privett's play about homosexual betrayal, called Sir John and Sir Ralph, are to vie for the attention of René, a French acrobat who will replace the young actor being coached in the affections of the two Sirs. At the play's end the subtext asserts itself as the director, who may be making a play for the young actor, says, "Can't you see how important your part is?" To which he answers, "Yes—and no." [10]

Also published in 1983 *For Whom the Bell Chimes,* a three act farce in the manner of Joe Orton's *What the Butler Saw* and *Loot,* opens on a modern omnibus studio flat, "a place for everything and everything in its place." [11] The bell chimes and a middle-aged con man enters to convince the flat's occupant, simply named X, to contribute to the cause of child polio victims. X cons Masterson, the con man, instead, taking his shabby clothes and to a certain extent his identity. Masterson soon discovers the body of X's mistress, performed by a wax dummy, in the disappearing bed which replaces the bedroom doors of conventional farce. Another bell chime brings Colonel Fenwick on stage to investigate the con man who is masquerading as a representative of the Anti-Child-Polio Campaign. Fenwick in searching for Masterson, disguised as X, had demolished the wall of the adjoining flat, bringing in yet another character to add to the confusion. Subsequent bell chimes bring in a police sergeant and his inspector, the inspector turning out to be Ginger, Masterson's old friend and lover, who has had a sex change, having finally made up his mind as to what sex to be. She has moved into police investigation: "They say at Scotland Yard that I combine the intellect of a man with the intuition of a woman" (86). X returns, Fenwick is taken away by the police who believe he has committed the crime, a stranger for the RSPCA arrives to investigate a report about a dead bitch, and reveals that X's murdered mistress, Felicity Harwich, is Branch Secretary for the RSPCA. The Inspector and Masterson, reunited, leave the flat as the bell chimes once more.

Frenzied as farces are wont to be, *For Whom the Bell Chimes* is distinguished by the emphasis placed on the grotesque and the macabre, elements not unusual to Greene's oeuvre. Here they are sustained by a full awareness of their hilarious potential as they delight and shock at one and the same time.

Chapter Eight

‐The Short Stories

In his introduction to the *Collected Stories* Graham Greene states that at one time he thought of his short stories as "scraps" salvaged from the novels. The form, he felt, limited him insofar as it precluded a knowledge of the end at the beginning of the composition:

> In the far longer work of the novel there were periods of great weariness, but at any moment the unexpected might happen—a minor character would suddenly take control and dictate his words and actions. Somewhere near the beginning, for no reason I knew, I would insert an incident which seemed entirely irrelevant, and sixty thousand words later, with a sense of excitement, I would realize why it was there—the narrative had been working all the time outside my conscious control. But in the short story I knew everything before I began to write—or so I thought.[1]

The form offered him, nevertheless, a way of escape from the tedium and uncertainty of living for a protracted period of time in the world of those characters who both challenged and intrigued him. Eventually he came to understand that the short story offered its own surprises: "in the unexpected shaping of a sentence, in a sudden reflection, in an unforeseen flash of dialogue; they came like cool drinks to a parched mouth" (viii). Short fiction, he further discovered, because of its brevity permitted not only a respite from the emotional immersion in the world of the novels, but also a greater precision as to character definition and event inasmuch as it allowed for the refining and polishing that the novel's length frequently forbade. By the time he came to revise his novels Greene felt that he had become a different person: not only had the characters of the novel developed, but their author had changed as well.

Because of such considerations, the novel, Greene feels, unlike the story, must inevitably give an appearance of roughness. He came to appreciate the delicate possibilities that the story's narrow ground offered and saw the stories not only as escapes from the novels but "even, if you like, escapades." He found that he could reread them

G.G. himself created to avoid
destruction; created story of destruction
to create happy mood away from
destruction

"more easily because they do not drag a whole lifetime in their wake" (x).

He does admit to certain favorites in the three volumes that comprise the *Collected Stories.* He likes "I Spy" (1930) for its simplicity in conveying "the sense of life as it is lived" (viii), and he feels that he has not written anything better than "The Destructors" (1954), "A Chance for Mr. Lever" (1936), "Under the Garden" (1963), and "Cheap in August" (1967). In preparing the volume for publication he discovered that humor had entered the stories with World War II, "very late and very unexpectedly," not only as an escape from the blitz and the catastrophes of war, but also as a refuge "from the thought of death" (xii). Yet there is humor in at least two of the stories written before the late thirties. It is difficult to read "Proof Positive" (1930) as anything but a humorous vindication, perhaps unintentional, of Philip Weaver's belief that the spirit can exist beyond the body; and certainly Mr. Chalfont is hoist with his own petard at the conclusion of "Jubilee" (1936). Yet Greene is correct in his assertion that humor as such becomes accessible with the stories that use the war as background.

Twenty-One Stories

Graham Greene's first volume of stories was published in 1935. Entitled *The Basement Room and Other Stories,* it collected, along with a novel fragment entitled "The Other Side of the Border," eight other tales. *Nineteen Stories,* published in 1947, eliminated the story entitled "The Lottery Ticket" and added nine new pieces to make up the nineteen of the title. Published in 1954, *Twenty-One Stories,* reprinted in the Collected Edition along with the two later collections, *A Sense of Reality* (1963), and *May We Borrow Your Husband?* (1967), omits the novel fragment and adds "The Destructors" (1954), "Special Duties" (1954), and "The Blue Film" (1954).

The arrangement of the tales in both *The Basement Room and Other Stories* and *Nineteen Stories* appears arbitrary. *Nineteen Stories,* for example, begins with "The Basement Room" (1936) and concludes with "Alas, Poor Maling" (1940). But *Twenty-One Stories* begins with "The Destructors" and proceeds chronologically in a backward fashion, from the immediate present to 1929, the date of "The End of the Party." *May We Borrow Your Husband?* and *A Sense of Reality* precede *Twenty-One Stories* in *Collected Stories* respectively. The reverse

chronology of the *Collected Stories* in the Collected Edition consequently allows the reader to examine and appreciate Greene's development as a story teller, while offering an implicit comment on
the techniques, devices, and preoccupations that remain, for the
most part, constants in his work.

The stories of the fifties, from "The Destructors" through "Alas,
Poor Maling" in 1940 make use of the war as background and
symbol, until with "A Little Place Off the Edgeware Road" (1939)
the thematic interest shifts to abnormal psychology and melodrama.
"A Little Place Off the Edgeware Road" makes use of usual Greene
imagery as it employs dream and the supernatural to develop a
theme of death-in-life. "Across the Bridge" (1938) employs the
Mexican border as the symbolic boundary that separates Mr. Calloway, "worth a million" (420), from the United States and the
police who are attempting to extradite him to England where the
law seeks to punish him for the crime he has committed. "The Case
for the Defence" (1939) and "A Drive in the Country" (1937) employ
melodrama and sensationalism in a lower middle-class milieu and
suggest the economically deprived period of the thirties. The violence implicit in the former is directed through the criminal who
may or may not escape justice—he is a twin—to the innocent
woman who has witnessed his crime; and the suicide pact of "The
Case for the Defence" reflects on Pinkie Brown's attempt to trick
Rose into a similar bargain in *Brighton Rock*. Fred's motives, however, are not explicated as Pinkie's are; yet he is as much a victim.
Fred says to the girl who escapes him, "Of course we neither of us
believe in God, but there may be a chance, and it's company, going
together like that," adding, "It's a gamble" (443).

"The Innocent" (1937) both anticipates and reflects upon "The
Basement Room," which follows immediately in the collection, in
its emphasis on the past as a factor shaping the future. "A Chance
for Mr. Lever" (1936), presents an African setting as the protagonist
discovers three days of happiness before he dies of yellow fever, the
victim of his dream as well as of the mosquito that has infected
him. Elements of Conrad's "Heart of Darkness" can be discerned
in the tale as Mr. Lever works his way through the jungle to discover
Mr. Davidson, whose endorsement he needs before he can sell his
machinery to those who are mining for riches in Africa. The tale
to a certain extent looks forward to *A Burnt-Out Case*. "Brother"
employs a civil insurrection to make the point that all men are

brothers, while observing that Communists at least are equal to one another whereas those who live under more traditional political systems are arbitrarily subject to class restrictions. "A Day Saved" (1935), a haunting tale of obsession, schizophrenia, and paranoia, employs, ambiguously, a doppelganger motif. It is followed by "I Spy" (1930) which bears on the early traumatic and scarring incident common to many of the novels and entertainments: a boy sneaking a cigarette witnesses his father being taken away by the police. "Proof Positive" in its use of the supernatural comments on the seance in *The Ministry of Fear;* and "The Second Death" (1929) in its first-person account of the narrator's restoration to sight by "a man like a tree" (55), comments on the miracles of both *The End of the Affair* and *The Potting Shed.* "The End of the Party" (1929), which concludes the collection, points to the spiritual and psychological affinities that exist in twins, the relationship which Greene examines in *England Made Me.*

Whereas several of the stories are pertinent to the thematic concerns of the novels, others reflect their tone, mood, and ambiance. "When Greek Meets Greek" (1941) replicates the war ambiance common to both *The Ministry of Fear* and *The End of the Affair,* but its humorous presentation of two sly old men conned by their younger counterparts insists on a suitable comic ending. The young people, thrown together by their elders, discover in their mutual appreciation of deception a meaningful love. "Across the Bridge" presents the symbol of the border, a constant in Greene's fiction, while it develops the yearnings of the individual to find acceptance and understanding despite his fall from grace. "The Destructors," the most ambiguous of the tales, appears at first reading to employ gratuitous malice as its theme, but upon reflection the story is more properly understood as an absurdist comment on the concepts of justice, natural law, and the creative act. As the boys determine to destroy, systematically and ruthlessly, the only building in their neighborhood left standing by the blitz, the reader becomes aware that the energy expended in the act of total destruction is in fact liberating. That Old Misery's house alone was spared by the blitz becomes an unacceptable absurdity to the boys, who deal it the same kind of rude justice that the bombs had rendered the other houses of the block. They intend no bodily harm to Old Misery, although in the course of their demolition they burn his savings and deprive him of a bed on which to rest his rheumatic bones. His unhappiness becomes an irrelevant consequence of the justice the boys are determined to bring about. Their energy and inventiveness in the destruction of the premises amounts, perversely, to an act of creation. " 'All this hate and love,' " says T, the chief architect of their design, " 'it's soft, it's hooey. There's only things, Blackie,' and he looked round the room crowded with the unfamiliar shadows of half things, broken things, former things" (338). All that matters to him and the boys he directs is the disinterested creative action. The story moves with the relentless and inexorable logic of a nightmare.

The stories in the collection for the most part employ third person narration, allowing Greene to comment as necessary on motivation and character. The most obvious example of authorial comment occurs at the end of "A Chance for Mr. Lever" as Greene directly addresses the reader, advising him that the events of the narrative might well have encouraged him as author to speak to the point of loving omniscience if his faith had not been shaken by "personal knowledge of the drab forest through which Mr. Lever now went so merrily, where it is impossible to believe in any spiritual life, in anything outside the nature dying round you, the shrivelling of the weeds. But of course, there are two opinions about everything . . ." (509).

The best known of the stories in the collection, "The Basement Room," also uses third person narration, but here the narrator's intrusions serve to supply a single and unifying focus for the story's meaning. The immediate action is presented by the omniscient author as he dramatizes the events that ultimately inhibit the boy Philip from fulfilling himself as an individual in later life. The narrative shifts from an intense and psychologically acute emphasis on the boy's unwitting betrayal of Baines, whom he loves, to a horrifying view of the old dying man who has been unable to be more than a "dilettante," an observer of the flow of events that the traumatizing experience immediately portrayed has kept him from participating in. The focus contracts and expands to allow the reader to understand the immediate situation and to appreciate its results on the man Philip becomes. Past events and present time fuse in the story's final words, as Philip remembers the girl Emmy who had unwittingly released the evil that excited the bitter Mrs. Baines to revenge: "Who is she? Who is she? dropping lower and lower into death, passing perhaps on the way the image of Baines: Baines

hopeless, Baines letting his head drop, Baines 'coming clean' "
(489).

"The Basement Room" also serves as an epitome of Greene's
symbols and psychological preoccupations. The house in Jungian
terms symbolizes the integrated personality. The green baize door
through which the boy passes on his way to the basement room
where the butler Baines lives with his housekeeper wife serves as a
means of distinguishing between the conscious and the subconscious;
the world above stairs and the world beneath epitomize the light
and the dark, the possibility of good and the reality of evil. The
world beyond the house, to which Philip twice escapes, becomes
mundane reality, where good and evil can exist in compatible tolerance of one another. Outside the house Philip agrees to keep
Baines's secret about his love for Emmy, but inside the house, in
his bedroom, Mrs. Baines invades his dreams and commits him to
an adult world of experience and fear. Philip becomes her unwitting
accomplice; as a consequence he suffers the death of the heart. Dream
and nightmare form a coherent imagery that enhances the idea of
waste and loss.

Three of the stories, "The Hint of an Explanation," "The Innocent," and "A Day Saved" employ first-person narration and so
comment on Greene's use of the technique in *The End of the Affair*
and *The Comedians*. The narrator of the first of these recounts his
experience on a train. His companion tells him a strange tale about
himself as a boy. A baker in the neighborhood, obsessed with the
Roman Catholic notion of transubstantiation, attempts to seduce
him into bringing him a consecrated host. The boy agrees, accepting
the baker's bribe of a toy train. But in his room, the wafer mushed
under his tongue, the boy suddenly intuits the metaphysical meaning of the symbol. The narrator remarks at the story's conclusion
that his companion, the happy man who has told him the tale, had
become a priest as a result of his adventure on the dangerous edge
of things.

The narrator of "The Innocent," by contrast, describes a re-
demptive effect achieved through memory as he returns to Bishops
Hendron, the town in which he grew up. As he retraces his years
of innocence he remembers his first love—"she must have been on
the point of eight. I loved her with an intensity I have never felt
since" (454). He remembers leaving messages for her in the wood-
working of the gate that led to their dancing school. He looks for

the hole and discovers a message he had left in the past in the form
of a "childish inaccurate sketch of a man and a woman" (456). At
first horrified, he recovers a sense of the purity of his feelings, "the
deep innocence," that had prompted him to leave the drawing.

The narrator of "A Day Saved" is a schizophrenic in shadow-
pursuit of an enemy whose crime or sin is not disclosed. At the
story's end the obsessed speaker curses his prey for having revealed
himself as "stupid and good-natured and happy," and for having
had the impertinence "to display himself like that to me." He resents
the man he has pursued for having cost him a day, lost because he
had flown to the Continent instead of going by sea, for having cost
him the 86,400 seconds of pursuit. The narrator then identifies
himself with his doppelganger, hoping that the moment will come
when the pursued will doubt himself as he, the pursuer, now doubts
himself. The motif of flight and pursuit, of course, reflects on one
of Greene's favorite structuring devices as does the doubling device.

A Sense of Reality

Published in 1963, *A Sense of Reality* collects seven stories which
are linked by fantasy; the reality suggested by the title is reality as
glimpsed through the distorting lenses of dream, illusion, and
memory.

The longest and the best of the tales, "Under the Garden," is
remarkable for its handling of point of view and for its ability to
present in a fresh and moving manner the yearnings and hesitations
of childhood. The first section, narrated in the third person, presents
as protagonist William Wilditch, a man in his early sixties who is
told by his doctors that his x-rays reveal a cancerous obstruction in
the lungs that demands surgical removal. "I don't want to appear
dialectical," he says, "but I do have to decide, don't I, whether I
want my particular kind of life prolonged" (170). The theme of the
story concerns the morality of choice, or free will. In an oblique
and occasionally whimsical manner "Under the Garden" recapitulates one of Greene's favorite preoccupations. Wilditch informs his
doctors that he is not a religious man, and admits to no curiosity
concerning the future. The burden of the story is to reveal what has
brought him to this point of apathy.

In returning to Winton Halt, where he has spent the happy
summers of his most impressionable years with his mother and

brother, Wilditch revisits the past in an effort to understand himself and to make his decision about life or death. He recalls an adventure that took place under the garden adjoining the house when he was seven years old, in Roman Catholic terms the age of consent. Surprised that the grounds and the lake and the island that figure so prominently in his adventure are smaller than his imagination has made them, he next discovers in the bookcase adjoining his bed a correspondence between his mother and the school authorities about a story he had later written and called "The Treasure of the Island." Rereading a portion, he wonders why as a thirteen-year-old he had reduced to platitudes the adventure that has haunted him through most of his life. He is not surprised, however, to discover that his mother's objection had been over the story's religious implications. Through Wilditch's reflections upon his earliest meaningful experience, Greene directs his reader's attention to the tale's metaphysical meaning.

Part two shifts from third-person narration to first-person as Wilditch reconstructs the cherished adventure. He remembers, or so he thinks, the smallest details of his descent into the world beneath the garden, where he had confronted a one-legged giant who called himself Javitt and his consort Maria. Beneath the garden he had discovered a world of slow time that admitted all possibilities. There he had learned of sexual beauty, represented by Javitt's daughter, Miss Ramsgate, the winner of beauty contests.

The adventure amounts to a descent into the self, and the process of self-discovery becomes a redaction, in childlike terms, of the grail mystery. The grail becomes the golden po, or chamberpot, upon which the boy sits in Manichaean splendor as he learns about the possibilities of life and beauty from Javitt, who himself sits on a gigantic toilet.

The next morning, in the present, Wilditch returns to the site of his adventure and finds an old battered chamberpot, which had once been yellow. He understands that his dream of beauty is still potent and that he can continue to follow the gleam about which he had learned from Javitt. Denied the knowledge of a traditional god by his Fabian mother, the child had out of his need constructed his own divinities. In finding the chamberpot Wilditch rediscovers the innocence and joy of his earliest years. The third section of the story returns to objective third-person presentation. Wilditch knows that there is yet choice: "Curiosity was growing in him like the cancer. . . . Poor mother—she had reason to fear . . ." (237).

"A Visit to Morin" presents as narrator a wine merchant who as a schoolboy had once been challenged by the novels of a once-famous writer named Morin. He meets the no-longer popular writer at a midnight Christmas mass, and in the conversation that follows discovers that the once devout writer has lost his belief but not his faith. In his introduction to *A Burnt-Out Case* Greene notes that the architect-protagonist of the novel was in some ways a redrafting of the Morin of the story.

"The Blessing," a mildly satirical vignette, is reminiscent of "Special Duties" of *Twenty-One Stories* in which the Roman Catholic concept of the storing up of indulgences is made fun of through Mr. Ferraro who employs an assistant to perform the good works necessary to a lessening of punishment in purgatory and to transfer the benefits to him. "The Blessing" comments on the illogicality of an archbishop blessing tanks and other apparatuses of warfare. But an old man explains to the skeptical newspaperman-protagonist that "if you have a desire to bless, you bless. . . . It's when you want to love and can't manage it. You stretch out your hands and say God forgive me that I can't love this thing anyway" (262–63).

"Church Militant," a first-person account of the attempt of a group of French women to wrest a plot of African soil as a base from which to do their good works, is more remarkable for its presentation of two believably drawn priests than for its religious satire.

"Dream of a Strange Land" is, as Greene informs his reader in the introduction to the volume, an almost direct transcription of a dream. A Swiss physician who is treating a bank clerk on the verge of retirement for leprosy informs his patient that he will have to find his cure in a sanitarium. The patient, reluctant to separate himself from the few comforts left him, returns that night to offer the doctor an alternative: he will isolate himself from life rather than go to a hospital. He discovers that the house has been transformed into a miniature casino, and that the physician is as out of place in the study, now transformed into a *salle priveé,* as he is outside its windows. The physician has allowed himself to be intimidated by the military into letting them use his home to please the whim of a senile general. The patient falls victim to a stray bullet at the same time that a champagne cork explodes. Unsure at first which of the characters from the dream represents himself, Greene has concluded that he is probably the doctor and perhaps the patient too.

"A Discovery in the Woods" is unique in Greene's works insofar as it is science fiction. The tale suggests a new beginning after a devastating calamity, and the events of the narrative redact the myth of Noah's Ark. The boy Pete, in his curiosity and desire to explore the unknown, represents the future, and the girl Liz intuition and the promise of beauty. Either seven or nine, depending on which of his parents is to be believed—the father wants Pete to work the sea as he does, the mother wants to keep him with her a while longer—the boy leads his small group across the border of safety into the danger of the woods. They discover the vessel "France" and the skeleton of a man who, unlike them—dwarfish and stunted— had once been straight and tall. Implicit in the action of the story, as the children search first for raspberries, then for treasure, is the biblical theme of the futility of human vanity. As he sees the child Liz nestling in the lap of the skeletal remains of a once-godlike man and hears her keen for the loss of a world, Pete discovers "for the first time a sensation of love" (322), and offers hope to the future.

May We Borrow Your Husband? and Other Comedies of the Sexual Life

The twelve stories that comprise the collection were written in a "single mood of sad hilarity" as Greene was moving into a two-room apartment in Antibes. Although the situation of the title story had actually occurred in St. Jean-Cap Ferrat, he transferred it to nearby Antibes, thus unifying several of the tales by means of locale as well as sexual theme. Several of the principal characters in the stories are, furthermore, writers—in "May We Borrow Your Husband?" the narrator is completing a biography of Rochester—and it becomes tempting to identify them with the author. The stories, however, are sufficiently and objectively presented so as to preclude direct identification. Yet, as Greene implies, the subjects grew from direct observation or out of dreams. The situation in "Cheap in August," for example, he remarked in Kingston, Jamaica, and "The Root of All Evil," the one story in the collection "which does not belong to the same world," in which jealousy and transvestism figure, grew from a dream. "I cannot remember changing a single incident," he writes, "though I suppose there must have been some lacunae which had to be filled in" (x–xi).

"May We Borrow Your Husband?", both farcical and tragic in its implications, presents two homosexual interior designers observed by a knowing narrator as they set about the seduction of a young man on his honeymoon. The situation is counterpointed by the narrator's awareness of the possibility of his seducing Poopy, the young and inexperienced wife of the young husband. The wisdom of age keeps him from the attempt, and the narrative ends with an implicitly understood comment: This is the way the world ends.

"Beauty" and "Chagrin in Three Parts" continue the theme of sexual perversion. The former comments on a rich and spoiled woman's obsessive love for her perfect Pekingese, who betrays her for the offal he discovers in a refuse barrel. The latter presents two middle-aged women, carefully observed by the narrator as he dines in a fashionable restaurant, about to embark on a lesbian relationship. Both women had been disappointed by their husbands, more than likely disappointing them in turn, and the story concludes with the narrator's awareness of the chagrin he feels for his own wasted opportunities.

"The Over-night Bag," a dark and macabre small comedy, describes the protagonist's air trip to London, his movement through customs, his return to his home somewhere near Knightsbridge as he jealously guards his over-night bag which, he says, contains his wife's dead baby. The events are given meaning by the Hieronymus Bosch reproduction which hangs on the sitting room wall in the apartment Henry Cooper shares with his mother. The reference to the little toe he had found in his marmalade on his European sojourn adds a further nuance to the morbid obsession that Cooper and his mother share.

"Mortmain," or inalienable ownership, records a mistress's ruthless tenacity in holding on to a lover who has married another woman. Josephine leaves "loving" notes throughout the apartment she had shared with Carter who, at the age of forty-two, thinks that he has found sexual and domestic contentment with his wife, Julia. The fact that Greene uses the name Carter disparagingly in other works suggests that the man gets what he deserves.

"Cheap in August," perhaps the best piece in the collection, in some ways Chekhovian, presents the difficulties of a thirty-nine year-old wife in having an affair in the off-season. Mary Watson is picked up by a man in his early seventies who is lonely and unhappy. She is moved to compassion and tenderness by "the fat old frightened man whom she almost loved," by his fear of death, "the certain-sure business, closing in on you, like tax inspectors . . ." (108–9).

The funniest of the stories, a delicate balance of farce and pathos, "A Shocking Accident" presents a macabre incident which builds to an hilarious conclusion. Jerome is called into his housemaster's room and told that his father, whom he loves and has romanticized into a mysterious adventurer, has died in a freak accident: a pig has fallen on him from the fifth story of a Neapolitan tenement. "Apparently," the housemaster tells the boy, barely restraining his amusement, "in the poorer quarters of Naples they keep pigs on their balconies. . . . It had grown too fat. The balcony broke" (111–12). As he grows older the boy, fearing the laughter that an account of the event always brings forth, becomes more and more reluctant to describe how his father, a writer of travel guides, had died. In his twenties, now an accountant, he meets and falls tepidly in love, but is afraid to tell the girl about his father's death for fear of her reaction. An old aunt does so, however, and Jerome is excited into a passionate tenderness when the girl asks him the same question he had asked the housemaster, ". . . what happened to the pig?" To which he answers happily, "They almost certainly had it for dinner . . ." (117).

"The Invisible Japanese Gentlemen" a tale of mismatched lovers, presents a young woman about to publish her first novel complimenting herself on her powers of observation as she attempts to convince her husband-to-be to give up a certain livelihood as a wine merchant and follow her into the bohemian world of literature. Failing to notice the group of ceremonious Japanese gentlemen dining at a nearby table until the young man comments on them, she understands his reference to them as a revelation of his reluctance to accept her terms: "Sometimes you are so evasive I think you don't want to marry me at all" (123).

"Awful When You Think of It" toys with one of Greene's favorite notions—the child as father of the man. An alcoholic minds a baby and reads into the infant's future his own present.

"Doctor Crombie" presents a comic first-person account of a boy's friendship with the school physician, offering a variation on the

Victorian notion that masturbation induces insanity, in this case cancer. Dr. Crombie insists that all sexual "congress," even in marriage, brings about the dread result. He has irrefutable statistics to prove his contention: "Almost one hundred percent of those who die of cancer have practised sex" (134). The narrator who has had four marriages discovers in his sixties that he has cancer of the lungs: "Of course the doctors attribute the disease to my heavy indulgence in cigarettes," he says, "but it amuses me all the same to believe with Doctor Crombie that it has been caused by excesses of a more agreeable nature" (135).

The collection concludes with "Two Gentle People," an account of a man and a woman in their middle years who meet on a park bench, touch for a moment, and then return to their separate tragedies, Marie-Claire Duval to her homosexual husband, Henry C. Greaves to his neurotic wife, Patience.

The stories in *May We Borrow Your Husband?* are, as are the majority of Greene's tales, in the tradition of de Maupassant. For the most part they begin realistically, achieve their climaxes through emphasis on scene and dialogue, make their point, and then conclude quickly, the moral either underscored or strongly implied. The unity of the collection resides in the fact that the stories present observed life, which accounts to a certain extent for the presence of the narrator-artist in several of them. "Cheap in August," however, presents a felt as much as observed experience. Even those stories that begin as dreams suggest the detachment of the controlling artist examining human behavior as a psychologist does, perversely savoring the unhappiness we bring to one another.

Chapter Nine
The Catholic as Novelist Once More

François Mauriac's position as a writer who happened to be a Catholic was similar to and yet unlike Greene's. In 1936 he wrote an account of the development of his religious convictions to refute the charge leveled at him by André Gide that he sought permission to be a Catholic without having to burn his books:

If I refuse to accept this reproach of Gide's it is not because I think I am innocent. I am probably more guilty than a man who is tugged both ways, who wants to write his books without missing heaven and to win heaven without foregoing his books. It is putting it too mildly to say that I "do not lose sight of Mammon." The fact is that I am in the front line of his besiegers. But the impossibility of serving two masters does not necessarily mean the forsaking of one for the other to the extent of losing sight of the forsaken One or losing awareness of His presence and power. And even if this sight and awareness were lost, we would still be wearing the untearable livery of the Master we had betrayed; we would still, by force or free will, belong to His house.[1]

And then he added: "Above all I liked to be persuaded by Pascal that a search was always possible, that there could always be a voyage of discovery within revealed truth" (19).

In *God and Mammon* Mauriac told his reader that early in life he became aware that, born a Catholic, he could not live outside the boundaries of his religion. This knowledge led him to criticize his religion inadvertently, and many readers detected ambiguities of point of view in his early works. Nevertheless, he continued to write within the borders of Catholicism and became the object of mistrust and contempt to many of his fellow-Catholics: "I knew that the Christian God demanded everything. I knew that he had no part in the flesh and that the world of nature and the world of grace were two and inimical. Pascal taught me this with an almost excessive ruthlessness, and I knew it to be terrifyingly true" (20).

His Catholic critics, therefore, were not as Mauriac told his reader, unjust in detecting and censuring the tendency toward Jansenism and Manichaeism that is to be found in such novels as *Flesh and Blood* and *Thérèse Desqueyroux;* he admitted that he too could discern an element of corruption prowling over his work "in the way it prowls over cemeteries which are nevertheless dominated by the Cross." And he went on to say: "I always put myself on guard against the aesthetic side of present-day Catholicism, and its emotional appeal, however sublime, at once excites my mistrust. I long with all my soul for the 'consolations of religion,' but I know at what price they must be bought. I know all about peace in suffering, and I know that bitterness with which past sins penetrate through present grace" (25).

Greene, like Mauriac, is aware of the difficulties inherent in writing against a Roman Catholic background, and is also aware of the fact that, to render the highest justice to God, the force of evil must be appreciated—even if, at times, appreciating the beauty of evil seems a questioning of the orthodox preachings of his Church. Greene, like Mauriac, is concerned not only with observing life but with creating a meaningful experience of it. He brings characters into the world—complex, inscrutable, and made unhappy by their lack of identity with the source of good. Both Greene and Mauriac, in a very real sense, within their novels lose their identity in the subjects of their creation; hence the charge that they "connive" with the devil. Mauriac wrote: "If there is a reason for the existence of the novelist on earth it is this: to show the element which holds out against God in the highest and noblest characters—the innermost evils and dissimulations; and also to light up the secret source of sanctity in creatures who seem to us to have failed" (59).

Speaking of *The Power and the Glory,* Mauriac said of Graham Greene in *Great Men:* "The work of an English Catholic novelist— of an Englishman returning to Catholicism—such as Graham Greene's *The Power and the Glory,* at first always gives me the sensation of being in a foreign land. To be sure, I find there my spiritual fatherland, and it is into the heart of a familiar mystery that Graham Greene introduces me. But everything takes place as though I were making my way into an old estate through a concealed door. . . ."[2]

Mauriac pointed out that the French Catholic enters the edifice of his religion by the front door; that, as a schoolboy, he is versed in the various schisms and heresies that comprise the official history of his Church. The convert to Roman Catholicism, on the other hand, enters the edifice of his religion through an archway of first impressions and early religious training. The religious influences felt as a child and a catechism so like and yet so unlike the Roman Catholic's unconsciously interfere and intrude when the man makes his choice later on. Mauriac may have envied Maritain and other converts to Catholicism for their freedom of choice, as he told the reader in the second chapter of *God and Mammon,* but he was, nevertheless, confused when reading Greene. Greene's world seemed alien to him, although its mysteries were clear. The explanation of this strangeness is perhaps not too difficult.

The melodrama, the key to much of Greene's work, perhaps that very aspect that made Mauriac feel an alien, was set by early reading in the romantic stories of Marjorie Bowen and Rider Haggard; but Charles Dickens, Joseph Conrad, Henry James, and Ford Madox Ford taught him how to handle his themes and to develop his plots. His early apprenticeship as movie critic for *Night and Day* and the *Spectator* sharpened his perceptions of the nature of melodrama and what could be achieved through it. The political activities of the 1930s perhaps indicated to him that melodrama was the best means of echoing the times. In *Journey without Maps,* he wrote:

> To-day our world seems peculiarly susceptible to brutality. There is a touch of nostalgia in the pleasure we take in gangster novels, in characters who have so agreeably simplified their emotions that they have begun living again at a level below the cerebral. We, like Wordsworth, are living after a war and a revolution, and these half-castes fighting with bombs between the cliffs of skyscrapers seem more likely than we to be aware of Proteus rising from the sea. It is not, of course, that one wishes to stay forever at that level, but when one sees to what unhappiness, to what peril of extinction centuries of cerebration have brought us, one sometimes has a curiosity to discover if one can from what we have come, to recall at which point we went astray.[3]

Greene's conversion to Roman Catholicism seems to have been a logical step in an intellectual development; his emotional attachment occurred, he has written, when he witnessed the Socialist persecutions of Roman Catholics in Mexico. In the teachings of the Roman Church, he found a hint of an explanation, to use his own term, for the problems that vexed him as a child and as a man, and a partial explanation for suffering and misery; hence come the questioning and the probing that so many readers remark in such mature works as *The Heart of the Matter* and *The End of the Affair*. The mixture of melodrama and specifically religious background first appeared in Greene's works in *Brighton Rock*, but his attitudes were discernible in earlier books.

Ultimately Greene differs from Mauriac in method rather than in theme, for Greene writes his novels and entertainments within the traditional forms of the English novel. Greene's reading of Dickens's novels accounts for many of his seedy characters and for his grotesque children, his Else and young Parkis; it also accounts in part for the social commentary and for the mixture of sentimentality and social ire of such works as *England Made Me, It's a Battlefield,* and *Brighton Rock*. Greene's reading of Conrad taught him the nature of allegory—as did his reading of Bunyan—and the importance of ethical choice. Lord Jim stands behind the whiskey priest, just as Axel Heyst, who cultivates pity as a form of contempt, stands behind Arthur Rowe and Major Scobie; and Marlow and Heyst stand behind Fowler and Querry. Moreover, Conrad's antiheroes relate in the same way to Pinkie Brown and James Raven. It is not surprising, therefore, that Greene says of Conrad in his travel book *In Search of a Character:* "Reading Conrad—the volume called *Youth* for the sake of *Heart of Darkness*—the first time since I abandoned him about 1932 because his influence on me was too great and too disastrous. The heavy hypnotic style falls around me again, and I am aware of the poverty of my own. Perhaps now I have lived long enough with my poverty to be safe from corruption. One day I will again read *Victory*. And *The Nigger*" (31).

Greene's reading in Henry James taught him concern for style, for point of view, for correctness, for the dissection of human motive; James also taught him how to manipulate the stuff of evil while unfolding the complexities of character:

There was no victory for human beings, that was his conclusion; you were punished in your way, whether you were of God's or the Devil's party. James believed in the supernatural, but he saw evil as an equal force with good. Humanity was cannon fodder in a war too balanced ever to be concluded. If he had been guilty of the supreme egotism of preserving his own existence, he left the material, in his profound unsparing analysis, for rendering even egotism the highest kind of justice, of giving the devil his due.[4]

With the death of James, Greene wrote in his essay on Mauriac, the English novel lost "the religious sense," and with it "the importance of the human act."[5]

Furthermore Greene, unlike Mauriac, is in the unenviable position of writing his books for a predominantly Protestant audience—one that still nourishes a distrust of Catholicism that goes back to the English Reformation. If Greene once seemed belligerent and insistent about the Roman Catholicism of his characters, it is perhaps because he was aware of, remembering his origins, the hostility of his readers. The fact that so many Protestant readers have seen fit to question Greene's personal orthodoxy is in itself an indication that he has achieved some measure of success in fabricating controversial stories of violence and suspense within a framework of Roman Catholic belief, a belief that suggests treachery to the spiritual fitness of many Protestants. But it also seems so to many Catholics as well.

François Mauriac, on the other hand, wrote to a predominantly Catholic audience—to one aware of the implications of Jansenism, the religious controversy between Bossuet and Fenelon, and the hundreds of years of Church influence on the hearts and intellects of Frenchmen. Mauriac wrote eloquently in *Great Men* of the influence of Pascal, Voltaire, Rousseau, Maurice de Guérin, and others on his works. But in *God and Mammon* he said revealingly: "I can say with truth that no book has moved me more deeply than a simple and innocent novel called *Feet of Clay* which I adored when I was fourteen. It was the work of an old and virtuous woman called Zenaide de Fleuriot, and it was full of imagination and sensibility" (52). Imagination and sensibility are keynotes of the Mauriac novels, just as melodrama and suspense are keynotes of the Greene novels. Like Greene—whose indebtedness to Beatrix Potter and to Charlotte M. Yonge's *The Little Duke,* a work of innocence, testified to by *The Ministry of Fear*—Mauriac's youthful sensibilities were moved by the exploits of innocence abroad in a black and white universe, the innocent taking the form of a freckle-faced girl with the lovely name of Armelle Trahec. Yet Mauriac admitted in the same passage that, when asked to name the writers who had most influenced him, he replied automatically "Balzac and Dostoyevsky."

This is to say that a youthful imagination, stimulated by the innocent exploits of Mlle. Trahec, was disciplined by a rigorous training in the classics of the French novel and in the psychological analyses of the pre-Freudian psychologist, Dostoevski—an influence that can also be ascribed to Greene. In *Great Men* Mauriac told his reader that he read avidly the writings of the iconoclastic Anatole France; that, despite Flaubert's anti-Catholicism, that writer's skill and understanding impressed him deeply, particularly Flaubert's liking for those who threw themselves into emotional extremes, perhaps as do Thérèse Desqueyroux and Maria Cross, as do Jean Pélouèyre and old Villenave. Stendhal stood behind the partly romantic, partly realistic love scenes of *La Pharisienne,* as he did in those many many scenes in which the psychology of the characters seems to shape itself on the very page. And Balzac and Zola behind those many novels that are centered on the Bordeaux countryside— novels in which the traditions of French family life, its greed and hypocrisy, its humor and dignity, are carefully and poignantly developed.

Mauriac was not a realist, however, in the sense that Zola was a realist; rather, he was a realist in a moral sense. As do the works of Balzac, the writer who automatically sprung to his lips when his literary influences were called into question, Mauriac's works move quietly, the observations keenly made and the scenes fully realized, the religious and moral implications rising insistently above action that might at times verge on the sensational. Even the melodramatic aspects of the Desqueyroux murder trial seem folded into the fabric of the novel in *Thérèse Desqueyroux,* for there the emphasis falls on the instinctive evil of the heroine whose face reveals the pitilessness of her character only in moments of lethargy; a heroine in whom, nevertheless, her author found the germs of spirituality, and through whom the power of grace could be felt.

The traditions of the French novel ultimately defined the method that Mauriac followed in portraying themes that are animated by a Roman Catholic understanding of the effects of sin on the soul and of the all-pervasive power of grace. No wonder he felt an alien when he first read Greene. The mystery was the same, but the approach had been determined by the conventions of the English novel and Greene's English literary heritage. The similarities that exist in the works of these two writers, startling enough at first, become curious contrasts in the final analysis.

There is one more point, however, that needs to be made. It would be foolish to say that Greene has not read Mauriac's novels and that Mauriac did not read his. And it is interesting to observe the reciprocal influences that can be seen in their works. It would seem that Greene borrowed more from Mauriac than Mauriac from him. Greene's drama *The Living Room,* for example, shows a remarkable similarity of theme and character to *La Pharisienne.* Greene's drama concerns the efforts of Helen Browne, the elderly and misguided Catholic, to keep her niece Rose from abandoning her religion by becoming the common-law wife of a married man. *La Pharisienne* recounts the exertions of a stepmother, Brigitte Pian, to impose the precepts of Roman Catholic dogma on her wards. Mauriac described with brilliant insight and a penetrating awareness of religious considerations Brigitte's gradual recognition of herself. The lady of the Pharisees gradually sees her image; but she is not appalled. She slowly becomes aware of her hypocrisy, but she feels that she is not evil. And this is much the situation that Mauriac developed in *The Desert of Love,* and that Greene himself has come extremely close to in *The End of the Affair.* For the heroine of *The Desert of Love,* Maria Cross, is in some ways like Sarah Miles before her conversion. Maria is promiscuous, but she is also tender, human, loving. After an accident she recognizes her hypocrisy and gives up an attempt to seduce her physician's son, the impressionable Raymond Courrèges. Maria finds at the end of her youth an ambiguous awareness of the love of God in her relationship with Bertrand de Larouselle, her husband's son by another wife. She succeeds in convincing herself that her love for Bertrand is a love of the god he loves. And perhaps it is. The important fact is that her hypocrisy, if it is hypocrisy, makes others aware of the reality of God. One knows who Brigitte Pian and Maria Cross are, and is better for recognizing the grain of holiness that is covered by the crust of hypocrisy. Mauriac's triumph is that he made his people come alive. And Greene's Helen Browne is such a character.

These characters are studies in misguided and, to some extent, unintentional hypocrisy (as is Lady Marchmain in Waugh's *Brideshead Revisited*); and they indicate Greene and Mauriac's concerns with similar themes. Further similarities could be drawn, but they would prove little more than that Greene has read Mauriac and Mauriac Greene; that within their works both deal with expressions of life within a Roman Catholic framework; that their works are different because as writers they experienced different backgrounds.

Both novelists, dealing with individuals in their relationship to God, and, consequently, to their fellow men, developed their themes according to their own geniuses. And in this realm all comparisons prove fruitless. The point is that within the confines of the novel form the uniqueness of two Catholic writers has been determined by their origins, their cultural traditions, and the times.

Chapter Ten
Literary Opinions

Greene criticism and scholarship divides, by and large, into two categories: that before the mid-1960s which extrapolates from the texts those philosophical, theological, and psychological elements that formulate a rationale for the characterization and action; and that since about 1965 which examines form, techniques, and texture that define the tradition within which Greene writes and lend artistic unity to the oeuvre. These two approaches are, however, frequently interdependent since religious concerns are more than a hobby with Greene. The later criticism takes Greene pretty much as he asks to be taken—as a novelist who happens to be a Catholic and not as a Catholic writer. There are of course exceptions to these generalizations. In many of the books and essays written on Greene such terms as Manichaeism, Augustinism, quietism, Pelagianism, Jansenism, and existentialism have been employed to describe Greene's bent or stance vis à vis his materials. These terms, perhaps, need clarification, and I here refer to explanatory Greene scholarship while commenting briefly on these perspectives and on the problems of genre implicit within the canon.

In *Esquisses anglaises*[1] Claire Eliane Engel discusses the possibility that the Greene oeuvre is tinged with Jansenism. Engel states that it has been possible to discern in Greene's novels both fatality and predestination, and that many have put the theme of flight and pursuit down to this Calvinist orientation, that is, God's choice for certain individuals. In other words, the man who throws himself into sin is dedicated to evil, and death is the wages of sin, but God can liberate the sinner through grace.

The Calvinistic ethic, then, may be interpreted as the raison d'être for the chase motif found in a good many Greene novels. However, this argument fails to consider sufficiently that the chase motif is a standard device of the detective story; indeed, that it is a traditional motif in the literature of many cultures, and that Greene, especially in the entertainments, remains within the conventions of the type of novel he writes. Accepting Jansenism as a ruling philosophy

189

would lead to the conclusion that the plight of the Greene hero is not of his own making, that it is predetermined, and that a particular sinner is doomed to hell or to be expedited to heaven according to the destiny God has ordained for him. Engel admits, however, that Greene's religion is not "une question de formalisme," that his ideas, whether or not they tend to Jansenism, are not rigid. Engel's observations, apply, of course, primarily to those novels written before 1949.

Evelyn Waugh in his review of *The Heart of the Matter* finds the theological climate that pervades the Greene world to be one of quietism, which, however, is defined as a tendency to religious devotion rather than a definite theological belief. It stresses Christian perfection as a state of uninterrupted contemplation of God, and it insists that the soul remains passive under a divine influence. Contemplation, quiet and serene, does not necessarily depend on the tenets of orthodox belief; rather, it succeeds by eliminating the thought of punishment or reward in another life. The quietist makes faith the paramount consideration, and he insists that contemplation of God makes the necessity of works negligible to produce a condition for salvation.

Waugh says of Major Scobie: "We are told that he is actuated throughout by the love of God. A love, it is true, that falls short of trust, but a love, we must suppose, which sanctifies his sins. That is the heart of the matter. Is such a sacrifice feasible? . . ."[2] Such an attitude, Waugh insists, would mean that one has to be as wicked as Pinkie Brown before he runs into the danger of being damned. This estimate of Greene's "devotional" tendencies in his novels would, if carried further, deprive the novels of dramatic conflict, of psychological motivation.

Walter Allen, in a characteristically provocative essay, first published in *Penguin New Writing*,[3] discusses the theology that informs Greene's novels in terms of Augustinism and Pelagianism. Augustinism accepts something of the Manichaean heresy which insists on a duality of nature. The Manichaean believes that all matter is evil and that man is therefore and consequently evil. (Man is, however, sometimes rescued by an arbitrary selection on the part of God.) St. Augustine adds to this the idea of the fortunate fall: there is evil in the world, but it is put there so that man can rise above it; and, by rising above it, he proves his kinship to God. Greene himself in the epigraph to *The Lawless Roads* quotes from Cardinal

Newman, and in the quotation the basis of the Christian aspects of Augustinism is apparent: "I can only answer, that either there is no Creator, or this living society of men is in a true sense discarded from His presence . . . *if* there be a God, *since* there is a God, the human race is implicated in some terrible aboriginal calamity." Nineteenth-century echoes are also heard herein.

In a world with no hope and in one without God, Allen goes on, all that man sees about him impresses him with a sense of the profound mystery that is beyond human solution. For the average person, Augustinism in its human aspects will appear nasty, seedy, unlikable, brutish, often cruel, often despicable. This attitude, then, in great part, accounts for Greene's grotesques, his Acky and his Prewitt, his Minty and his Farrant, his Pinkie and his Lime.

Pelagianism, on the other hand, insists that man is naturally good, "but is perverted by external factors, by society as such if he is an anarchist, by the capitalist system if he is a Marxist, or by the family" (149). The Pelagian would go so far as to deny the reality of evil, for his emphasis would be placed on man as one who has within himself the power to control his destiny.

Allen maintains that Greene has adopted in his works the Augustinian concept of evil and that this affords him a basis for evaluating the ills of the world. He adds that Augustinism offers the same possibilities for heroism in the twentieth century that its non-Christian counterpart offered for the sixteenth and early seventeenth centuries:

In the understanding and assessment of the human situation in such an age of violence as our own the Augustinian, for whom evil is endemic in man's nature, is at a tremendous advantage. How tremendous may be seen if we compare the present age with an age of similar violence, the Elizabethan period and the first half of the seventeenth century. England had its burnings and its martyrdoms, its civil wars, yet in comparison with continental Europe was relatively peaceful. But how the Englishman reacted to those years of violence may be seen in the plays of the great Elizabethans: Marlowe, Shakespeare, Jonson, Webster, Tourneur, Ford, are horrified but fascinated; yet they can assimilate violence, the evil; it is part and parcel of their emotional world; it is what happens to man when the order, the natural and the supernatural, that curbs him, is broken. It does not surprise them, because the jungle is, as it were, man's natural state. (150)

Allen's appraisal seems most logical, for it allows the possibility of heroic adventure. The Greene universe is not limited to the evil that Manichaeism advocates as the prevailing aspect of life, nor to the predetermined world of Jansenist thought. By allowing for the possibility that man may rise above the evil that is endemic to his nature, Greene's hero may find heaven at the end of his journey. If not heaven, then in his death he may find heroism—perhaps not the magnificent and bragging heroism of a Tamerlane, but at least the pitiful heroism of the Duchess of Malfi.

Not all of Greene's critics, however, are disposed to label him primarily a religious writer. George Woodcock[4] and Arthur Calder-Marshall maintain that Greene's principal concern is not with religion but with the relationship of man to society, "with the individual as victim, and society the villain."[5] Their claim is that Greene is a good man fallen among Catholics.

Kenneth Allott and Miriam Farris,[6] in what is still one of the best books of Greene criticism, admit the strong religious tone that pervades the novels; but they indicate that this concern is merely a facet of the Greene universe. They correctly stress the idea that Greene's preoccupation with good and evil made itself apparent in his early youth, long before he adopted Roman Catholicism. They insist on the idea of the corrupted childhood leading to a predilection for horror and violence in later life, and they define the Greene canon in terms of "obsessions."

The obsessions that Allott and Farris discuss in their critique are, first, those depending on the divided mind—the world of *The Man Within;* second, those dealing with the fallen world—*Stamboul Train* and *It's a Battlefield;* third, those in which the theme of pity is exploited—*The Ministry of Fear, The Power and the Glory,* and *The Heart of the Matter.* The central obsession, that which lends unity to the others, is to Allott and Farris the terror of life and its origins in the early years; it is the corruption of the state of innocence that is the dominating motif in the work of Greene. Fear of life accounts for the theme of damnation; and this theme finds particular expression in the sin of the whiskey priest of *The Power and the Glory* and in Scobie's suicide in *The Heart of the Matter.*

Since Allott and Farris prefer to deal with Greene's "obsessions," they fail to reckon with the power of the religious theme as a structuring aspect of the novels. Certainly the preoccupations that they define in Greene's work are evident in the novels, but the religious element cannot be dismissed quite so easily. The theme of childhood betrayal which Greene so brilliantly develops in "The Basement Room" seems to be a secondary rather than a principal consideration in the mature novels where it is related to the fall from grace.

In a provocative study, *Graham Greene: témoin des temps tragiques,*[7] Paul Rostenne discusses the novels in terms of Sartrian existentialism, an aspect of Greene scholarship developed in chapters 4 and 5. According to Sartre, existentialism insists on the cult of the individual, what he labels "le culte du moi." Sartrian existentialism denies God and makes atheism the ruling philosophy. In his novels Sartre has caught the conflict of a hero versus a society that does not foster heroism. There is little reason, it seems, for judging the Greene hero as uniquely the exponent of such a philosophy, although there are certain superficial resemblances, particularly in Scobie, Fowler, and Brown. The Greene hero chooses, despite his egotism, not so much "le culte du moi" as what can loosely be referred to as "le culte des autres"; when Major Scobie commits suicide he does not deny the existence of God and glorify the idea of self; paradoxical as it may seem to the existentialist, he affirms his relationship to God.

Gaétan Bernoville in an introductory essay to a study of the Catholicism of François Mauriac indicates strongly his disapproval of those who would label Greene primarily a theologian or even one whose preoccupations in his novels are exclusively religious. Bernoville indicates that in the 1940s a religious preoccupation replaced the psychoanalytic preoccupation that dominated much of the literature of the 1920s and the 1930s. Bernoville considers Greene, as Greene considers himself, to be primarily and essentially a novelist; the Catholicism involved in the books is merely a device used to render his fable "captivating."[8]

One of the most sensible books of comparative criticism is Jacques Madaule's *Graham Greene,* which discounts the influence of Claudel, Mauriac, and Bernanos; Madaule insists that Greene's chief problem as a writer who uses Catholicism as a theme in his work is the predominantly Protestant audience for which he writes; and he sees Greene's use of religion as flexible:

The Christianity of Graham Greene is a realistic Christianity, which does not at all signify that he is superstitious. Greene has a horror of idealism and optimism, which Protestantism has paradoxically developed in the Anglo-Saxon world. This produces, finally, the Ida Arnolds and, in an infinitely more sympathetic register, such beings as Miss Lehr and her brother, who very charitably receive the fugitive priest, but who do not at all understand his "mummeries."[9]

In the 1960s John Atkins and Francis Kunkel's critiques of Greene are noteworthy. Atkins's *Graham Greene*[10] purports to be a biographical study, but since Greene is characteristically reticent about his life, Atkins can offer only conjectures. In *The Labyrinthine Ways of Graham Greene*[11] Francis Kunkel explains the use of religious symbols, traces character development and themes, and analyzes provocative situations as he evaluates both literary and religious influences on Greene as a maturing artist.

Two books of outstanding merit published in the 1970s are Gwen Boardman's *Graham Greene: The Aesthetics of Exploration*[12] and Peter Wolfe's *Graham Greene the Entertainer*. Boardman begins with a discussion of Greene's interest in the theme of lost innocence, which she discovers in most of his work, then moves into a discussion of Greene's search of uncorrupted imagination, the dominant motif of his first travel book, *Journey without Maps*. The voyage into Africa is for Boardman one into the heart of darkness. She takes Greene's description of Africa, a continent shaped like the human heart, and proceeds to discover in this image a basis for the spiritual odyssey that explains Greene's aesthetic exploration. Wolfe's study of the entertainments, primarily one of genre, is lucid and persuasive. He is fully aware of the fact that "Greene's belief in original sin carries the entertainments beyond the crime-puzzle formulas," and that the hunted man and the avenger of society are frequently the same.[13]

In the 1980s Gangeshwar Rai's *Graham Greene, An Existential Approach*[14] addresses once again the proposition that Sartrian existentialism exerts a controlling influence on the oeuvre, and he compares Greene's "heroes" to Sartre's and Camus's counterparts. The approach works better in *The Quiet American* and *The Comedians* than it does in many of the earlier novels. K. C. Joseph Kurismmotil's *Heaven and Hell on Earth: An Appreciation of Five Novels of Graham Greene*[15] sees, correctly, a pattern of development from *Brighton Rock* through *The End of the Affair,* and argues that *A Burnt-Out Case* is an epilogue to a study of damnation or salvation. Henry J. Donaghy in *Graham Greene: An Introduction to His Writings*[16] presents a brief but accurate comment on the major works while offering comments of the film adaptations whenever applicable.

Two bibliographies of Greene criticism published recently are indispensable to those pursuing a keener awareness of Greene's canon—R. A. Wobbe's *Graham Greene: A Bibliography and Guide to Research* (1980)[17] and A. F. Cassis's *Graham Greene: An Annotated Bibliography of Criticism*[18] in 1981. These are necessarily incomplete, for Greene continues to be a prolific writer in his later years.

The very best of all recent criticism available on Greene is that written by himself. *Ways of Escape* continues the memoirs of *A Sort of Life* which ends with Greene in his late twenties, and the introductions written for the Collected Edition supply insights into the works that dazzle and humble those who consider Greene, as I do, the finest living writer in our language. His conversations with Marie-Françoise Allain entitled *The Other Man*—there seems to be in fact an imposter who travels the world as the original—is a book that readers and critics will refer to again and again inasmuch as it reveals provocative aspects of the private man that affect the works.

Notes and References

Preface

1. Thomas Merton, *The Seven-Storey Mountain* (New York: Harcourt, 1948), 128.
2. Bertrand Russell, *The Impact of Science on Society* (New York: Simon and Schuster, 1953), 91–92.

Chapter One

1. Evelyn Waugh, *Brideshead Revisited,* Uniform Edition (London: Chapman and Hall, 1949), 69.
2. "François Mauriac," in *The Lost Childhood* (London, 1951), 69.
3. Bernard Blackstone, *Virginia Woolf: A Commentary* (London: Hogarth, 1949), 69.
4. See Lionel Trilling, *E. M. Forster* (Norfolk, 1943), 113–15.
5. See William York Tindall, *D. H. Lawrence and Susan His Cow* (New York: Columbia, 1939), 173–74.
6. T. S. Eliot, *After Strange Gods* (London: Faber, 1934), 54.
7. Ibid., 54.
8. Ibid., 59.
9. Ibid., 60.
10. William York Tindall, *Forces in Modern British Literature: 1885–1946* (New York: Knopf, 1947), 122.
11. Ibid., 186.
12. André Gide, *The Journals of André Gide,* trans. Justin O'Brien (New York: Knopf, 1949), vol. 3, *1928–1939,* 126. The last paragraph quoted above is particularly interesting in view of Waugh's attitude to the Catholic aristocracy in England. Compare Theresa Marchmain in *Brideshead Revisited.*
13. Ibid., 3:259.
14. Ibid., 3:226.
15. See Tindall, *Forces* 186 ff.
16. Elizabeth Bowen, Graham Greene, and V. S. Pritchett, *Why Do I Write?* (London, 1948), 29–30. Subsequent references are included parenthetically in the text.
17. Rex Warner, "Freedom in Literary and Artistic Creation," in *Freedom and Culture* (New York: Columbia, 1951), 210–11.
18. Marie-Françoise Allain, *The Other Man: Conversations with Graham Greene* (New York, 1981), 91. Subsequent references are included parenthetically in the text.

19. Kathleen Nott, *The Emperor's Clothes* (London: Heinemann, 1954), 310–11.

20. Ibid., 309.

21. Jacques Maritain, *Art and Scholasticism* (New York: Scribner's, 1949), 171.

22. "Henry James: The Religious Aspect," in *The Lost Childhood,* 39.

23. *In Search of a Character* (New York, 1961), 13–14.

24. "Henry James, The Religious Aspect," in *The Lost Childhood,* 39.

25. François Mauriac, *God and Mammon* (London: Sheed and Ward, 1946), 59.

26. "The Lost Childhood," in *The Lost Childhood,* 16.

27. Ibid., 15–16.

28. Ibid., 17.

29. *The Lawless Roads* (London, 1939), 11–12.

30. "The Revolver in the Corner Cupboard," in *The Lost Childhood,* 174.

31. *A Sort of Life* (New York, 1971), 168.

Chapter Two

1. *A Gun for Sale* (London, 1973), v. Subsequent references are to the Collected Edition.

2. Evelyn Waugh, "Felix Culpa," *Commonweal* 48 (16 July 1948):323.

3. "Henry James: The Private Universe," in *The Lost Childhood,* 24.

4. "Henry James: The Religious Aspect," in *The Lost Childhood,* 39.

5. *Stamboul Train* (London, 1974), ix. Subsequent references are to the Collected Edition.

6. *The Confidential Agent* (London, 1977), viii. Subsequent references are to the Collected Edition.

7. *The Ministry of Fear* (London, 1973), x–xi. Subsequent references are to the Collected Edition.

8. Gwen Boardman, *Graham Greene: The Aesthetics of Exploration* (Gainesville, 1971), 79.

9. *The Third Man* (London, 1976), 8. Subsequent references are to the Collected Edition.

10. T. S. Eliot, "What the Thunder Said," in *The Waste Land,* ll. 359–65. Eliot says in a note to the poem that the passage was stimulated by ". . . the account of one of the Antarctic expeditions: . . . it was related that the party of explorers, at the extremity of their strength, had

the constant delusion that there was *one more member* than could actually be counted."

11. Gavin Lambert, "The Double Agent," in *The Dangerous Edge* (New York, 1976), 159.

12. Peter Wolfe, *Graham Greene the Entertainer* (Carbondale, 1972), 126.

13. *Loser Takes All* (London, 1976), 123. Subsequent references are to the Collected Edition.

14. *Our Man in Havana* (London, 1977), vii–viii. Subsequent references are to the Collected Edition.

15. *Ways of Escape* (New York, 1980), 296. Subsequent references are included parenthetically in the text.

16. *An Impossible Woman: The Memoirs of Dottoressa Moor of Capri* (New York, 1975), 199.

17. *The Comedians* (London, 1976), 46. Subsequent references are to the Collected Edition.

18. *Travels with My Aunt* (New York, 1971), 305.

Chapter Three

1. *The Man Within* (London, 1976), v. Subsequent references are to the Collected Edition.

2. *It's a Battlefield* (London, 1970), x. Subsequent references are to the Collected Edition.

3. *England Made Me* (London, 1970), x. Subsequent references are to the Collected Edition.

4. *Nineteen Stories* (New York, 1949), 211.

5. Francis Kunkel, *The Labyrinthine Ways of Graham Greene* (New York, 1959), 43–56. Kunkel astutely points out those aspects of Pinkie Brown's character that derive from Minty.

Chapter Four

1. *Brighton Rock* (London, 1970), viii. Subsequent references are to the Collected Edition.

2. Sean O'Casey, *Rose and Crown* (New York: Macmillan, 1952), 272.

3. *The Power and the Glory* (London, 1971), vii. Subsequent references are to the Collected Edition.

4. "The Young Dickens," in *The Lost Childhood,* 56.

5. "Frederick Rolfe: Edwardian Inferno," in *The Lost Childhood,* 93.

6. The rose is, more than likely, a reference to Dante's multifoliate rose and to the rose in Eliot's "Ash Wednesday."

7. Evelyn Waugh, "Felix Culpa," *Commonweal* 48 (16 July 1948):324.

8. See the chapter called Literary Opinions.

9. *Why Do I Write?*, 32. One is reminded of James's urgent plea to an acquaintance that he not finish an anecdote, for in it James had found the germ of a story and foreknowledge of the ending might have encouraged him to influence the actions of his characters.

10. *The Heart of the Matter* (London, 1971), vii. Subsequent references are to the Collected Edition.

11. Kenneth Allott and Miriam Farris, *The Art of Graham Greene* (London, 1951), 214.

12. Martin C. D'Arcy, "The Anatomy of a Hero," in *Transformation Three* (London: n.p., n.d.), 16–18.

13. *The End of the Affair* (London, 1974), viii–ix. Subsequent references are to the Collected Edition.

14. Boardman, *Aesthetics of Exploration,* 91.

15. *The End of the Affair* bears striking similarities to *The Desert of Love.*

16. "François Mauriac," in *The Lost Childhood,* 69.

17. Evelyn Waugh, "The Heart's Own Reasons," *Commonweal* 54 (17 August 1951):458.

18. Georges Bernanos, *The Diary of a Country Priest,* trans. Pamela Morris (New York: Macmillan, 1937), 123–24.

Chapter Five

1. *The Quiet American* (London, 1973), ix. Subsequent references are to the Collected Edition.

2. Gangeshwar Rai, *Graham Greene: An Existential Approach* (Atlantic Highlands, N.J., 1983), 76.

3. Compare Paul Rostenne, *Graham Greene: témoin des temps tragiques* (Paris, 1949), 218 ff., and Robert Evans, "Existentialism in Graham Greene's *The Quiet American,*" *Modern Fiction Studies* 3 (Autumn 1957):241–48 for differing approaches to the existential problem.

4. *A Burnt-Out Case* (London, 1974), xii–xiii. Subsequent references are to the Collected Edition.

5. Joseph Kurismmotil, *Heaven and Hell on Earth: An Appreciation of Five Novels of Graham Greene* (Chicago, 1982), 151.

6. Orville Prescott, "Books of the Times," *New York Times,* 17 February 1961, 25.

7. Ibid.

Chapter Six

1. Michael Routh, "Greene's Parody of Farce and Comedy in *The Comedians,*" *Renascence* 36, no. 3 (Spring 1974):150.

2. Rai, *An Existential Approach,* 82.

3. Alan Kennedy, *The Protean Self: Dramatic Action in Contemporary Fiction* (New York, 1974), 239.

4. Paul Hernadi, "On the How, What, and Why of Narrative," in *On Narrative,* ed. W. J. T. Mitchell, 197–99 (Chicago: Chicago, 1981).

5. *The Honorary Consul* (New York, 1973), 168. Subsequent references are included parenthetically in the text.

6. *The Human Factor* (New York, 1978), 23. Subsequent references are included parenthetically in the text.

7. Julian Symons, in his review of *Monsignor Quixote, Times Literary Supplement,* 8 October 1982, 1089, has observed that Greene's knowledge of chess is not all it might be. Subsequently referred to parenthetically in the text.

8. George Steiner, review of *The Human Factor, New Yorker,* 8 May 1978, 153.

9. *Doctor Fischer of Geneva or The Bomb Party* (New York, 1981), 153.

10. *The Tenth Man* (New York, 1985), 11–13. Subsequent references are included parenthetically in the text.

Chapter Seven

1. *The Living Room* (London, 1953), 23.

2. *The Living Room,* introduction by Peter Glenville (London, 1957), ix.

3. "The Second Death," in *Collected Stories* (London, 1974), 549–50. Subsequent references are included parenthetically in the text.

4. *The Potting Shed* (London, 1957–58), 69. Subsequent references are included parenthetically in the text.

5. Jacob H. Adler, "Graham Greene's Plays: Technique Versus Value," in *Graham Greene: Some Critical Considerations,* ed. Robert O. Evans (Louisville, Ky., 1963), 225.

6. *The Complaisant Lover* (London, 1959), 69. Subsequent references are included parenthetically in the text.

7. *Carving a Statue* (London, 1972), 11. Subsequent references are included parenthetically in the text.

8. *The Return of A. J. Raffles* (New York, 1975). Subsequent references are included parenthetically in the text.

9. Martin Esslin, review of *The Return of A. J. Raffles, Plays and Players* 23 (February 1976):30.

10. *Yes and No: A Play in One Act* (London, 1983), 21–22.

11. *For Whom the Bell Chimes* (London, 1983), 32. Subsequent references are included parenthetically in the text.

Chapter Eight

1. *Collected Stories* (London, 1974), vii. Subsequent references are to the Collected Edition.

Chapter Nine

1. Mauriac, *God and Mammon,* 37. Subsequent references are made parenthetically in the text.
2. François Mauriac, *Great Men,* trans. Elsie Pell (London: Rockcliff, 1952), 10.
3. *Journey without Maps* (London, 1978), 9.
4. "Henry James: The Private Universe," in *The Lost Childhood,* 30.
5. "François Mauriac," in *The Lost Childhood,* 69–74.

Chapter Ten

1. Claire Eliane Engel, *Esquisses anglaises: Charles Morgan, Graham Greene, T. S. Eliot* (Paris, 1949), 69.
2. Evelyn Waugh, "Felix Culpa?" *Commonweal* 48 (16 July 1948):324.
3. Walter Allen, "The Novels of Graham Greene," *Penguin New Writing* 18 [1943]:148–60. Subsequent references are included parenthetically in the text.
4. George Woodcock, *The Writer and Politics* (London, 1948), 151–52.
5. Arthur Calder-Marshall, "Graham Greene," in *Living Writers,* ed. Gilbert Phelps, 39–47. (London, 1947).
6. Allott and Farris, *Art of Graham Greene,* 24–25.
7. Rostenne, *Greene: témoin des temps tragiques,* 218. The discussion of Greene as a novelist is very hazy. Rostenne prefers to use Greene as a stalking horse so that he can move into all sorts of philosophical and religious discussions pertinent to the modern French novel. The discussion on Greene compares him to Bernanos, Sartre, and Céline. Although his reading is wide, he fails to appreciate the force of Roman Catholicism as an important factor in what he terms "la vision Greenienne." His explanation of existentialism, especially when it is relative to Roman Catholicism, appears tenuous. The discussion by Marcel Gabriel in H. J. Blackman, ed., *Six Existentialist Thinkers* (London: Macmillan, 1952), 68–85 is much more illuminating.
8. Robert J. North, *Le Catholicisme dans l'oeuvre de François Mauriac,* introduction by Gaetan Bernoville (n.p.: 1950), xii–xvi.
9. Jacques Madaule, *Graham Greene* (Paris: Editions du Temps Présent, 1949), 368; my translation.
10. John Atkins, *Graham Greene* (London, 1957).

11. Kunkel, *Labyrinthine Ways.*

12. Boardman, *Aesthetics of Exploration.*

13. Wolfe, *Greene the Entertainer,* 14.

14. Rai, *An Existential Approach.*

15. Kurismmotil, *Heaven and Hell on Earth.*

16. Henry J. Donaghy, *Graham Greene: An Introduction to His Writings* (Amsterdam, 1983).

17. R. A. Wobbe, *Graham Greene: A Bibliography and Guide to Research* (New York, 1979).

18. A. F. Cassis, *Graham Greene: An Annotated Bibliography of Criticism* (Metuchen, N.J., 1981).

Selected Bibliography

There are many editions of Greene's works available; and what I have done below is to list chronologically and as exactly as possible the facts of original publication. Greene's work has been assembled, but not fully, into a Collected Edition by Heinemann and the Bodley Head, and I have indicated these dates in square brackets for the benefit of the reader. I have also listed those books and articles about Greene that I feel the interested reader would find most useful in the section entitled Secondary Sources.

PRIMARY SOURCES

1. Major Works

Babbling April. collected poems. Oxford: Basil Blackwell, 1925.

The Man Within. London: Heinemann, 1929. [Collected Edition, 1976.]

The Name of Action. London: Heinemann, 1930. [Withdrawn.]

Rumour at Nightfall. London: Heinemann, 1931. [Withdrawn.]

Stamboul Train; an entertainment. London: Heinemann, 1932. Published in the United States under the title of *Orient Express* (Garden City: Doubleday, 1932). [Collected Edition, 1974.]

It's a Battlefield. London: Heinemann, 1934. [Collected Edition, 1975.]

The Basement Room. London: Cresset Press, 1935. Includes: "The Basement Room"; "Brother"; "A Chance for Mr. Lever"; "A Day Saved"; "The End of the Party"; "I Spy"; "Jubilee"; "The Lottery Ticket"; "The Other Side of the Border" (unfinished novel); "Proof Positive."

England Made Me. London: Heinemann, 1935. Published in the United States as *The Shipwrecked* (New York: Viking, 1953). [Collected Edition, 1970.]

Journey without Maps: A Travel Book. London: Heinemann, 1936. [Collected Edition, 1978.]

A Gun for Sale; an entertainment. London: Heinemann, 1936. Published in the United States under the title of *This Gun for Hire* (Garden City: Doubleday, 1936). [Collected Edition, 1973.]

Brighton Rock. London: Heinemann, 1938. [Collected Edition, 1975.]

The Confidential Agent; an entertainment. London: Heinemann, 1939. [Collected Edition, 1977.]

The Lawless Roads. London: Longmans, 1939. Published in the United States under the title *Another Mexico* (New York: Viking, 1939). [Collected Edition, 1978.]

The Power and the Glory. London: Heinemann, 1940. Published in the United States as *The Labyrinthine Ways* (New York: Viking, 1940), and reissued in 1946 under the original English title. [Collected Edition, 1979.]

The Ministry of Fear; an entertainment. London: Heinemann, 1943. [Collected Edition, 1973.]

Nineteen Stories. London: Heinemann, 1947. Contains the stories published in *The Basement Room and Other Stories,* listed above, plus the following: "Across the Bridge"; "Alas, Poor Maling"; "The Case for the Defence"; "A Drive in the Country"; "The Innocent"; "A Little Place Off the Edgeware Road"; "Men at Work"; "The Second Death"; "When Greek Meets Greek."

The Heart of the Matter. London: Heinemann, 1948. [Collected Edition, 1975.]

The Third Man; an entertainment. New York: Viking, 1950. Published as a story in *American Magazine* 147 (March 1949):142–60. [Collected Edition, 1976.]

The Fallen Idol; an entertainment. In *The Third Man and The Fallen Idol.* London: Heinemann, 1950. A retitling of "The Basement Room."

The Lost Childhood and Other Essays. London: Eyre & Spottiswoode, 1951. Contains the following essays: "At Home"; "Beatrix Potter"; "Bombing Manoeuvre"; "Book Market"; "Burden of Childhood"; "Dr. Oates of Salamanca"; "Domestic Background"; "Don in Mexico"; "Eric Gill"; "Fielding and Sterne"; "Film Lunch"; "Ford Madox Ford"; "Francis Parkman"; "François Mauriac"; "Frederick Rolfe: Edwardian Inferno"; "From Feathers to Iron"; "George Darley"; "Great Dog of Weimar"; "Harkaway's Oxford"; "Henry James: The Private Universe"; "Henry James: The Religious Aspect"; "Herbert Read"; "Hoax on Mr. Hulton"; "Invincible Ignorance"; "Isis Idol"; "Last Buchan"; "Lesson of the Master"; "Lost Childhood"; "Man Made Angry"; "Mr. Cook's Century"; "Plays of Henry James"; "Poker-face"; "Portrait of a Lady"; "Portrait of a Maiden Lady"; "Remembering Mr. Jones"; "Revolver in the Corner Cupboard"; "Samuel Butler"; "Saratoga Trunk"; "Ugly Act"; "Unheroic Dramatist"; "Unknown War"; "Vive le Roi"; "Walter de la Mare's Short Stories"; "Young Dickens."

The End of the Affair. London: Heinemann, 1951. [Collected Edition, 1974.]

The Living Room; a play in two acts. London: Heinemann, 1953.

Twenty-One Stories. London: Heinemann, 1954. [Collected Edition, 1974.] Contains the same stories published in *Nineteen Stories,* listed above, substituting for "The Lottery Ticket" and "The Other Side of the Border" the following: "The Blue Film"; "The Destructors"; "The Hint of an Explanation"; "Special Duties."

Loser Takes All; an entertainment. London: Heinemann, 1955. [Collected Edition, 1976.]

The Quiet American. London: Heinemann, 1955. [Collected Edition, 1973.]

The Potting Shed; a play in three acts. London: Heinemann, 1957–58.

Our Man in Havana; an entertainment. London: Heinemann, 1958. [Collected Edition, 1970.]

The Complaisant Lover; a comedy. London: Heinemann, 1959.

A Burnt-Out Case. London: Heinemann, 1961. [Collected Edition, 1974.]

In Search of a Character: Two African Journals. London: Bodley Head, 1961.

A Sense of Reality. London: Bodley Head, 1963. Contains the following stories: Under the Garden; A Visit to Morin; Dream of a Strange Land; A Discovery in the Woods. [Collected Edition, 1972.]

Carving a Statue. London: Bodley Head, 1964.

The Comedians. London: Bodley Head, 1965. [Collected Edition, 1976.]

May We Borrow Your Husband? and Other Comedies of the Sexual Life. London: Bodley Head, 1967. [Collected Edition, 1972.]

Collected Essays. London: Bodley Head, 1969.

Travels with My Aunt. London: Bodley Head, 1970.

A Sort of Life. London: Bodley Head, 1971.

Collected Stories, Collected Edition. London: Bodley Head, 1972. Contains *Twenty-One Stories; A Sense of Reality;* and *May We Borrow Your Husband? and Other Comedies of the Sexual Life.*

The Honorary Consul. London: Bodley Head, 1974.

Lord Rochester's Monkey. London: Bodley Head, 1974.

An Impossible Woman: The Memories of Dottoressa Moor of Capri, London: Bodley Head, 1975.

The Human Factor. London: Bodley Head, 1978.

Ways of Escape. London: Bodley Head, 1980.

Doctor Fischer of Geneva or The Bomb Party. London: Bodley Head, 1980.

The Great Jowett. London: Bodley Head, 1981.

Monsignor Quixote. London: Bodley Head, 1982.

J'Accuse: The Dark Side of Nice. London: Bodley Head, 1982.

Yes and No and *For Whom the Bell Chimes.* London: Bodley Head, 1983.

Getting to Know the General: The Story of an Involvement. London: Bodley Head, 1984.

The Tenth Man. London: Bodley Head, 1985.

2. Other Stories by Graham Greene

"The Bear Fell Free." London: Grayson & Grayson, 1935. [Grayson Books.]

"The Escapist." *Spectator* 162 (13 January 1939):48–49.

"The Lieutenant Died Last." *Colliers* 105 (29 June 1940):9–10.

"News in English." In *Alfred Hitchcock's Fireside Book of Suspense,* edited by Alfred Hitchcock (New York: Simon & Schuster, 1947).

"Voyage in the Dark." *Spectator* 161 (16 September 1938):437.

3. Children's Books

The Little Fire Engine. London: Parrish, 1950. Published in the United States as *The Little Red Fire Engine.* New York: Lothrop, Lee & Shepard, 1952.

The Little Horse Bus. London: Parrish, 1952.

The Little Steam Roller. New York: Lothrop, Lee & Shepard, 1955.

4. Nonfiction

The Best of Saki. Selected and with an introduction, "The Burden of Childhood," by Graham Greene. London: British Publisher's Guild, 1950.

British Dramatists. London: W. Collins, 1942. ["Britain in Pictures" series.]

Graham Greene on Film. Edited by John Russell Taylor. New York: Simon & Schuster, 1972.

Essais Catholiques. Paris: Editions de Sevil, 1953.

The Old School, Essays by Divers Hands. Edited and with an introduction and essay, "The Last Word," by Graham Greene. London: Jonathan Cape, 1934.

Why Do I Write? An exchange of views between Elizabeth Bowen, Graham Greene, and V. S. Pritchett. London: Percival Marshall, 1948.

SECONDARY SOURCES

Allain, Marie-Françoise. *The Other Man: Conversations with Graham Greene.* New York: Simon & Schuster, 1981. Indispensable to any study of Greene. He answers questions concerning his craft with charm and wit.

Albères, R. M. "Graham Greene et résponsibilités," 157–85. In his *Les hommes traqués.* Paris: Nouvelle Editions, 1953. Discusses the problem of the individual's responsibility to a religious ethic.

Allen, Walter, "Graham Greene." In *Writers of To-day,* edited by Denys Val Baker, 15–28. London: Sidgwick, 1946. (Previously published as "The Novels of Graham Greene." *Penguin New Writing* 18 [1943]:148–60.) Discusses philosophy of Greene's novels in terms of Augustinism and Pelagianism.

————. "Awareness of Evil: Graham Greene." *Nation* 182 (21 April 1957):344–46.

————. *Tradition and Dream: The English and American Novel from the Twenties to Our Time.* London: Phoenex House, 1964. Places Greene in a 1930s context and sees *Brighton Rock* as the most original and archetypal of Greene's novels.

Allen, W. Gore. "Evelyn Waugh and Graham Greene." *Irish Monthly* 77 (January 1949):16–22. A comparison of the two writers' approaches to Catholicism. Says the driving impulse of Greene's world is evil; not so, Waugh's.

Allott, Kenneth, and Miriam Farris. *The Art of Graham Greene.* London: Hamish Hamilton, 1951. Sees Greene's work in terms of obsessions such as "the divided mind," and "the fallen world."

Atkins, John. *Graham Greene: A Biographical and Literary Study.* New York: Roy Publishers, 1958. Studies themes and relates early novels and characters to later works. Includes biographical information.

Beebe, Maurice. "Criticism of Graham Greene: A Selected Checklist with an Index to Studies of Separate Works." *Modern Fiction Studies* 3 (Autumn 1957):281–88.

Bernoville, Gaétan. "Introduction." In *Le Catholicisme dans l'oeuvre de Fran-çois Mauriac,* by Robert J. North. Paris: Editions du Conquistador, 1950. Says that Greene makes his fable pleasing by utilizing the figure of the pathetic Christian.

Birmingham, William. "Graham Greene Criticism: A Bibliographical Study." *Thought* 27 (Spring 1952):72–100.

Boardman, Gwen. *Graham Greene: The Aesthetics of Exploration.* Gainesville: Univ. of Florida, 1971. Sees journeys as means of aesthetic discovery.

Bouscaren, Anthony T. "France and Graham Greene versus America and Diem." *Catholic World* 181 (September 1955):414–17. Discusses French attitude toward Catholicism.

Boyle, Alexander. "Graham Greene." *Irish Monthly* 77 (November 1949):519–25. Discusses Greene's Catholic point of view.

————. "The Symbolism of Graham Greene." *Irish Monthly* 80 (1952):98–102. Discusses Greene's use of traditional and private symbols.

Braybrooke, Neville. "Graham Greene." *Envoy* 3 (September 1950):10–23.

————. "Graham Greene, a Pioneer Novelist." *College English* 12 (October 1950):1–9. A good discussion of themes in *Brighton Rock* and *The Heart of the Matter.*

————. "Graham Greene as Critic." *Commonweal* 54 (6 July 1951):312–14.

Buckler, William E., and Arnold B. Sklare. *Stories from Six Authors.* New York: McGraw-Hill, 1960. General introduction to the art of Greene for the student.

Burgess, Anthony. "The Greene and the Red: Politics in the Novels of Graham Greene." In *Urgent Copy: Literary Studies*. New York: Norton, 1968. Considers the political climate of *The Quiet American* and *The Comedians;* warns against identifying Greene with the narrators.

————. "More Comedians." *Spectator* 218, no. 7243 (21 April 1967):454. Speaks to the bittersweet qualities of *May We Borrow Your Husband?*

————. "Religion and the Arts: The Manicheans." *Times Literary Supplement* 3340 (3 March):153–54. Considers the dialectical problem of sin and sainthood in *The Heart of the Matter*.

Calder-Marshall, Arthur. "Graham Greene." In *Living Writers: Being Critical Studies Broadcast in the B. B. C. Third Programme*, edited by Gilbert Phelps. London: Sylvan Press, 1947. Says Greene's chief concern as a novelist is social.

Cassis, A. F. *Graham Greene: An Annotated Bibliography of Criticism*. Metuchen, N.J. and London: Scarecrow, 1981. Excellent and careful annotations of Greene scholarship through 1979.

Codey, Regina. "Notes on Graham Greene's Dramatic Technique." *Approach*, no. 17 [1955?]:23–27. Discusses Greene's use of religiously oriented subject matter.

Connolly, Francis X. "Inside Modern Man: The Spiritual Adventures of Graham Greene." *Renascence* 1 (Spring 1949):16–24. Discusses Greene's concern with Roman Catholicism.

Costello, Donald P. "Greene and the Catholic Press." *Renascence* 12 (Autumn 1959):3–28. Discusses Greene's reception by the contemporary Catholic press.

Cottrell, Beekman W. "Second Time Charm: The Theatre of Graham Greene." *Modern Fiction Studies* 3 (Autumn 1957):249–55. Discusses Greene's handling of religious themes in his dramas.

DeVitis, A. A. "Allegory in *Brighton Rock*." *Modern Fiction Studies* 3 (Autumn 1957):216–25. Explanation of form of *Brighton Rock*.

————. "The Church and Major Scobie." *Renascence* 10 (Spring 1958):115–20). Considers Scobie as modern tragic hero.

————. "The Entertaining Mr. Greene." *Renascence* 14 (Autumn 1961):8–24. Looks at themes and characters in the entertainments.

Donaghy, Denis. *Graham Greene: An Introduction to His Writings*. Amsterdam: Rodopi, 1983. Useful introductions to major works with comments on film adaptations.

Ellis, William D., Jr. "The Grand Theme of Graham Greene." *Southwest Review* 41 (Summer 1956):239–50. Discusses the problem of Greene's heroes and their sense of sin.

Engel, Claire Eliane. *Esquisses anglaises: Charles Morgan, Graham Greene, T. S. Eliot*. Paris: Editions Je Sers, 1949. Sees Greene's work as tinged with Jansenism; the Calvinist ethic becomes a dominant motif.

Evans, R. O., ed. *Graham Greene: Some Critical Considerations.* Lexington: University of Kentucky Press, 1963. Essays by different authors on varying subjects.

————. "Existentialism in Graham Greene's *The Quiet American.*" *Modern Fiction Studies* 3 (Autumn 1957):241–48. Sees the novel as conforming to certain aspects of existentialism.

Findlater, Richard. "Graham Greene as Dramatist." *Twentieth Century* 156 (June 1953):471–73. Looks at Greene's use of the stage as vehicle for his themes.

Gardiner, Harold C. "Graham Greene, Catholic Shocker." *Renascence* 1 (Spring 1949):12–15. Discusses the disquieting effect of Greene's work on many readers.

Gaston, George M. A. *The Pursuit of Salvation: A Critical Guide to the Novels of Graham Greene.* Troy, N.Y.: Whitson, 1984. Contains useful remarks on the various stances Greene has taken toward his religiously oriented subject matter.

Gregor, Ian. "The New Romanticism: A Comment on *The Living Room.*" *Blackfriars,* September 1953, 403–6. Good discussion of characterization.

Grubbs, Henry A. "Albert Camus and Graham Greene." *Modern Language Quarterly* 10 (March 1949):33–42. A view of Greene against existentialist philosophy.

Haber, Herbert R. "The Two Worlds of Graham Greene." *Modern Fiction Studies* 3 (Autumn 1957):256–68. The two worlds are the world of the spirit and the world of men.

Herling, Gustav. "Two Sanctities: Greene and Camus." *Adam,* no. 201 (1950):10–19. The problem of existentialist background is looked at critically.

Hoggart, Richard. "The Force of Caricature: Aspects of the Art of Graham Greene, with Particular Reference to *The Power and the Glory.*" *Essays in Criticism* 3 (October 1953):447–62.

Jerrold, Douglas. "Graham Greene, Pleasure-Hater." *Harper's* 205 (August 1952):50–52. Calls Greene "the finest living novelist, bar one, in our language."

Karl, Frederick R. *The Contemporary English Novel.* New York: Farrar, Straus & Cudahy, 1962. Looks at Scobie as tragic hero.

Kunkel, Francis L. *The Labyrinthine Ways of Graham Greene.* New York: Sheed & Ward, 1960. An examination of Greene's maturing artistry.

Kurismmotil, K. C., S. J. *Heaven and Hell on Earth: An Appreciation of Five Novels of Graham Greene.* Chicago: Loyola, 1982. Sees novels from *Brighton Rock* through *The End of the Affair* as possessing thematic unity, and *A Burnt-Out Case* as an epilogue to those four.

Lambert, Gavin. "The Double Agent." In *The Dangerous Edge*. New York: Grossman, 1975. Brisk and witty analysis of the technical and thematic aspects of the entertainments.

Lewis, R. W. B. "The Fiction of Graham Greene: Between the Horror and the Glory." *Kenyon Review* 19 (Winter 1957):56–75. Considers the plan of *The Power and the Glory*.

————. "Graham Greene: The Religious Affair." *The Picaresque Saint: Representative Figures in Contemporary Fiction*. New York: Lippincott, 1959.

————. "The 'Trilogy' of Graham Greene." *Modern Fiction Studies* 3 (Autumn 1957):195–215. Considers the themes that lend unity to the three novels published between 1938 and 1948.

Lodge, David. *Graham Greene*. Columbia Essays on Modern Writers, no. 17. New York: Columbia, 1971. Analyzes the rhetorical element in Greene's novels; concludes that *The End of the Affair* is his best.

McCarthy, Mary. "Graham Greene and the Intelligentsia." *Partisan Review* 11 (Spring 1944):228–30. Discusses Greene's appeal as a popular writer.

Madaule, Jacques. *Graham Greene*. Paris: Editions du Temps Présent, 1949. Says one of Greene's chief problems as a writer is the Protestant audience for which he writes; that Greene has a horror of the optimism that Protestantism has developed in the Anglo-Saxon world.

Marshall, Bruce. "Graham Greene and Evelyn Waugh." *Commonweal* 51 (3 March 1950):551–53. Points out obvious points of difference in approach to religion.

Mesnet, Marie-Beatrice. *Graham Greene and the Heart of the Matter*. London: Cresset Press, 1954. Looks at the major novels and comments on characterization, themes, and techniques.

Newby, P. H. *The Novel, 1945–1950*. London: Longmans, 1951. Places Greene in a literary perspective.

O'Donnell, Donat. "Graham Greene: The Anatomy of Pity." In his *Maria Cross: Imaginative Patterns in a Group of Modern Catholic Writers*. New York: Oxford University Press, 1952. Sees Greene from a rather narrow point of view; discusses the problem of grace.

O'Faolain, Sean. "Graham Greene: I Suffer; Therefore, I Am." In his *The Vanishing Hero: Studies in Novelists of the Twenties*. London: Eyre & Spottiswoode, 1956.

————. "The Novels of Graham Greene: *The Heart of the Matter*." *Britain Today*, no. 148 (August 1948):32–36. Discussion of Scobie's role in the novel.

Osterman, Robert. "Interview with Graham Greene." *Catholic World* 170 (February 1950):356–61.

Pange, Victor de. *Graham Greene.* Paris: Editions Universitaires, 1953. Excellent discussion of the role of the lieutenant in *The Power and the Glory.*

Patten, Karl. "The Structure of *The Power and the Glory.*" *Modern Fiction Studies* 3 (Autumn 1957):225–34. Looks at the novel in terms of symbolical identifications and spatial patterns.

Phillips, Gene D., S. J. *Graham Greene: The Films of His Fiction.* New York: Teachers College Press, 1974. Lucid and careful observations concerning the transformations from novel and entertainments to motion pictures.

Prescott, Orville. "Comrade of the Coterie." In his *In My Opinion,* 92–109. Indianapolis: Bobbs-Merrill, 1952. Discusses Greene's Roman Catholic orientation.

Pritchett, V. S. "The World of Graham Greene." *New Statesman,* 4 January 1958, 17–18. Discussion of Greene's unhappy world.

"Propos de table avec Graham Greene." *Dieu Vivant,* no. 16 (1950):127–37. Transcript of conversation between Greene and several French critics.

Rai, Gangeshwar. *Graham Greene: An Existential Approach.* Atlantic Highlands: Humanities Press, 1983. Flexible approach to the existential problems implicit in certain of the novels and short stories.

Reed, Henry. *The Novel Since 1939.* London: Longmans, 1947, pp. 15–18. Places Greene in literary perspective.

Rewak, William J., S. J. "*The Potting Shed:* Maturation of Graham Greene's Vision." *Catholic World* 186 (December 1957):210–13. Comments on action and structure and Greene's thematic material.

Rischik, Josef. *Graham Greene und Sein Werk.* Bern: Verlag A. Francke Ag., 1951. Discusses Greene's predilection for the "seedy," the unhappy, and the disoriented.

Rostenne, Paul. *Graham Greene: témoin des temps tragiques.* Paris: Juillard, 1949. Discusses the novels as possible existentialist exemplifications.

Roy, Jean-H. "L'Oeuvre de Graham Greene ou un christianisme de la damnation." *Les Temps Modernes* 52 (1950):1513–19.

Sharrock, Roger. *Saints, Sinners and Comedians: The Novels of Graham Greene.* Turnbridge Wells and Notre Dame: Burns and Oates and University of Notre Dame, 1984. Valuable comments on Greene's adaptation of cinematic techniques and the development of his style.

"Shocker." *Time* 58 (29 October 1951):98–104. (Anonymous profile.) Brief résumé of Greene's career to publication of *The End of the Affair.*

Shuttleworth, Martin, and **Simon Raven.** "The Art of Fiction III: Graham Greene." *Paris Review* 1 (Autumn 1953):24–41. (Interview.) Questions posed to Greene concerning the craft, philosophy, and theory of the artist.

Stratford, Philip. *Faith and Fiction: Creative Process in Greene and Mauriac.* Notre Dame: Univ. of Notre Dame Press, 1964. Compares Greene and Mauriac and the religious milieux from which they create their fictions.

Traversi, Derek. "Graham Greene." *Twentieth Century* 149 (1951):231–40, 319–28. Discusses themes in *Brighton Rock* and in *The Heart of the Matter.*

Turnell, Martin. "The Religious Novel." *Commonweal* 55 (26 October 1951):55–57. Discusses Greene's Catholicism as rationale for the novels.

Voorhees, Richard. "Recent Greene." *South Atlantic Quarterly* 62 (Spring 1963):244–55. Comments on later fiction; says Greene's later work is compelling because of the dilemma by which it is plagued.

———. "The World of Graham Greene." *South Atlantic Quarterly* 50 (July 1951):389–98. Says Greene's combination of naturalistic description and Christian sense of sin makes him a moralist as well as a novelist.

Wansbrough, John. "Graham Greene: The Detective in the Wasteland." *Harvard Advocate* 136 (December 1952):11–13, 29–31. Discusses technique.

Wassmer, Thomas A. "The Problem and Mystery of Sin in the Works of Graham Greene." *Christian Scholar* 43, no. 4 (Winter 1960):309–15. Examines Greene's use of Roman Catholic themes.

Waugh, Evelyn. "Felix Culpa?" *Commonweal* 48 (16 July 1948):322–25. Discusses Scobie's suicide and Roman Catholic implications.

West, Anthony. "Graham Greene." In his *Principles and Persuasions.* New York: Harcourt Brace, 1957.

Wobbe, R. A. *Graham Greene: A Bibliography and Guide to Research.* New York and London: Garland, 1979. Information about Greene and the criticism about him up to 1977. Includes references to works reviewed by Greene.

Wolfe, Peter. *Graham Greene the Entertainer.* Carbondale: Southern Illinois Univ. Press, 1972. Lucid and sensible approach to the problems and techniques in Greene's thrillers.

Woodcock, George. "Graham Greene." In his *The Writer and Politics,* 125–53. London: Porcupine Press, 1948. Discusses Greene and communism.

Wyndham, Francis. *Graham Greene.* Bibliographical Series of Supplements to *British Book News on Writers and Their Work,* no. 67. London: Longmans, 1955.

Wysard, Anthony, ed. *Wheeler's Review.* Vol. 24, nos. 1, 2. London: Wheeler House, 1978. Published by the famous fish restaurant; a useful picture history of Berkhamsted, with special reference to a "mellowing" Greene.

Zabel, Morton Dauwen. "Graham Greene: The Best and the Worst." In
his *Craft and Character in Modern Fiction.* New York: Viking, 1957.
(Earlier versions of this essay were included in *Forms of Modern Fiction,*
edited by William Van O'Connor [Minneapolis: University of Min-
nesota Press, 1948], 287–93; in *Critiques and Essays on Modern Fiction
1920–1951,* edited by John W. Aldridge [New York: Ronald Press
Co., 1952], 518–25; and in *Der Monat* [Berlin], in 1953.) One of
the best treatments of Greene that has been written.

Index

DATE DUE
